SPEED ON SKATES

BARRY PUBLOW

Human Kinetics

Library of Congress Cataloging-in-Publication Data

Publow, Barry, 1970-
   Speed on skates / Barry Publow.
      p.   cm.
   Includes bibliographical references and index.
   ISBN 0-88011-721-4
   1. Speed skating. 2. In-line skating. 3. Speed skating—
   Training. 4. Skating—Training. I. Title.
GV850.3.P83 1999
   796.91'4—dc21   98-39168
                                                                                   CIP

ISBN-10: 0-88011-721-4
ISBN-13: 978-0-88011-721-0

Developmental Editor: Syd Slobodnik; **Managing Editor:** Katy Patterson; **Copyeditor:** Anne Mischakoff-Heiles; **Proofreader:** Jim Burns; **Indexer:** L. Pilar Wyman; **Graphic Designer:** Robert Reuther; **Graphic Artist:** Kimberly Maxey; **Photo Editor:** Boyd LaFoon; **Cover Designer:** Jack Davis; **Photographers (cover):** © H. Barry Giles and Tim Hanrahan; **Illustrators:** Tom Roberts and John Hatton; **Printer:** Versa Press

All photos in Chapters 1 and 4 by Tim Hanrahan unless otherwise noted. Chapter 3 photos by Tim Hanrahan. All photos in Chapters 2 and 7-9 by Barry Giles.

Human Kinetics books are available at special discounts for bulk purchase. Special editions or book excerpts can also be created to specification. For details, contact the Special Sales Manager at Human Kinetics.

Printed in the United States of America   10   9   8   7

Human Kinetics
Web site: www.HumanKinetics.com

United States: Human Kinetics, P.O. Box 5076, Champaign, IL 61825-5076
800-747-4457
e-mail: humank@hkusa.com

Canada: Human Kinetics, 475 Devonshire Road, Unit 100, Windsor, ON N8Y 2L5
800-465-7301 (in Canada only)
e-mail: orders@hkcanada.com

Europe: Human Kinetics, 107 Bradford Road, Stanningley
Leeds LS28 6AT, United Kingdom
+44 (0) 113 255 5665
e-mail: hk@hkeurope.com

Australia: Human Kinetics, 57A Price Avenue, Lower Mitcham, South Australia 5062
08 8372 0999
e-mail: liaw@hkaustralia.com

New Zealand: Human Kinetics, Division of Sports Distributors NZ Ltd.
P.O. Box 300 226 Albany, North Shore City, Auckland
0064 9 448 1207
e-mail: info@humankinetics.co.nz

To my son Brayden
for helping me realize the true meaning of
patience and perseverance.

Contents

Preface

Speedskating is among the most beautiful sport activities one can watch. As a teenager, before I became involved in the sport, I watched speedskating on television, and I remember my awe in witnessing the sheer power of the skaters. Their smooth, graceful, and coordinated motions propelled them around the track with apparent ease and simply amazing speed.

The rhythmic, fluid, almost hypnotic motions of speedskaters continue to entrance me even now that I have become an experienced skater and coach. Whether I witness the raw sprint power of Bonnie Blair, the effortless efficiency of Johann Koss, or the enduring speed of Derek Parra, watching great skaters at work can be an almost religious experience. For me, speedskating represents the ultimate athletic endeavor. Few sports require such a balance of power, speed, endurance, coordination, self-determination, and dedication. Knowing these challenges, I have an ever-growing appreciation and respect for the sport and its athletes, coaches, and developers.

Though equally as beautiful to watch as ice speedskaters, in-line speedskaters are typically a little more rough around the edges. In-line speedskating shares most of the enduring technical and aesthetic qualities of ice speedskating, but by nature has some distinct differences. In-line racing is a pack sport, which may detract from the overall finesse and beauty of the technique. Yet a draft line of skaters moving in synchronicity can reveal the visual attractiveness of the technically perfect ice skater.

The first edition of this book was a short training outline that I wrote in 1992 as an exercise physiology paper at the university. I had given it out to a few skaters whom I knew, but it otherwise collected dust along with my numerous other papers related to speedskating. In January 1996, a former coworker asked if I would write a relatively simple training program for a skater in Michigan. One idea spawned another, until I realized that I had enough information to write this book. Hence, the impetus for *Speed on Skates* was realized.

Any skater can implement the information within these pages to benefit their skating, regardless of ability. Likely the most comprehensive and thorough accumulation of information ever compiled for the in-line and ice speedskater, this book has a fourfold purpose: first, it is intended to serve as a practical and sound reference guide that provides specific technical and training information for both coaches and athletes. Second, it is designed to help all skaters improve the overall quality of their workouts, using macro-planning to incorporate a timely application of training for the appropriate energy system. Third, this book is intended to fill the ever-growing need that skaters have for a training and resource manual specifically for the sport of speedskating. Last, this book allows me to pass along to other skaters the knowledge I have gained through years of experience as a kinesiologist, coach, and fellow skater.

Speed on Skates takes an in-depth look at the essential components necessary to achieve heightened levels of performance. It provides specific information, detailed instruction, and technical guidelines to assist developing skaters in their quest for personal excellence.

Gaining a solid, theoretical framework and basic direction related to the principles and processes of physical adaptation will allow you to systematically implement some of the most contemporary training methods now available to athletes. Each chapter incorporates theory with specific training methodology and application. Whether you are a novice competitor or an elite racer, the information in this book is guaranteed to make you a better, faster, and more well-rounded skater.

You will be reading an amalgamation of modern scientific principles, proven research, personal experience, insight, and observation. I have taken a practical, yet scientific and balanced, approach to training. It is my hope that *Speed on Skates* presents this mixture of technique, illustration, and practical application in a logical, easy-to-follow manner.

This book divides essential information into three broad parts. The first explains important mechanical aspects and technical parameters basic to the development of efficient skating form. Part II, the largest section, examines the requisites, training methods, and techniques to develop the physical attributes that lead to performance success. Each chapter in it describes the role and relevance that a component can offer in the overall conditioning process. Part III describes racing and many of the strategic elements that speedskaters use in both in-line and ice-skating disciplines. It also provides information on speedskating equipment.

Although each chapter is designed to complement the others, each is also a discrete or independent entity. Thus, even though I recommend your following the chapters in the order in which they appear, this format also allows you to browse through these pages in a random, independent order.

Improvements in equipment, technique, and training methods are likely to pave the way for tomorrow's athletes to surpass the level of accomplishment now displayed by top speedskaters. Until then it is my hope that *Speed on Skates* will represent the best source of specific technical and training information available for the developing athlete. It is my sincere wish that this book will significantly assist each and every skater who chooses to explore the information within these covers.

Acknowledgments

This book would never have come to fruition without the ongoing support of a few key people. A heartfelt thanks goes out to Sandy Nimmo, friend and director of the Canadian In-line and Roller Skating Association (CIRSA), for your direction, guidance, and encouragement over the years and to Valerie Gaston for your hours of brainstorming, editing, and continuous encouragement. Thanks also goes to the Toronto In-line Speedskating Club (TISC) members for providing me with the appropriate medium to develop and pursue my love for in-line racing and to Wayne Burrett, friend and TISC president, for your compassion, generosity, understanding, and ongoing friendship. Thanks to members of the Ottawa Inline Speedskating Club for being such great students, training partners, and friends; to Jennifer Publow for your profound overall influence on the direction of my sporting life; and to my parents for nurturing me during the more difficult times. And last of all, to Jocelyn Martin Sicotte, my former coach and mentor. If it had not been for your inspiration, vision, and commitment to the sport of speedskating, I would likely never have reached the point I am at today.

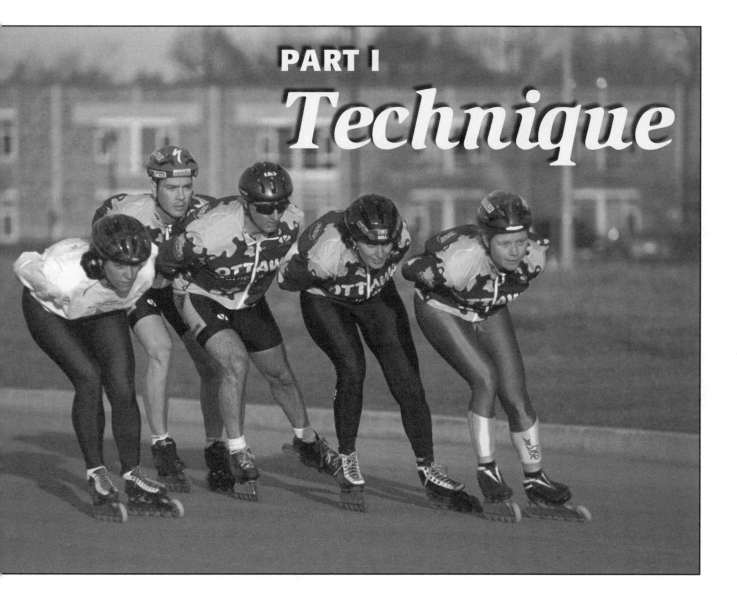

PART I

Technique

1

In-Line Speedskating

The Speedskater is a balance of energy and power. This image depicts three entities, frozen in a moment of time. The ebb and flow of the bodies is echoed by an eerie sound. It is the sound of the singing bearings. They sing with every motion, all twenty of them in a choir of hisses and intermittent screams of ecstasy. This is the dance of the Speedskater.

Eric Gee

In any sport we usually admire those athletes who are the best. With speedskating, they are the athletes who go the fastest. If we look at the ten fastest speedskaters in the world, whether on ice or in-line, we find that the majority skate with superior technical prowess. A few individuals can skate fast simply by taking advantage of an inherent genetic capacity for incredible power output. The rest of us, however, must muddle through years of practice, development, and refinement of the technical elements of skating. Speedskating is one of the few sports I know of whose seasoned, elite skaters continue to dedicate enormous time to honing technique.

Once the technical aspects are all in place, we can focus more on the physiologic qualities that allow us to go fast. This doesn't mean that skaters cannot (and should not) be working on conditioning early on, but rather that technique should be the primary focus for any developing skater. Novice skaters are likely to progress more rapidly by positively modifying technique than by achieving adaptations in physical ability. In other words, technique is probably the most important component of success in speedskating. Without appropriate technique, any amount of strength and power is largely wasted through inefficient motion.

In this chapter you will read about the basics of skating mechanics and those essential components that lead to efficient technique for in-line speedskating. The mechanics described here involve the more classically oriented technique that has evolved from speedskating on ice. Later in the chapter you will find a description of the more modern (and still evolving) method of skating known as the double-push technique, which almost all elite skaters now use. The double-push appears to be a far superior way of generating propulsion and executing skating mechanics with maximal efficiency. It is recommended that all skaters first master the finer points of classic technique, however, before attempting to learn the double-push. Classic technique will give you a more solid foundation for bodily feedback, as well as a greater appreciation for the overall beauty and complexity of the skating movement pattern.

THE SPEEDSKATING MOVEMENT PATTERN

The objective in speedskating, as in all speed sports, is to travel from point A to point B as quickly as possible. Speed is a product of how effectively one can apply power in the face of external resistance. Technique dictates to what extent an individual can channel energy in a useful way to generate force and speed. That is, technique is a vehicle that determines how effectively the skater can use power to achieve speed through propulsion.

$$\text{Speed} = \frac{\text{Power} \times \text{Effectiveness (Technique)}}{\text{Resistance}}$$

Gaining speed through propulsion requires overcoming resistance. The resistance component refers to two variables:

- There are *frictional* forces both between the asphalt and wheels and an internal resistance within the wheels and their bearings. Because in-line skating generates a great deal more surface friction than does a hard steel blade on slippery ice, speeds achieved on in-line skates are about 10 percent lower than those attained on ice.
- *Air resistance,* or *drag,* is created by the frontal surface area of the skater. Drag relates to the velocity of travel, as shown by the exponential equation $R = v^2$, where resistance increases with the square of the velocity.

The entire movement pattern for speedskating is a dynamic and uninterrupted motion that is difficult to describe verbally or to illustrate in a single photograph. Because of its complex and fluid nature, the sequence of motion is best described by breaking up the overall pattern of movement into five phases. Usually these phases are differentiated as follows:

1. Basic body position
2. Push-off
3. Glide
4. Stroke recovery
5. Weight transfer

Each of these phases demonstrates certain necessary, mechanical characteristics inherent within the overall pattern of movement. It is important to remember that these phases are not separate or discrete in appearance, but involve considerable overlap in their sequential application.

BASIC BODY POSITION— THE TEN COMMANDMENTS

Proper technique allows a skater to exploit certain biomechanical advantages, thus maximally utilizing the muscular and physiologic capabilities. The components of basic body position serve as the raw foundation for virtually all further developmental aspects of speedskating technique. That is, the basic position defines important joint angles that must be maintained during most of the movement pattern. The position acts as a sort of template on which to add the more dynamic aspects of technique that form the entire stride. Many mechanical discrepancies occur during the skating motion, which can be traced back to small but discernible errors in basic body position.

The angles at three joints are essential in the basic body position. These involve the hip (trunk), the knee, and the ankle joints (see figure 1.1), which you can read about later in more detail. What you will find here are only the 10 most essential details of speedskating's basic position (figure 1.2, a and b).

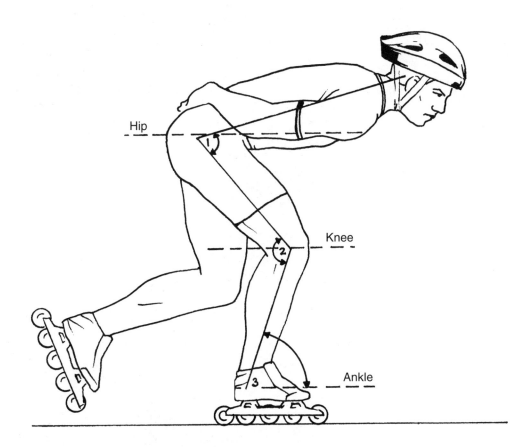

1.1 The three important angles in speedskating: hip, knee, and ankle.

1.2a Basic position from the front.

1.2b Basic position from the side.

1. KEEP THE FEET SHOULDER-WIDTH APART, PROVIDING A STABLE BASE OF SUPPORT.

2. MAINTAIN THE ANKLES IN A NEUTRAL POSITION SO THAT YOU ARE DIRECTLY ON TOP OF (OVER) THE WHEELS.

It is permissible, even advisable, to have the ankles collapsed slightly outward so that the skates rest on the outside edge.

It is worth dedicating time to ensure that this neutral, or outward, wheel position can be maintained comfortably without fear or hesitation. Control over the wheels' "edges" is paramount for maintaining stability during the glide and developing force through the push-off. Many skaters have thought, "I can't stay on top of the wheels. My ankles just aren't strong enough." Inexperienced skaters often complain of insufficient ankle strength and stability. However, the truth is that most skaters *do* have enough strength at the ankle to prevent the joints from canting either inward (inversion) or outward (eversion). Higher-cut boots can provide additional support to prevent undesired canting movements, but often at a cost: they limit the range of motion about the ankle.

Most cases of poor ankle stability stem from insufficient knee flexion rather than from true weakness in the shin muscles. The simplest solution is to squat lower, making the ankle joint structurally more stable. Over time, too, there is no better way to strengthen the shin muscles than to log skating mileage.

3. POSITION BOTH SKATES PARALLEL, POINTING STRAIGHT AHEAD IN THE DIRECTION OF TRAVEL.

4. FLEX THE KNEES TO ABOUT 110 DEGREES, PLACING THE THIGHS ALMOST PARALLEL TO THE GROUND.

The knees must be flexed so that the skater assumes a deep-seated position. Although the actual degree of knee bend will vary somewhat, depending on the distance or duration one is skating, the knees should be flexed about 110 to 120 degrees (still deeper for a sprint). Most new skaters, not yet having well-defined perceptions of body movement, mistakenly believe their knees are bending more than they actually are. Since speedskating is one of the few sport activities that require this deep-seated position, it is natural for new skaters to feel awkward. As a general rule of thumb, the knees are considered sufficiently flexed when the kneecaps (patellae) are vertically aligned directly over the toes.

Although deep knee flexion during speedskating is necessary to achieve a long push displacement, an excessively low knee angle (bend) can adversely affect mechanical efficiency. Studies show that a knee bend deeper than 110 degrees does not improve external power output because the increased muscle tension interferes with the movement of certain metabolic substances such as lactic acid.

5. KEEP THE BODY WEIGHT BACK TOWARD THE HEELS.

The center of gravity must be located about one-half to two-thirds of the way toward the heels. To focus the body's weight away from the balls of the feet in this manner, you bend the knees, lower the rear end, and sit back slightly. Exactly where the line of gravity falls is vital for both the push-off and glide phases; the location dictates from which part of the push-off action the forces will be concentrated. If the center of gravity is too far forward, excessive body weight is applied on the front wheels, reducing the overall effectiveness of both push and glide. This increased pressure on the front of the skate will also interfere with proper push-off mechanics by reducing the effectiveness of force application, leading the skater to push from the toes. Wheel wear patterns can provide valuable insight in regard to center of gravity. A heavily worn front wheel often indicates that body weight is too far forward.

6. FLEX THE TRUNK FORWARD FROM AN UPRIGHT POSITION BETWEEN 45 AND 60 DEGREES (I.E., IT SHOULD BE 30 TO 45 DEGREES ABOVE THE HORIZONTAL PLANE), WITH A SLIGHT ROUNDING IN THE BACK.

Lowering the trunk facilitates performance by reducing total frontal surface area. Since this surface constitutes the largest factor influencing air resistance, remaining too upright (having too little forward trunk flexion) imposes an unnecessary amount of drag. Leaning forward excessively, however, can interfere with the ease of breathing, decrease efficiency during push-off (by shifting the center of gravity too far forward on the skate), and place increased tension on the lower back muscles.

7. REST BOTH ARMS COMFORTABLY ON THE MIDDLE OF THE LOWER BACK.

Typically, the right hand should be on top of the left hand when resting on the back. Since track skating and many race courses rely heavily on left-hand turns, having the right hand on top makes the transition much easier from two hands on the back to a single, right arm-swing. This is a small detail, however, and you should place the hands in whatever position is comfortable.

When both hands are placed on the back, the shoulders and arms should remain as relaxed as possible. Tension in the limbs and shoulders can interfere with technique. At the same time, the arms should be held neatly behind the back with the elbows tucked in *close to the body* to minimize frontal surface area.

8. HOLD THE SHOULDERS LEVEL (AS VIEWED EITHER FROM BEHIND OR IN FRONT) AND POINTED STRAIGHT AHEAD (I.E., THERE SHOULD BE NO ROTATION OF THE SPINE AND UPPER BODY).

It is permissible to have a slight dropping or tilting of the shoulders during skating as the hips move during the weight transfer. However, since execution of the basic position serves as a calibration exercise, it is important to ensure that the shoulders are in a neutral horizontal position with no discrepancy in height.

Regardless of the specific phase of the speedskating movement, it is vital to avoid rotating the spine. Securing this particular aspect is an important part of the basic position, and any rotation should be corrected immediately.

9. HOLD THE HEAD UPRIGHT, WITH THE EYES LOOKING AHEAD.

Perceptual awareness and being able to rapidly interpret sensory information from the surroundings are important for all skaters. Keeping the head upright and scanning the terrain ahead is a vital safety skill to develop. Learning this early on helps develop superior spatial awareness and body perception, since vision alone should not be relied on to detect errors in technique.

10. KEEP THE BODY AS RELAXED AS POSSIBLE.

Feeling stable in the basic position is very important, and even experienced skaters should spend time focusing on refining this aspect. Needless active tension in the muscles can interfere with stability, further disrupting mechanics that make up the entire movement sequence of speedskating.

PUSH-OFF

The push-off phase is characterized by a smooth and powerful accelerated push that exhibits a definite snap of power at the end of the extension. Skaters spend much time on the precise mechanics of the push-off, since (with classic technique) it constitutes the sole means of applying force for propulsion. The two main components that determine the effectiveness of the push-off are the direction of the push and the knee angle prior to extension.

Direction of Push

Although the precise direction of push will vary slightly, depending on the velocity the skater has and on the degree of surface incline or decline, the push should be directed in general at a right angle to the direction of travel. That is, the push should be straight to the side. During this phase, there should occur simultaneously an extension of the hip and knee and a slight external (outward) rotation of the hip joint as the muscles push through their full range of motion. (See figure 1.3.)

1.3 Complete extension of the pushing leg.

Knee Angle Prior to Extension

A deeply-seated knee angle prior to push-off heightens the ability to develop explosive power and acceleration. This is accomplished by lengthening lateral push displacement and by increasing the muscles' working range. This results in a higher degree of control in the push and an increased ability to generate propulsion by keeping the wheels on the road for as long as possible.

The most common errors of the push-off phase involve the variables of the direction of push and the knee angle. Novice skaters often push back excessively. In order to correct this backward tendency, the skate can be pushed in a slightly forward direction during the extension. This exaggeration drill not only helps direct the push in the desired direction, but also ensures that the push is originating from the back half of the skate. If a skater concentrates on pushing the extension leg slightly forward, momentum will actually carry it back slightly. The result will be a push directed almost completely sideward.

Here are some key points to remember about the mechanics of the push-off:

- As the push-off leg extends, the body's weight and center of gravity move over the support leg, allowing for a smooth weight transfer and a long, stable glide.
- Once the weight has been transferred and the push progresses, maintain the support leg in the same deep knee bend throughout the entire glide.
- Keep the shoulders essentially in the same basic position (that is, without any rotation of the trunk), allowing only a minimal dropping of the shoulders as the hips tilt slightly during the weight transfer.
- Keep the upper body as relaxed as possible, since energy unnecessarily spent contracting muscles in the upper body (other than those necessary to ensure good position) is wasted—it does not contribute to the overall effectiveness of the push.
- Hold the head upright and directed straight ahead.
- There should be no vertical displacement of the center of gravity (that is, no "bobbing" of the hips or shoulders during the push or any phase of the skating stride). The only displacement to the center of gravity during push-off should be horizontal, as the weight transfer occurs.
- The push-off should occur in an accelerated fashion. Almost all the force that the muscles generate during the push develops during the first one-third of the range of motion.

GLIDE

The glide phase begins the moment the pushing leg is lifted off the road for recovery, and it terminates the moment the support leg initiates force into a lateral push. Although the glide is essentially static with respect to support-leg activity, the free leg uses this time to regroup. For improving the glide phase, the important facets to explore are the time spent on the support leg and the orientation of the wheels on the road.

Glide Time

Air resistance (drag) and rolling resistance (both friction from the wheel-to-road contact and resistance within the wheel and its bearing assembly) cause a fairly rapid deceleration after a propulsive pushing force has been applied. Because of this, the glide time with in-line skating is comparatively shorter than it is with skating on ice. So a higher stroke cadence (more strides per minute) is used for in-line skating than for ice skating.

Wheel Orientation—Edge Control

From the moment the skate is set down on the road following the stroke recovery, the skater should glide on the *outside* of the wheels. It is important to ensure that this outward angle is already achieved during the set-down because it maximizes gliding time and the effectiveness of the subsequent weight transfer and the onset of pushing force. The glide proceeds on the outside wheel edge until the weight transfer occurs. At this point, the hips of the skater move laterally *away from* the direction of push and the wheels roll over the top for the onset of pushing force. The wheel orientation during the glide is illustrated in figure 1.4, a and b.

1.4a During the early glide, the recovery skate must be set down on the outside wheel edge.

1.4b The skate of the glide leg rolls on the outside wheel edge until the weight transfer occurs.

STROKE RECOVERY

The purpose of the recovery phase is to regroup the push leg in preparation for the all-important weight transfer. The transition from push-off to stroke recovery begins the instant the pushing leg reaches full extension to the side. In order for this process to proceed smoothly, the support leg at the terminal point of the push must carry all of the weight. The best way to describe the pattern followed by the recovery leg is as a semicircle around the back. Although the recovery phase constitutes one of the best areas to add personal expression to one's technique, there are a few important points to bear in mind when developing this component of the skating stride.

Skate Lift-Off

As the push leg reaches maximal extension, the skater initiates the recovery process by lifting the wheels horizontally and gently off the road, with the skate frame parallel to the ground and pointing directly ahead. This is illustrated in figure 1.5. The most common error in making the skate lift-off is a pronounced toe flick. This involves rotating the ankle externally and pointing the toes at the end of the push so that the skate does not remain parallel to the road.

1.5 The skate should lift off the road with the wheels maintained in the horizontal plane.

Several points are important to remember about the skate lift-off:

- The skate should be kept as low to the ground as possible during the entire recovery process, lifted just high enough to clear the road.
- The upper and lower leg should move together, in general, as a unit. As the leg begins to circle around the back, the knee flexes slightly while pointing in a downward direction.
- The toe of the boot should lead the semicircular path that the skate follows. Most importantly, the skate should point directly ahead as it moves under the body. It is advisable to *turn the foot slightly inward* to ensure that you place the skate down pointing straight ahead.
- As the leg progresses through the semicircle, gradual flexion of the knee occurs so that the skate can assume an angle close to 90 degrees to the road.

Set-Down

As the skate passes under the body after completing the recovery phase, the skater's knee should drive forward forcefully. The set-down of the wheels should occur a few inches ahead of the support leg skate, angling slightly on the outside edge. This set-down step is a necessary precursor to the remaining chain of events: weight transfer, push, and glide. The set-down of the skate comprises one of the most critical aspects of the skating stride: incorrect execution of it can dramatically reduce skating efficiency and disrupt all following stages of the stride. The weight transfer, set down, and onset of pushing force occur simultaneously. Here are two important points of set-down to explore:

- The recovery phase is the only time the leg has to rest! Allow the leg to remain in a relaxed state as it regroups. Pay conscious effort to ensure that muscle tension dissipates to allow the blood flow to be restored, at least momentarily, to near-normal levels.
- Above all, the recovery process should be a single, fluid motion, a natural and continuous extension of the push-off.

WEIGHT TRANSFER

The weight transfer is probably the most difficult skill for a developing skater to attain. It is also the most difficult concept for a coach to explain accurately or correct for misalignments in application.

The lateral transfer of weight is not a single, discrete moment during the stride. Conceptually, it is more a transitory process somewhere between the recovery and push-off phases. It coincides with the end of the recovery, the rolling over of the support skate wheels from the outside to inside, and the initial force development of the push-off leg. The weight transfer continues until the pushing skate reaches full extension, when the recovery skate then carries all the weight as it sets down.

The weight transfer helps supplement force generated on the inside edge of the wheels during push-off, thereby minimizing the muscular effort necessary to generate propulsion. To understand this process, it is useful to consider the weight transfer in three separate steps: the glide, the roll, and the force initialization. These steps correspond to the changes in applied pressure from the outside to inside of the wheels and the corresponding lateral movements of the hips and center of gravity.

Glide

During the glide phase, the body's weight is carried entirely by the support leg. During this time, the free leg goes through its active recovery and regrouping process. At the beginning of the glide phase, the wheels of the support skate are angled on the outside (that is, pressure is applied on the outside aspect of the wheels). See figure 1.6a. This causes a slight shift in the skater's balance toward the side of the glide leg. Equilibrium is maintained, however, because balance is offset by the still-regrouping push leg.

Roll

As the recovery leg begins to move under the body, the skater's balance begins to shift back toward the side of the recovery skate. As this occurs, the center of gravity also begins to move in this direction. This slight shift in the center of gravity causes the wheels to roll inward over the highest point (apex) of the wheel. See figure 1.6b. For a split second, the skater is rolling directly on top of the wheels. It can now be seen that it is imperative to ensure that the glide begins on the outside of the wheels.

1.6a Late recovery/weight transfer: the glide—outside edge roll.

1.6b Late recovery/weight transfer: rolling over the wheel's apex onto the inner edge.

Force Initialization

The critical point has now been reached whereby the hips and center of balance continue to fall over the midline and toward the side of the recovery leg. As this occurs, the shoulders should remain stable with only a slight dropping of the shoulder on the side of the recovery leg. At this point, the knee of the recovery leg is being driven forward and ahead of the glide leg's skate. The glide leg skate has now rolled over the top of the wheels, so that pressure is applied on the inside edge of the pushing wheels. See figure 1.6c. As the set-down occurs, the glide leg has begun to accelerate into push-off. During the first instant of push-off, the recovery leg is now set down beside and slightly ahead of the push leg. For a brief instant, an imaginary line drawn down from the center of gravity would lie inside both legs.

Timing makes the weight transfer a difficult skill to master. It must be exact, and if the weight transfer is *too early,* the recovery leg will not have sufficient time to regroup: the center of gravity will not have time to "prime." Since the weight transfer helps minimize the efforts required of the push-off muscles, without good timing more force will be needed to get a strong extension. In addition, an early weight transfer will not allow a skater to experience the rolling over of the wheels from the outside and top to the inside, where more leverage and force can be applied toward the push.

If the weight transfer is *too late,* on the other hand, the skater essentially "misses the boat." Optimal lateral momentum is not generated, and too much time is spent on the inside edge of the wheels. The late timing limits glide time drastically—and

1.6c Late recovery/weight transfer: onset of force application.

ultimately reduces speed. Speedskating is all about efficiency, and the timing of the weight transfer is vital for efficient technique.

Proper transfer of the weight also ensures that there is no wasted movement in the hips. Adequate muscular strength is required to maintain integrity in the hip and trunk area during push-off. Pelvic instability, common in young and inexperienced skaters, results in a notable "dipping" of the hip during push-off; energy is disbursed through the needless, absorbing effect of hip motion. This is illustrated in figure 1.7. Instruction, practice, and strengthening of the pelvic, hip, and torso musculature, however, can often remedy such misalignment.

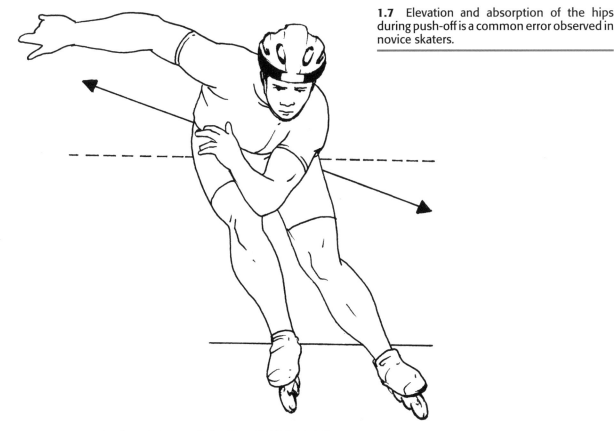

1.7 Elevation and absorption of the hips during push-off is a common error observed in novice skaters.

STRAIGHTAWAY ARM SWING

Up to 80 percent of an in-line race may be covered with both arms placed on the back. Often, however, a single- or double-arm swing is more appropriate. Swinging the arms aids balance, maintains tempo, and increases the power applied through the legs during push-off. To work effectively, the arm swing must precisely counter the motion of the legs. This section will describe the mechanics that lead to effective complementary arm movement, whether with a single- or double-arm swing. Although there are certain mechanical aspects of the movement pattern that should be executed correctly, the arm swing is a movement that allows for some personal flair.

Throughout the arm swing, the shoulder complex should be as relaxed as possible. The arm movement can be forcefully initiated at the beginning of the swing, allowing momentum to then carry it through most of its range of motion. Overall, the arm's swing should act as a sort of metronome for the legs' action, complementing their pushing.

One-Arm Swing Mechanics

All arm swings have a forward and backward movement. The forward part of the arm swing must coincide with the extension of the same-side leg's push and the lateral shift in the center of gravity toward the opposite side. The backswing, on the other hand, is timed to coordinate with the extension of the opposite leg's pushing and the shift in the center of gravity toward the same side. Precisely coordinating these events with the push-off and recovery mechanics can be a surprisingly difficult task, even for experienced skaters. The single-arm version is probably the less common form of arm swing, with most in-line racers opting to use the more powerful and stabilizing two-arm swing. However, an effective single-arm swing is a good supplementary tool to have in one's arsenal of skills.

Forward Swing

As the arm swings forward from the backswing, the hand should pass very close to the hip, with the arm tucked in close to the body. This helps keep the body compact, minimizes air resistance by reducing frontal surface area, and decreases the risk of "rubbing" with other competitors. The elbow joint should have only a very slight bend as it brushes past the pelvis. As the arm continues forward, it may either cross the midline of the body or remain entirely on the same side of the body. Swinging the arm obliquely across the midline is often preferable because it more directly opposes the push-off forces being applied from extension of the leg and allows for better lateral control over the center of gravity. The actual amounts of overlap across the midline can vary considerably between individuals. A general rule is that the hand should cross no farther than the opposite shoulder.

A forward swing should end no higher than the chin. As the arm proceeds forward from the hip, the elbow joint increasingly flexes, reaching a final joint angle of some 150 to 170 degrees at the top of the swing. Timing is everything with an arm swing. The arm should reach its terminal position just as the same-side leg reaches its maximum extension. See figure 1.8a.

Backswing

The transition from forward swing to backswing occurs during the recovery phase of the same-side leg. Since the center of gravity takes a moment to fall back toward the recovery side, the arm is held in a static position at the top of the forward swing for an instant. As the arm moves into the backswing, it falls back across the midline, and the elbow joint begins to gradually straighten out. Keep the hand and arm close to the upper body; they should pass near to the hip (figure 1.8b). As the opposite leg continues to extend to the side, the arm begins to move back behind the shoulder. Once past the hip, the arm should continue to follow a similar oblique line, but reach maximal extension in a position tucked neatly behind the body. The arm should go as far as roughly the height of the same shoulder in its rearward extension. At this point, the elbow should have no noticeable bend. See figure 1.8c.

Exact timing of the backswing is also critical for the arm's movement to fully aid push-off forces. Your arm should reach the terminal point of the backswing at the same time that your opposite-side leg reaches its maximal extension. This highest point of the backswing is held only an instant. Make the transition to the forward swing as the opposite leg goes through recovery and the center of gravity once again begins to shift laterally.

1.8a Single-arm swing: terminal foreswing position.

1.8b Single-arm swing: transition to backswing.

1.8c Single-arm swing: terminal backswing position.

Two-Arm Swing Mechanics

The two-arm swing is used often during an in-line race, and utilizes some of the same mechanics as the single-arm swing. However, it distinctly differs from the mechanics of the one-arm swing in three ways:

- The arms tend to display significantly more lateral displacement as they cross over in front and behind the body. Neither hand, however, should pass the point of the opposite shoulder during the forward swing.

- Since the two-arm swing is used primarily for *intense* efforts, the maximal height of the *backswing* may reach up to the level of the head.

- With the two-arm swing, the elbows are bent slightly more at the farthest extension points, both in the forward swing and the backswing. The two-arm swing is illustrated in figure 1.9.

Coordinating a two-arm swing with the legs can be difficult. With practice, however, coordination will occur. You should feel as though the arms' action leads the legs, determining their tempo, degree of lateral displacement, and overall output of power.

1.9 Two-arm swing.

CROSSOVER STEPS AND TURN MECHANICS

Crossover steps allow a skater to take the shortest route through a corner, counteract the centrifugal force that pushes the body away from the center of the curve, and build speed and acceleration through a turn. Crossover steps allow each skate to apply force toward the outside of the turn by recovering the outer skate in front of the inner. Some might argue that mastery of crossover steps is a relatively low priority for an outdoor in-line skater. It's true that some courses are so straight that crossovers may not even be necessary. Most road courses do have corners, however, that would be most effectively negotiated using crossover technique. Consequently, skaters who have developed their ability in this area have an enormous advantage over those who have not.

Successful skaters must be proficient at turning both ways, which makes in-line racing interesting. Gaining this proficiency requires practice time and versatility in technique. Many racers prefer left-hand turns, because the counterclockwise direction is the direction of rotation for track skating. On the other hand, many racecourses have several right-hand turns as well.

Lacking skill or confidence in turning technique is a recipe for disaster. It means an increased likelihood of crashing as you mix skates with fellow competitors. Furthermore, having poor cornering technique often means losing place in the pack after each turn. Many a distraught skater has been heard to moan, "If I could hold my own in the turns, I would be fine" or "After every turn, I was sprinting for a hundred meters to catch the pack again!" Both these statements reflect the importance of turn technique for outdoor in-line racing. On the track, turn technique is everything.

It is impossible for a skater to excel without having developed exceptional crossover ability. Indoor skaters who later move to the road have a major advantage over the competition in this regard. Outdoor purists, having less-defined crossover ability, may be able to hold their own through some turns, but they lack any real advantage over their indoor-trained competition. Though some races may not demand superb crossover technique, it takes only one technical course to realize just how important this skill is—and to wish you had spent time practicing it.

The mechanics of good turn technique on in-line skates are essentially identical to those on ice skates. A detailed breakdown of upper- and lower-body position for ice speedskating, as well as crossover arm-swing mechanics, is described in chapter 2. Regardless of the similarities in technique between ice and in-line, significant differences also exist between them. This short section discusses these discrepancies and focuses on specific crossover issues as they relate to in-line speedskating.

Versatility Is Essential

Track skaters, although heavily dependent on turn technique, have at least one major advantage: predictability. The track never changes. The radius of each turn is the same, the surface is uniformly smooth, each corner can essentially be set up the same every time, and the direction is always counterclockwise. With outdoor road skating, the situation is entirely different. Outdoor racers must be able to turn in both directions. Moreover, no two turns are ever the same, which complicates things further. Outdoor corners vary in turn radius, length, and the *amount* of change in radius. Road conditions (such as cracks, sewer grates, or uneven pavement) and environmental factors (such as wind and moisture) also affect cornering execution. Being versatile is probably the single greatest skill a skater can strive for. The best skaters have developed not only exceptional cornering technique, but also a keen sense of perception that allows them to prestructure all aspects of a turn in advance so as to best negotiate the corner.

Ice Technique for In-Line Skating?

Effective ice techniques are clearly not always the best ones for in-line skaters. First, in-line skates have no rocker, or blade bend, as ice skates do. Because of this, in-lines have no "high point" through which force can be concentrated to allow tight turning. This changes the desired push specifics only marginally, but it dramatically affects the sensory perceptions if you are used to ice skating.

A second difference between ice and in-line crossover technique has to do with power output through the turn. A skater's power output results from both how hard he pushes each stride and from the frequency, or cadence, of the strides. To generalize, in-liners push less hard through most turns, but they have a considerably higher rate of turnover during the crossover steps. This difference is due in part to the decreased traction of wheels as compared with a blade. In-line speedskaters have a higher crossover rate partly because they participate in a pack sport in which more regular crossover steps allow them greater versatility, agility, and control. A higher stroke rate is necessary in addition to maintain a high power output when they are not pushing with maximal effort.

Still another difference between ice and in-line crossover technique has to do with push displacement of the inner leg. Generally speaking, the inside leg does not "push through" to the same degree in in-line skating as in ice skating. Although traction is at issue with wheels, this difference is primarily attributed to the fact that shortening the push-through of the inner leg facilitates a more *rapid* crossover frequency. Figure 1.10, a and b illustrates the difference in crossover technique between ice and in-line skating.

Barry Giles

1.10a There exist subtle but important differences in crossover technique between ice and in-line skating.

1.10b An in-line crossover.

OVERVIEW OF CROSSOVER PRINCIPLES

Before leaving this introduction to in-line crossover techniques, review these following principles. Applying them to your practices will help make your skating more effective and efficient.

- Strive to apply pushing force from the middle wheel.
- The centrifugal force through a turn is best opposed by directing the pushing legs along a straight line radiating from the center of the turn.
- The pushing leg should progress through the full range of available motion.
- Both the left and right leg pushes should exhibit an equal rhythm, executed in the same time frame.
- Only the wheels' edges to the inside of the turn are used during crossover steps. That is, use the left edges for a left-hand turn and the right edges for a right-hand turn.
- Although traction on wheels is often limited, the pushing action of both legs should accelerate to reach peak velocity midway through the push.
- The recovery of both legs should be as close to the ground as possible. Set both skates down either flat or on the back half of the wheels.

- Keep the hips and upper body as stable as possible to provide a solid source of leverage for the legs.
- Align your shoulders and head with the tangent of the curve.
- Since there is no gliding period in the turns, your legs should apply a constant force during the crossover steps.
- The rate of leg turnover using crossover steps is always higher than straightaway leg tempo.

DOUBLE-PUSH TECHNIQUE—HISTORY

In-line racers have traditionally mimicked what is essentially a technique for speedskating on ice. To be effective on the road, nevertheless, in-line speedskating requires slight modifications of the mechanics in several areas. In Holland, a mecca for speedskaters, most serious athletes dabble in both cold- and warm-weather versions of the sport. Ice speedskaters are generally purists in their perspective: they adhere strictly to traditional technique. This protectionism, their mentality of preserving traditions, likely infiltrated slowly into other European nations where speedskating was popular.

In North America and most of the world, modern in-line racing takes its roots from four-wheel "quad" roller skating. Its racing athletes realized that in-lines were more versatile and faster. At the 1992 World Championships in Venice, Italy, in-line athletes dominated all events. The following year at the World Championships in Colorado Springs, almost all skaters had made the transition to five-wheeled in-lines. They were simply superior.

With the transition to in-lines in full gear, athletes strove to improve the sport's technical elements. Since four-wheel "quad" technique proved poor for in-line skating, athletes soon developed a style that closely mirrored that of the ice skaters. After all, ice speedskating is a time-honored sport whose athletes have long sought perfection, prowess, efficiency, and aesthetic beauty. Surely, years of practice, coaching, and development on the ice had developed a technique close to perfection.

The mechanics of in-line speedskating are quickly changing as this evolution changes the face of skating from its classic, ice-oriented technique to a superior method of skating called the *double-push technique*. Although science has not yet validated more recent theories, the ideas are founded on logical, proven mechanical principles and known processes of performance physiology.

1993

At the 1993 Junior North American Championships in Cambridge, Ontario, Canadian spectators unknowingly witnessed the beginning of a new technical era. The Canadians, taught to skate very "ice-like," watched in awe as teenage sensation Chad Hedrick of the U.S. demonstrated a radically different technique. His method was not only bizarre, but also went against all the basics of classical speedskating technique. Hedrick's new style was immediately given such descriptive names as "the scissors," "the crisscross," or simply "the Chad." See figure 1.11.

1994-1995

At the 1994 World Championships in France, Chad dominated the field not only with his seemingly effortless and graceful power, but also with his unique style. Within

© Bob Justice/Mach Five Sports

1.11 Chad Hedrick—the best double-push skater in the world.

seven months, at the 1995 Pan American Games in Argentina, most of the top skaters had already adopted, or perhaps copied, this technique. Skaters who were placing middle-of-the-pack the previous year now were vying for medals because of the double-push.

Present

Chad Hedrick continues to dominate the domestic and international racing scenes. Almost all top male skaters in the United States and abroad now skate using the double-push. However, female skaters have yet to adopt the double-push to the same degree as male skaters. Who first "invented" the double-push remains a topic of debate, but assigning that credit is irrelevant to this discussion. There is no question that Chad introduced this technique to the world, and he is largely responsible for the recent wave of athletes trying desperately to learn it.

Transforming a dynamic, complex movement pattern like speedskating into written words is a vexing task. A photo may be worth a thousand words, but it can depict only a static instant at a single point, and speedskating is a fluid motion. The photos included here have been taken to best illustrate and supplement verbal descriptions of specific points in the movement. Nevertheless, this technique may remain difficult to conceptualize.

Speedskating is about power output and how efficiently power can be applied through technique. But traditional technique often has limits in its application. Ice skaters execute whatever effective biomechanical events can be performed within the potential of the blade on ice. With wheels, however, the limits of possibility are much broader. Classic ice speedskating technique, which involves pushing and gliding from a relatively static position, is not the most effective technique on wheels. Switching to the double-push can, *and will*, directly improve speed, efficiency, and performance.

THE DOUBLE-PUSH MOVEMENT PATTERN

This technique involves two pushes instead of one. Although both actions are not pushes by definition, this technique allows a skater to apply external power in two ways. As in classic technique, power is applied during the normal pushing phase of the movement. The double-push is superior because supplementary propulsive force is applied during what is normally a static glide period.

Part of what makes the double-push a difficult technique to describe is the fact that the typical classic technique stages of push, glide, and recovery involve more overlap. During the double-push, there is much more going on simultaneously. A description of the double-push is further complicated by the fact that traditional terms such as "glide leg" take on new meaning because the glide leg is supporting the body *and* pulling inward toward the body. Because of this, the "glide leg" is hereby referred to as the pulling/support leg. Regardless of the increased complexity of this technique, a similar process of phasic breakdown is valuable for analyzing the movement pattern. However, it must be remembered that these are not stages that follow in discrete and independent sequence, but simultaneous actions which form a complex pattern of movement. The double-push is best described using the following phases:

- Push
- Set-Down
- Pull (i.e., Glide)
- Recovery

Push

With the double-push, the sideward extension of the push leg progresses in much the same manner as it does with conventional technique. However, the pulling motion of the support leg during the glide (described further later) results in a push that is initiated from a more inward position (i.e., closer to or across the midline of the body). This constitutes one of the main advantages of the double-push technique: starting the push from this more inward position effectively maximizes one's push displacement without necessitating a painfully low knee bend. This may sound confusing at first, and this is one of the problems inherent in discussing the technique. Since double-push becomes so complex when diluted into mere words, it is difficult to ascribe a logical starting point to begin the discussion.

Set-Down

After many years of trying to learn the double-push, perfect it, and then teach it to others, it has become apparent that one of the most difficult related skills to acquire is the set-down of the recovery skate. Classic technique involves setting the recovery skate down almost immediately beside and slightly ahead of the support leg skate as the weight transfer occurs. Refer back to figure 1.4.

With the double-push technique, the set-down is slightly delayed, and occurs significantly more to the outside of the body. This component of the movement pattern is so important that the remaining chain of events simply cannot be performed if the set-down is incorrect. Grasping the basic premise of the set-down mechanics is a first step, but applying it is an entirely different and more difficult matter. For this reason, a considerable amount of attention and illustration is dedicated to this phase of the double-push stride. The photo sequence in figure 1.12, a–e illustrates the set-down of the free (recovery) leg from its terminal recovery position beside or behind the support leg to the moment it is set down on the road. Notice that the set-down process occurs simultaneously with the pushing action of the other leg.

Figure 1.12a: The pulling/support leg has reached the farthest point under the midline of the body. Notice that at this point the wheels roll on the outside edge. The free recovery skate is in the final stages of regrouping behind the support leg.

Figure 1.12b: The support leg skate begins to track outward in the early stages of push, yet the wheels have not yet rolled onto the inside edge. In classic technique, the skate set-down would have already occurred almost immediately next to the pushing skate. In double-push skating, however, the recovery skate and center of gravity are moving *away from* the direction of push. The recovery leg's skate is thrown out to the side as the body's weight begins to move away from the pushing leg.

1.12 Double-push technique: the set-down/push phase.

a

b

c

d

e

Figure 1.12c: The support leg begins to accelerate outward into the push as the weight now moves in the opposite direction. Compare the previous frame with this one and notice that the wheels of the push skate have rolled onto the inner edge. The recovery skate continues to move with the body weight away from the direction of push.

Figure 1.12d: At the precise moment that the recovery skate touches the road, notice how the pushing skate is still in contact with the road as it completes its range of motion. The set-down occurs late in double-push skating, compared with classic technique (i.e. the push is almost complete by the time the recovery skate is set down). Because the center of gravity moves laterally with the push leg, almost full body weight is applied to the set-down skate the instant it touches the road. When this occurs, the set-down leg now becomes the support leg. This step is necessary to generate what will become force potential for pulling. Notice the outside angle of the set-down skate wheels.

Figure 1.12e: Now the skate has set down. With the set-down skate angled on the outside wheel edge, the body weight continues to move in the direction of the support leg. The powerful inward pulling action of the support leg can now begin. The skate also turns slightly inward toward the body to help generate pulling force and initiate the leg's inward motion. From observing the position of the hips and shoulders, it is apparent that full body weight is being applied to the pulling/support-leg skate. The continuing movement of the body weight (toward the support leg side) facilitates the force production of the pulling/support leg. In the short time between 1.12d and 1.12e (the last instant of push-off), both skates apply propulsive force, helping to conserve forward momentum. This creates a smoother transition between push and pull, and it dramatically reduces the subtle (but significant) deceleration that occurs during the recovery process of the classic technique.

Recovery

Before we delve into this component of the double-push movement pattern, it is important to note that the recovery of the pushing leg occurs simultaneously with the inward pulling action of the support leg. Overall, the recovery complements the pulling action of the support leg by facilitating balance, stabilizing the hips, and helping to optimize force generation. From a more practical standpoint, this process serves to set up the recovery skate for the next set-down and subsequent pulling action.

As opposed to the circle-around-the-back path of classic technique, the double-push recovery can be referred to as a *snap* recovery. This motion can be seen in figure 1-13, a and b. That is, the skate of the recovery leg is drawn almost directly inward until it reaches a position beside or behind the position of the support leg. This is accomplished by gradually lifting the skate off the road and progressively flexing the knee as the leg returns almost directly inward. This path is preferable to the traditional circle-around-the-back technique because it reduces recovery time. Since an in-line skater decelerates much faster that an ice skater, minimizing glide time (and having a faster stride frequency), is therefore advantageous. The snap recovery promotes a faster stroke cadence and more closely matches the coordination of the pulling support leg.

1.13 Double-push technique: snap recovery.

a

b

Pull (Glide Phase)

Classic speedskating technique involves a static glide. During the glide, the support leg is positioned directly under the body as the skate glides in a banana-shaped, outward arc and the muscles of the hip and leg are engaged in a static (isometric) contraction. The energy generated by these muscles is not used for propulsion; rather it is wasted on supporting the body's weight throughout the glide. These repeated contractions, which lower the mechanical efficiency of the movement and force muscles toward anaerobic metabolism, can prompt early muscle fatigue, and they determine to what extent a skater can use full aerobic capacity (van Ingen Schenau, de Groot, and Hollander 1983).

The static body position used in the classic technique causes velocity to gradually taper until power is again applied in the next push-off. Consider the analogy of paddling a canoe. Each time the paddle is moved through the water, the canoe accelerates. As the paddle is taken out of the water in preparation for the next stroke, the canoe begins to lose speed. Once the paddle is again moved through the water, the canoe will accelerate once again. Figure 1.14, a–c depicts body position in classic speedskating technique. Notice how the glide leg is held in a static position directly under the hip. The knee, nose, and toe all lie in the same vertical plane.

a

1.14 Classic technique: the glide phase.

In sharp contrast, the double-push technique finds a way around the negative impact of the classic technique's isometric contractions by transforming the usual static glide into a more dynamic movement. The inward pulling action of the support leg during the glide phase allows the skater to use some of this "support energy" to generate forward propulsion while also reducing the process of deceleration that naturally occurs during the glide. We now know that the biggest reason the double-push technique is superior to classic technique is that power output can be applied during the entire stride. As a result of the additional propulsive force generated, it is easier to accelerate and easier to maintain velocity by reducing minute fluctuations in speed that would normally occur during a static glide. Using the canoe analogy once again, double-push skating would be like having two paddles where another stroke could be initiated the instant the first paddle finished its movement and exited the water.

Body position must be exact for the pull to be effective. The set-down is crucial in this regard to allow the pull to occur in a smooth and natural fashion. Figure 1.15, a–e depicts changes in body position from the beginning of the set-down to the point where the pulling/support leg finishes its inward motion and makes the transition to push. As can be seen, there is a distinct difference in body position between classic and double-push skating. In the double-push, the support leg comes under the body and across the hip to the midline of the body. This is the main discernible difference between these two techniques.

Figure 1.15a: As the recovery skate sets down on the road (and becomes the support leg), the hip and the body weight continue to move away from the side of the pushing. This is crucial. This step, combined with the outer wheel angle and slight turning-in of the pull-leg skate, initiates the inward motion of the pull leg. The instant the skate begins to track inward, the continuing movement of the center of gravity (away from the push) combines with the active pulling force of the upper leg to generate propulsion. Notice that as the skate is set down, the push leg is finishing its range of motion.

Figure 1.15b: As the push leg reaches full extension, the hip and the body weight continue to move in the opposite direction. The support leg now carries almost all the body weight as the inward pulling action begins to move inward. As the support leg pulls inward, the skate will angle progressively more on its outside edge.

1.15 Double-push technique: pull/recovery phase.

a

b

c

d

e

Figure 1.15c: As the support leg continues to pull inward, the knee of the push leg now begins to flex as it goes through recovery. Notice that an imaginary line drawn from the pulling/support hip to the skate would be about 15-20 degrees from vertical. It is also important to note that as the support leg pulls inward, it begins to thrust forward and extend slightly at the knee so that the body weight is focused on the middle to the rear of the skate.

Figure 1.15d: The support leg has reached its most inward position where it has crossed under the midline and slightly ahead of the body. The recovery skate has been drawn almost directly inward as it approaches a position beside the support leg skate. An imaginary line drawn from the support hip to the skate would now be at its steepest position—about 25-30 degrees. At this point, the center of gravity has ceased to move in the direction of the support leg. If the skater were to hold this posture in a static position, he would topple over. This does not happen, however, because the position of the recovery leg helps offset balance, and the pulling/support leg is only in this position for a brief moment.

Figure 1.15e: Although still on the outside wheel edge, the support leg skate now begins to track outward again as the leg "primes" for the upcoming push. As this occurs, the center of gravity once again begins to move back toward the center of the body (away from the push). The recovery skate reaches its furthest point behind/beside the support leg as it prepares to move laterally with the shift in body weight. The wheels of the support leg skate will not roll over to the inside edge until the skate moves outside of the vertical line drawn down from the (same side) hip. This happens very rapidly because as the support skate moves outward into push, the center of gravity and hips continue to move in the opposite direction with the set-down of the recovery skate.

Style and Technique

Many athletes and coaches mistakenly use the terms *style* and *technique* interchangeably. It is important to this discussion to differentiate between these terms. Technique refers to the raw mechanical components that, when executed, produce the actual movement pattern. Style, on the other hand, refers to an individual's flare or signature, which is added to these basics. Two skaters with equally proficient technique can appear very different in form. It is style that distinguishes one from another.

Extremes

Another concept that is part of discussing technique is *extremes*. This term applies particularly to the double-push technique. Classic speedskating is precise in its application, especially when performed on the ice. The variability of movement possible within the scope of proper form is small. By contrast, the double-push opens a much broader range of possibility. In other words, its movement pattern allows a high degree of variability in performance. This range is an indirect performance advantage of the double-push: it allows a skater to wander among the possible extremes of application. Different situations (e.g., sprints, accelerations, steady tempo) seem to have an optimal set-point within these extremes. In other words, certain technical parameters can be manipulated by the skater to match the demands of the situation. This gives a skater more personal input into the manipulation of mechanical traits of the technique. Put another way, the double-push gives a skater a more diverse and effective arsenal of "gears" or tools to use under various race conditions.

UNLOCKING THE MYSTERY— WHY THE DOUBLE-PUSH IS BETTER

It should now be clear what the double-push is. To develop your own practice of it, it may be helpful to first understand the theoretical reasons explaining why the double-push is superior to classic technique for speedskating on wheels.

Two Pushes Are Better Than One

The great superiority of the double-push is that by using it, positive work can be performed during what is normally a static, energy-inefficient glide phase. The pulling of the inner thigh muscles leverages the outside wheels' edge to help generate propulsion, much as the lateral push produces forward motion using the inside wheels' edge. As a result, the double-push allows a skater to do more total work per stride cycle than does classic technique. See figure 1.16. One might think that the push-pull method would require twice the energy compared with the "single-push" of classic skating. It does not. The double-push simply makes constructive use of the available, contractile glide energy by using it for additional propulsion.

Increased Push Displacement (Stroke Length)

One of the best ways to go fast is to increase *push displacement* (i.e., the distance the skate travels sideways from the beginning to the end of the push). With classic technique, the only way to achieve a longer push displacement is to bend the knees (squat lower). Research shows, however, that such deep knee flexion increases the level of isometric tension in the quadriceps muscles. This tension is a major limiting factor in performance: it temporarily restricts blood flow in the muscles, resulting in a more rapid accumulation of metabolic substances (such as lactic acid) that interfere with the function of the muscle fibers. Deep knee flexion represents a classic catch-22 situation: sitting low is required to achieve a long push, but doing so is taxing and can cause the early onset of local muscle fatigue. The double-push doesn't entirely solve this problem, but it lessens it.

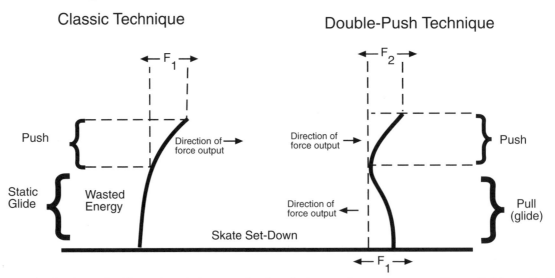

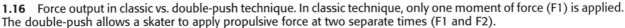

1.16 Force output in classic vs. double-push technique. In classic technique, only one moment of force (F1) is applied. The double-push allows a skater to apply propulsive force at two separate times (F1 and F2).

Allowing the support leg to come under the body and across the midline during the pulling part of the glide allows the push to be initiated from a more inward position. Given the same preextension (preparatory) knee angle, the total push displacement will be increased. Compared with a skater using classic technique, a double-push skater can either sit higher while equaling the push displacement of the classic skater—or can assume the same low knee bend of the classic skater and reach a greater push displacement. Either way, increased mechanical efficiency results, without claim to additional physiologic processes. Instead, a subjective feeling of enormous power results from the noticeable decrease of lactic acid in the muscles.

Reflex Potentiation—Stretch-Shortening Enhancement

A muscle that is quickly elongated due to a stretch or rapid eccentric (lengthening) movement produces a stronger and more powerful concentric (shortening) contraction. This rebound effect likely occurs with the double-push technique because the abductor muscles of the hip are rapidly stretched as the glide leg moves under the body's midline. The action stimulates muscle stretch receptors and gives the following push-off contraction a slight, but significant boost of power. The higher initial force level in the muscles also contributes to force production and increased mechanical efficiency:

- Increased strength and power can be observed with similar effort or energy expenditure.
- Less effort or energy is required to produce the level of force generated by the nonpotentiated push of classic technique.

Because muscles have elastic properties, the inward pulling of the support leg under and across the body takes advantage of the passive resistance developed in the stretched hip muscles. Like a rubber band, the stored energy, an elastic recoil, is released when the push-off begins.

Momentum

With the double-push technique, momentum, too, can be positively used to complement force production, maintain velocity, enhance efficiency, and save energy. Whereas classic technique involves pushing from an almost static position, the double-push allows a skater to use momentum from the legs to enhance push-off force. Rather than use a great deal of energy to initiate a push from a static glide, the continuous motion of the support leg and its transition from push to pull means that less energy is required to initiate movement. The recovery process of the free leg also helps conserve momentum and complements pushing force by being thrown away from the body as the push progresses.

Gear Selection

Without doubt, there are a great deal more skaters using the double-push today than there were only a year ago. However, the number of skaters who do it well and are able to extract the full potential this technique has to offer is still very small. Many skaters can execute *some* of the characteristics of double-push skating while at a moderate, steady speed. However, these same skaters have not yet developed the "full-blown" version: the ability to take advantage of the diverse range of movement possible, and to accelerate in an effortless and efficient manner unfathomable to a classic skater.

Classic technique, on the other hand, is very precise in its execution, and allows very little room for an individual to alter or customize technique. The only functional variables a classic skater can manipulate in order to adapt to different situations are knee bend and stride frequency. The double-push offers a skater greater means of altering technique to match each specific situation. In effect, the skater using the double-push has more "gears" available. By altering numerous technical parameters, the double-push skater can experiment until the right combination of elements creates a comfortable and customized style.

One of the profound advantages of the double-push is the economy of motion available during situations of mild to intense acceleration. One of the more interesting aspects of the double-push is the transition in movement dynamics from a steady speed to full-blown acceleration, and the actual changes in stroke mechanics that take place. With classic technique, all a skater can do is lower the knee bend and increase stride tempo. By contrast, several things happen during acceleration in double-push skating (see figure 1.17, a and b):

- The knee bend of both legs (i.e., push leg and pulling/support leg) deepens.
- The pulling/support leg crosses further toward or under the body's midline.
- There is a more noticeable forward thrust of the leg and extension (straightening) of the knee once the pulling/support leg reaches the furthest point inward.
- The skate is set down further to the outside of the body, providing more leverage for "pulling".
- Stride tempo increases.
- The amount of lateral upper body movement increases to contribute to, and enhance, the action of the legs.
- Both arms swing to complement push-off force and increase stability.

Maintenance of Velocity

If we look at the small fluctuations in velocity that occur during continuous cycles of the classic speedskating stride, we find a predictable and repeating pattern. Each time a skater pushes, there is a small, momentary acceleration with peak velocity reached soon after. During the glide phase and regrouping of the push leg, a small but visually discrete decrease in speed occurs. After all, during the glide phase of classic skating, no power is being applied through push-off—and, therefore, no propulsion. Surface friction and air resistance would both subtly scrub off speed. Velocity continues to fall until the next stride. Looking at the relationship between time and velocity on a fine scale, we discover a repetitive sinusoidal (S-shaped) pattern.

With the double-push, this pattern is markedly different. Because propulsive forces are generated and applied during the entire stride cycle, much less fluctuation exists in velocity. The amplitude of the velocity-time relation is smaller, but the oscillations are probably faster, indicating a more regular application of external force.

The implication of these fluctuations and patterns is that the double-push technique maintains speed better throughout the course of the stride's repeated cycles. Logically, this gives an individual skater a wider range over which to fine-tune power output and, therefore, speed. Because in-line racing is a pack sport that requires frequent, repeated small adjustments in speed, improved control and maintenance of velocity are favorable outcomes of technique. Although this fact likely plays a minor role in defining the superiority of the double-push, combined with other advantages, the overall effect is considerable.

1.17a Double-push technique: because of extremes of motion during acceleration, the recovery skate is set down further away from the midline.

1.17b Double-push technique: the range of "pull" by the support leg increases.

DOES THE DOUBLE-PUSH WORK ON ICE?

One might question why, the double-push technique being a superior way to skate, ice speedskaters didn't discover it a long time ago. The answer is that for various reasons true double-push skating just does not work on ice. Ice blades are hard, thin strips of steel that allow only a few inches of surface contact. Their placement on the ice must be extremely precise because they are sharpened to have a square profile on the bottom. The outer edge is used for maintaining traction and control during the glide, and the inner edge for pushing off. By contrast, wheels are forgiving and allow a broader scope of application. Their elliptical profile provides an entirely different surface contact: they deform easily, and they are wider and more stable. As a wheel rolls from side to side, the mechanics related to pressure points on the wheel also change. These structural points, combined with the fact that an in-line racing skate provides five separate areas of surface contact, likely explains why the double-push will work on wheels but not on ice.

CHAPTER

2

Ice Speedskating Technique

For many reasons, the technique for ice speedskating is much more precise than for in-line speedskating. Wheels are considerably more forgiving than a blade, and they provide a much broader range of possibility in the movement pattern. On in-lines, small discrepancies in application easily go unnoticed and usually don't disturb the perceived effectiveness, even of more important technical parameters. Conversely, on ice skates, even minute technical infractions lead to inefficient motion. Such nuances are more easily recognized because they affect sensory perception and decrease the effectiveness of movement.

Although the technique described in chapter 1 closely reflects the mechanics that produce efficient ice speedskating technique, there are some important differences between the techniques for in-line and ice speedskating. For skaters who dabble in both warm- and cold-weather versions of the sport, understanding these differences is imperative for achieving technical proficiency in both sport forms. This chapter summarizes the similarities between ice and in-line technique and outlines the necessary modifications to make to skate successfully on ice.

Despite some amazing similarities, ice and in-line speedskating are distinct forms of the sport. To aid comprehension and allow for direct comparison with the discussion in chapter 1, we will break down the movement pattern into the phases of establishing basic body position, push-off, glide, weight transfer, and recovery mechanics. For each aspect, the discussion will highlight differences in technique and what is necessary for ice speedskating.

BASIC BODY POSITION ON ICE— THE TEN COMMANDMENTS

As with in-line technique, the components of basic body position are the foundation for further developmental aspects of speedskating technique. See figures 2.1a and 2.1b for an illustration of the basic body position. The basic position defines the important joint angles and issues of upper-body alignment that must be maintained during the speedskating stride. Many errors in the skating motion can be traced back to small but discernible discrepancies in basic body position. Here are the important points of basic body position for speedskating on ice:

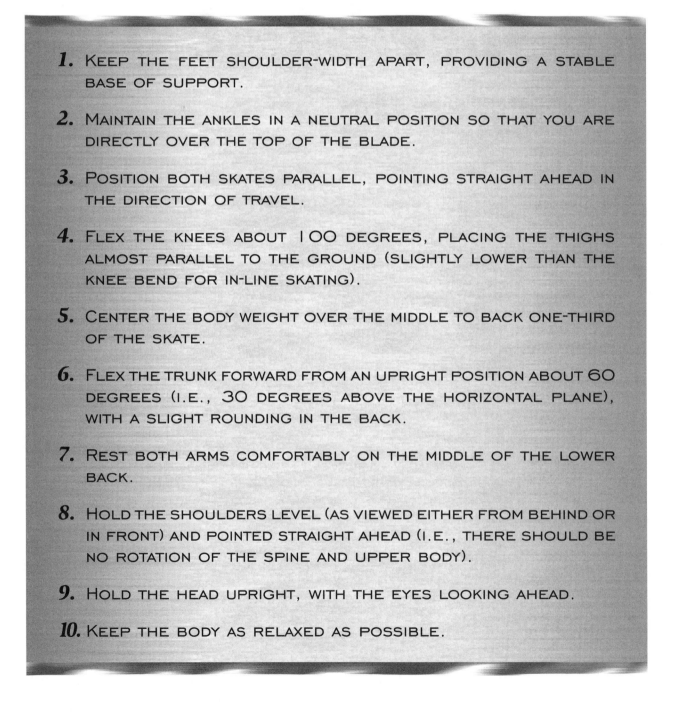

1. KEEP THE FEET SHOULDER-WIDTH APART, PROVIDING A STABLE BASE OF SUPPORT.

2. MAINTAIN THE ANKLES IN A NEUTRAL POSITION SO THAT YOU ARE DIRECTLY OVER THE TOP OF THE BLADE.

3. POSITION BOTH SKATES PARALLEL, POINTING STRAIGHT AHEAD IN THE DIRECTION OF TRAVEL.

4. FLEX THE KNEES ABOUT 100 DEGREES, PLACING THE THIGHS ALMOST PARALLEL TO THE GROUND (SLIGHTLY LOWER THAN THE KNEE BEND FOR IN-LINE SKATING).

5. CENTER THE BODY WEIGHT OVER THE MIDDLE TO BACK ONE-THIRD OF THE SKATE.

6. FLEX THE TRUNK FORWARD FROM AN UPRIGHT POSITION ABOUT 60 DEGREES (I.E., 30 DEGREES ABOVE THE HORIZONTAL PLANE), WITH A SLIGHT ROUNDING IN THE BACK.

7. REST BOTH ARMS COMFORTABLY ON THE MIDDLE OF THE LOWER BACK.

8. HOLD THE SHOULDERS LEVEL (AS VIEWED EITHER FROM BEHIND OR IN FRONT) AND POINTED STRAIGHT AHEAD (I.E., THERE SHOULD BE NO ROTATION OF THE SPINE AND UPPER BODY).

9. HOLD THE HEAD UPRIGHT, WITH THE EYES LOOKING AHEAD.

10. KEEP THE BODY AS RELAXED AS POSSIBLE.

2.1a Basic position from the front.

2.1b Basic position from the side.

PUSH-OFF

As with in-line speedskating, the push-off phase is characterized by a smooth and powerful accelerated push, exhibiting a snap of power at the end of the extension. The biomechanics of push-off during ice speedskating, however, demonstrate some of the key differences between the application of ice and in-line technique.

Knee Angle Prior to Extension

Ice skaters demonstrate a smaller preextension knee angle, in general, compared with in-line skaters: that is, a *deeper* knee bend. The lower knee bend and more deeply seated position affect the location of the center of gravity over the skate. Thus, the point of application of push-off forces differs between ice and in-line skating (de Boer, Vos, Hutter, de Groot, and van Ingen Schenau 1987b). Since the lower body position of the ice skater moves the center of gravity toward the rear of the blade, athletes who participate in both forms of speedskating must realize the effect that body position has on determining push-off force. Figures 2.2a and 2.2b illustrate the typical difference in body position between an in-line skater and an ice skater, and the resulting effect on the vertical line of gravity.

a

b

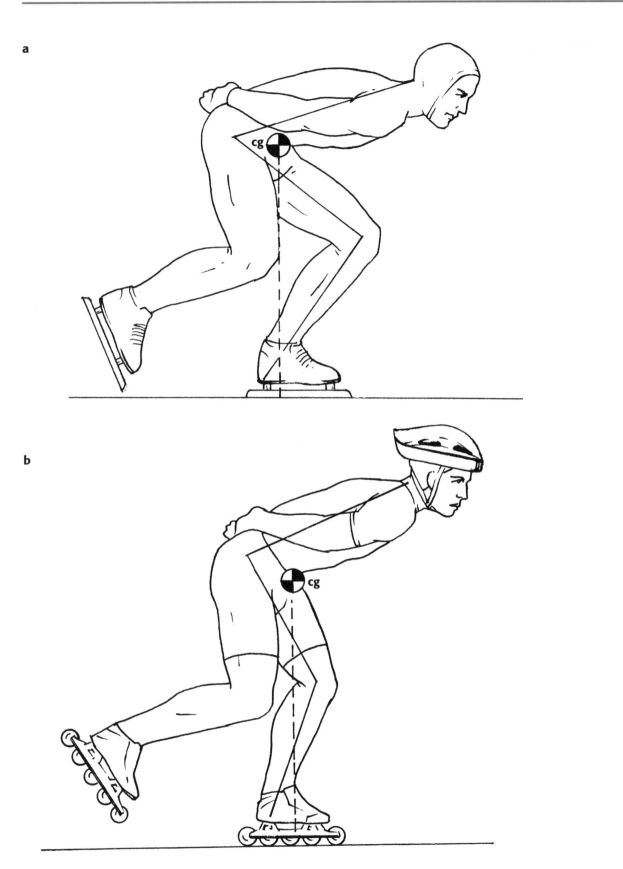

2.2 In ice skating *(a)*, the center of gravity (cg) should intersect the rear one-third of the skate. With in-line skating *(b)*, the more upright body position shifts this position forward slightly to roughly the middle of the skate.

2.3 The mean skating positions at different metric (long track) distances. In the 500m race *(a)*, the trunk is more vertical than any other distance. The thigh is held more vertical at longer distances *(b)* 1,500m, *(c)* 5,000m, (d) 10,000m.

Adapted, with permission, from G. van Ingen Schenau and K. Bakker, 1980, "A biomechanical model of speedskating," *Journal of Human Movement Studies* 6:12.

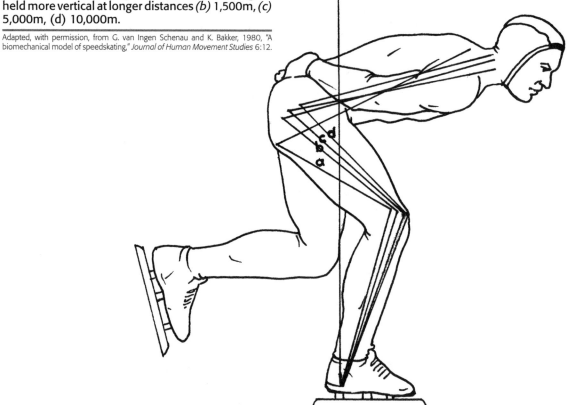

A deeper knee angle among ice skaters has a second major impact: it affects push displacement. Ice skaters tend to sit lower, resulting in a greater push displacement. This difference can be attributed in part to the fact that a metric ice race involves relatively shorter distances than does a typical in-line race. Since there is a direct correlation between one's knee angle and the distance one skates (lower knee bend for sprints; less bend or higher for distance races), this greater sideways displacement among ice skaters is not surprising. However, over identical distances ice skaters usually display a deeper knee bend than in-liners do. Van Ingen Schenau and Bakker (1980) concluded that there is a significant difference in body position in various metric long-track distances (see their results, which are graphically depicted in figure 2.3).

Direction of Push

With both ice and in-line speedskating techniques, the emphasis is on executing the push directly to the side. Surface friction is experienced differently on ice and asphalt, however, so the direction of push also varies between the two sport forms. With in-line skating, the sideward push begins to travel slightly rearward as the push progresses, partly because of velocity and partly because of frictional forces. On ice speedskates, the push-off should continue in a *more sideward trajectory throughout* the entire range of motion. In this way, the blade tip of the pushing skate should be only an inch or two behind the tip of the support leg's blade.

Stride Frequency

At any given velocity, stride frequency in ice skating is slower than in in-line skating. The low coefficient of friction of a blade with ice means that the degree of deceleration during gliding is minimal compared with wheels on asphalt. (In-line skaters therefore use a higher stroke cadence to overcome the higher frictional forces.) Ice skaters control velocity primarily through changes in stride frequency.

Push Specifics on Ice

Here are some key points to remember concerning the mechanics of the push-off for speedskating on ice.

- As the push-off leg extends, body weight and the center of gravity itself progressively move over the support leg.
- Once the weight has been transferred and the push progresses, maintain the support leg in a deeply bent position of about 100 degrees.
- Keep the shoulders the same as in the basic position (with no rotation).
- Keep the upper body as relaxed as possible, maintained in correct alignment (as described in the basic position).
- Hold the head upright, with the eyes focused straight ahead.
- Do not allow the hips and trunk to bob up and down. The center of gravity should be displaced only in a horizontal direction at the beginning of force application (as the weight transfer occurs).
- The push-off should occur in an accelerated fashion, with most of the muscular force developed during the first one-third of the extension.

GLIDE

Although the glide phase in ice skating is essentially static, key differences distinguish it in execution from the in-line glide. These relate to the amount of time spent on the support leg and the orientation of the blade on the ice.

Glide Time

Speedskating on ice involves a significantly longer glide phase than on wheels. Here the dramatic difference comes to play in the frictional forces from blade to ice, compared with from wheels to asphalt. Research has determined that on wheels some 45 percent of the generated power is lost to friction. On ice, the reduced level of friction produces a loss of only 18 percent of the power output (Kandou et al. 1987). Take advantage of these savings on ice by making gliding time optimal. Naturally, at a certain point a prolonged glide can detract from overall efficiency. Practice and experimenting usually will lead to developing an effective push–glide time relation that will maximize the value of your glide.

Edge Control

One of the greatest differences between ice and in-line speedskating is that edge control on ice must be extremely precise. On wheels there are no clearly defined

2.4 Early in the glide, the outside edge of the blade is used to grip the ice surface.

edges, merely a parabolic surface on which to push off and glide. On ice, on the other hand, the skater's blade is very thin and has a flat bottom and two sharp edges. Applying the optimal amount of pressure to either part of the blade at the right moment is crucial for achieving technical efficiency.

Through most of the glide phase, an ice skater appears to be riding on the flat part of the blade. Certainly, this area would present the least resistance to forward motion. However, the flat part of the blade has no edges to grip the ice, maintain glide trajectory, or provide control over the movement. The fact is that all parts of the blade are used at different times in the glide.

Early on in the glide phase, the blade of the support leg skate must be angled slightly to the outside so that the outer edge grips the ice (figure 2.4). As the free leg begins its recovery action, pressure is slowly released from the outside edge. During this, the skater's body weight shifts more toward the midline and the blade temporarily glides flat. This is ideal because resistance is lowest, but this state makes the blade difficult to control. The transition to the inside edge continues until the regrouping of the leg is nearly completed and the weight transfer has been initiated. At this instant, the blade rolls over, so that pushing force can be concentrated on the inner edge of the blade. The timing of these events is critical for optimizing glide time and maintaining control and stability.

STROKE RECOVERY

The transition from push-off to stroke recovery begins as soon as the pushing leg reaches full extension to the side. The mechanics of good stroke recovery on ice are essentially identical as for in-line technique (see chapter 1). The only significant difference with ice speedskating technique is that it requires greater precision.

Skate Lift-Off

Once the push leg reaches full extension, the skater initiates the recovery process by lifting the skate gently off the ice, with the blade remaining parallel to the surface and pointed directly ahead (see figure 2.5). Absolutely no toe flick should occur at the end of the motion. The most common error with skate lift-off is *toe flick*, a combination of external rotation of the leg or ankle (or both) and plantar flexion (pointing the

2.5 To initiate the recovery, the blade should lift off parallel to the ice. On klap skates, the blade will abruptly snap back toward the boot as it is lifted off the ice.

toes). This error usually results from incorrect body position, which places the center of gravity too far forward on the blade.

Remember these important points about the ice skate lift-off and recovery. Figure 2.6, a–c illustrates lift-off and recovery mechanics.

- To execute the recovery smoothly, all of the weight must be carried by the support leg at the end of the push (2.6a).
- The skate should be kept as low to the ice as possible during the entire recovery process.
- The upper and lower leg should move together as a unit. As the leg begins to circle around the back, the knee progressively flexes (2.6b) to the point where it may be pointing directly downward.
- The toe should lead the semicircular path that the skate follows. It is permissible, even advisable, to *turn the toe of the skate inward slightly* as the recovery proceeds (2.6c).
- As the skate finishes its push and lifts off the ice, you should hear very little sound. A raspy or scratching sound usually indicates that the body weight is focused too far forward on the skate blade.

2.6 Stroke recovery: the upper and lower leg should move together as one unit.

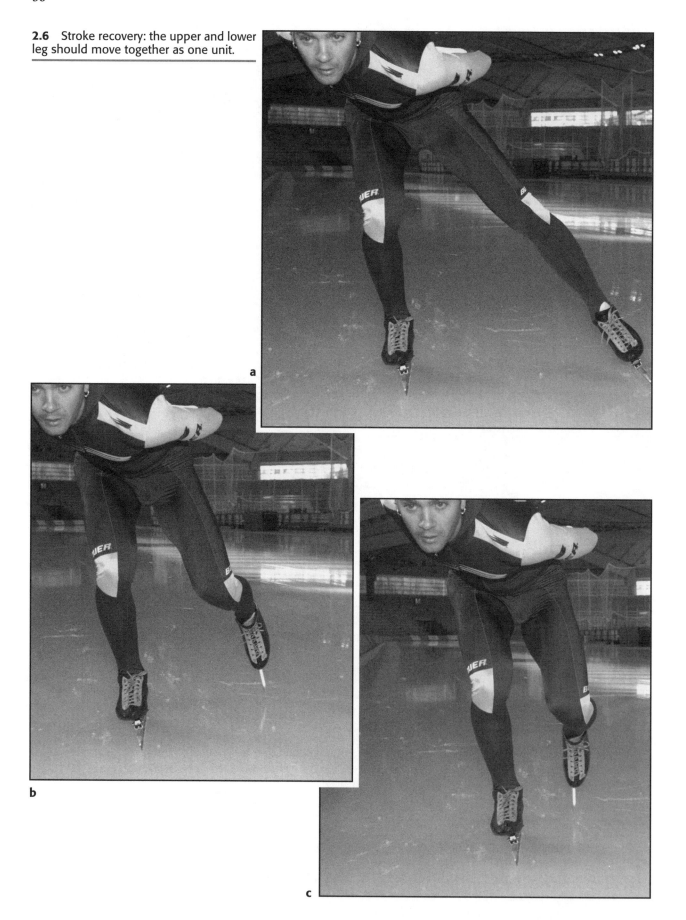

a

b

c

Set-Down

As the skate completes the semicircle around the back, the recovery leg is actively driven forward under the hips in preparation for the blade's set-down. The blade of the recovery skate should be set down a few inches ahead of the support leg's blade. This helps ensure that the back half of the blade contacts the ice first, keeping the center of gravity toward the rear of the skate. Equally important, the blade should be set down methodically so that its outside edge can grip the surface of the ice. You can help ensure this action, facilitated by the weight transfer, by placing the blade down with the *ankle turned slightly outward*. Set-down mechanics are shown in figure 2.7, a–c.

- The recovery phase is the only time to momentarily restore blood flow in the muscles to near-normal levels. Make sure that muscle tension dissipates as the leg regroups!
- The recovery process should be a single, uninterrupted motion—a continuous extension of the push-off phase.

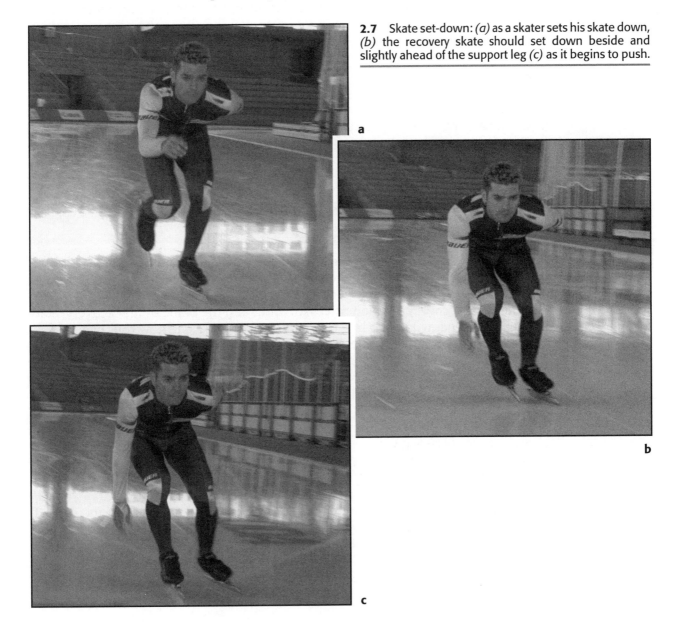

2.7 Skate set-down: *(a)* as a skater sets his skate down, *(b)* the recovery skate should set down beside and slightly ahead of the support leg *(c)* as it begins to push.

WEIGHT TRANSFER

The weight transfer supplements force generated on the inside edge of the blade during push-off. It minimizes the muscular effort needed to generate propulsion. A transitory process, the transfer of body weight links the recovery and pushing phases of the speedskating stride. The weight transfers for ice skating and for classically oriented in-line technique are virtually identical. In ice skating, however, the lateral shift in the center of gravity is more accentuated and defined. This phase of ice technique presents several important aspects to understand.

Glide

During the glide, the free leg goes through an active recovery and regrouping process. The blade of the support leg is very slightly angled to the outside early in the glide phase (see figure 2.8a). During the entire glide, the body's weight must be carried by the support leg in order to optimize gliding time and conserve forward momentum. A skater who glides on the inside blade edge may not have the center of gravity positioned completely over the support leg.

Blade Roll

As the recovery leg begins to move under the body, the skater's balance begins to shift away from the support leg and back toward the midline of the body. As this shift occurs, the center of gravity also begins to move back in this midline direction, and this slight shift causes the blade to begin rolling inward to actually glide on the flat section. This condition should be maintained for as long as possible (see figure 2.8b).

Force Initialization

You now reach the critical point: the hip and center of balance continue to "fall" over the midline toward the side of the recovery leg. As they shift, the hips and shoulders may dip slightly toward the recovery side, but you must avoid any lateral flexion of the trunk. The recovery leg then drives forward, and the blade of the recovery skate is about to be set down on the ice. The blade of the glide skate now rolls over, so that pressure is applied on the inside edge. As the set-down occurs, the glide leg begins to accelerate into push-off. During the first instant of push-off, the recovery leg finishes regrouping and is set down next to the push leg, very slightly on its outside edge. A line drawn down from the center of gravity actually would briefly lie inside both legs (see figure 2.8c).

   The weight transfer is difficult to master because its timing must be exact. If the weight transfer occurs *too early,* the recovery leg may not have had sufficient time to regroup and the center of gravity may fall inward prematurely. Since the weight transfer helps minimize the efforts of the push-off muscles, more force would then be required to get a strong extension. In addition, an early weight transfer will decrease glide time by causing the blade to roll over to the inside edge too early. If the weight transfer occurs *too late,* on the other hand, a skater misses the optimal time when lateral momentum can enhance push-off force. Excessive time would thus be spent on the inside edge of the blade, limiting glide time and ultimately reducing speed. Speedskating is all about efficiency, and the timing of the weight transfer is vital for efficient technique.

2.8 Glide mechanics on ice: *(a)* outside edge grips the ice; *(b)* the blade glides flat as long as possible; *(c)* at the beginning of force application both skates lie inside the vertical line of gravity.

Hip Stability

During the entire speedskating movement pattern, adequate muscular strength is required to maintain integrity in the hip and trunk area. Without it, much of the pushing energy is disbursed through the needless absorbing effect of hip motion. A skater with insufficient hip strength demonstrates a dipping of the hip to the same side as the pushing leg (see chapter 1, figure 1.7). Fortunately, instruction, practice, and strengthening of the trunk's musculature can remedy this type of technical misalignment.

During ice skating, absolutely no vertical displacement of the pelvis should occur as the push is initiated. The weight transfer should occur simultaneously with the onset of pushing force, and it should not disrupt body alignment. On in-line skates, elevating the center of gravity slightly can actually be effective by increasing kinetic energy during the weight transfer. In ice, however, such a movement can grossly disturb the execution of the push-off and rolling action of the blade on the ice surface. Avoid any such elevation of the hips during the stride!

CROSSOVER STEPS

Skaters use crossover steps to take the shortest route through a corner, counteract the centrifugal force that pushes the body away from the center of the curve, and build speed and acceleration through a turn. Lacking skill or confidence with respect to turn technique poses a huge liability to performance. Without proficient turns, a skater exits the corner with significantly lower velocity than he or she entered it. Such a skater would have to expend considerable energy on the straightaway in order to accelerate again. It is much better to build speed through the corner, so that exit velocity is equal to or greater than entry speed. This way, the skater can relax somewhat during the straightaway, striving mainly to minimize deceleration before the next turn.

Good technique for a turn differs markedly from the mechanics of a straightaway. Confidence in your ability is imperative for practicing the crossover stroke. Tension often leads to inhibition. Inhibition then leads you to hold back, creating hesitant and jerky movements. Developing fluid, smooth crossovers will take much time and practice. This next section outlines the important aspects of body position, turn mechanics, and principles of execution. Note that the discussion assumes a *counterclockwise* (left-hand) turn.

CENTRIFUGAL FORCE AND ROTARY MOTION

Just as certain laws of physics govern the straight, linear motion of an object, other laws of motion dictate the forces that act on an object traveling through an arc. It is not essential to understand these principles in depth, but a general overview of the laws of rotary motion will help you comprehend the reasoning behind certain aspects of turn mechanics.

A common and simple analogy to describe principles of rotary motion is a bicycle wheel. While the hub acts as the center of rotation, the spokes represent imaginary lines of direction (vectors) upon which centrifugal force acts. These lines of centrifugal force project directly outward from the axis in all directions (see figure 2.9). As the wheel spins progressively faster, centrifugal force becomes increasingly greater. What makes this interesting is that the centrifugal force becomes greater the farther one moves from the center of the wheel.

This analogy of a bicycle wheel to centrifugal force has several implications. To maintain control through a turn, a skater must be able to counteract and directly oppose the vector that represents centrifugal force. In fact, acceleration through a turn can only be achieved if the skater's power output is significantly greater than the centrifugal force. The skater must apply a counteracting force that is equal to or greater in magnitude than—and opposite in direction to—that of the centrifugal force.

Using effective crossover technique allows a skater to exit a turn with more velocity than the speed at which the skater enters the turn. Consider as an example a skater entering a turn at 30 kilometers per hour (kmh; 18 miles per hour). Once the turn begins, centrifugal force acts to push the skater outward from the center. To navigate through the radius, the skater must directly counter this centrifugal force. That is, to maintain the initial velocity of 30 kmh, the skater must apply more power than was needed to

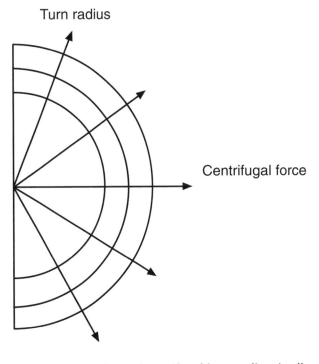

Turn radius

Centrifugal force

2.9 Imaginary lines of centrifugal force radiate in all directions from the turn center.

maintain this same velocity in the straight. On exiting the turn, however, the trajectory of the skater gradually straightens out, bringing a rather sudden dissipation of centrifugal force. The outward drag experienced in the turn is released, and this slingshot effect results in the skater being accelerated out of the turn with a noticeable increase in velocity (provided that power output remains high). The skater can then either relax momentarily so that velocity once again diminishes to 30 kmh or can effectively use this acceleration to increase race speed. In short-track, racing solid crossover technique can thus prove to be a valuable means of implementing strategy and applying tactics.

UPPER-BODY POSITION IN TURN MECHANICS

Although the powerful lower body essentially generates all the power output in the turn, the *position of the upper body* is vital to ensure that the mechanics of the legs are effective. Even slight misalignments in the upper body can adversely and dramatically affect the efficiency of the crossover steps. In this respect, the upper body is the primary stabilizer and guide for all actions of the lower limbs. Correct upper-body posture is illustrated in figure 2.10.

Head

The position of the head is actually quite significant because its alignment tends to lead the rest of the upper body. Throughout the corner, it is important that the head aims in the direction of the turn with no vertical displacement. Up-and-down motion of the head usually indicates improper execution of lower-body mechanics.

There should be little or no lateral flexion in the neck, and no rotation in it. Since the head usually positions itself according to the focal point of vision, it is important to look ahead about 10 meters (33 feet), rather than down at the feet or at the exit of the turn.

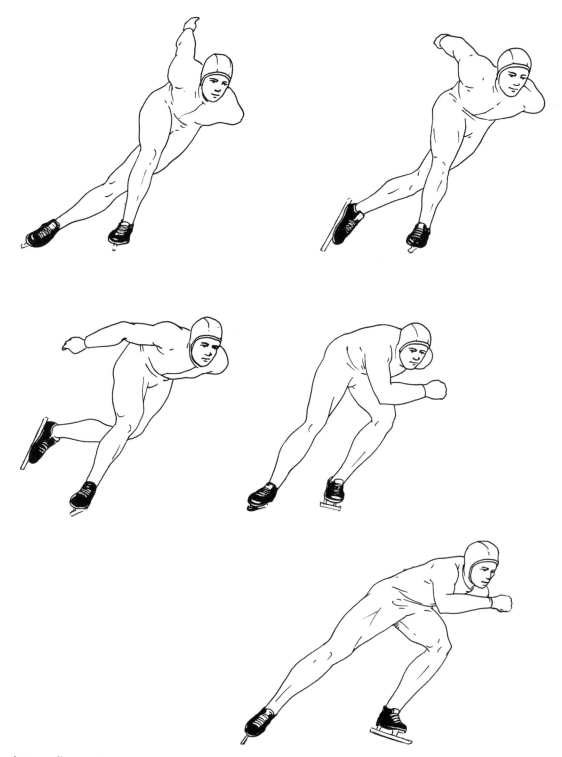

2.10 Upper-body turn alignment.

Shoulders

Of all aspects of upper-body alignment, that of the shoulders is undoubtedly the most important. Like the head, the shoulders should not experience up-and-down bobbing as the legs move through their steps. Rather, the shoulders should be maintained in a position parallel to the hips with absolutely no rotation. Rotating the shoulders in the turn is likely the most common upper-body misalignment, and it can have devastating effects on stroke efficiency. The most common problem is rotating the shoulders (and therefore the trunk) inward. Not only does this destabilize the hip area, responsible for providing a solid platform for the lower body, but it also results in a more rearward angle of push through the turn. Rotating the shoulders decreases force and the ability to counteract the effects of centrifugal force. This technical error is depicted in figure 2.11.

To maximize power and control, the shoulders should be in line with the pull of centrifugal force. Neither shoulder should drop from your flexing the trunk laterally—the shoulders should

2.11 Rotating the shoulders during crossover steps has devastating effects on mechanics.

be kept parallel with the hips. Depending on the turn velocity, and therefore the amount of angle as you lean into the turn, the inside shoulder may be slightly lower. It is okay if the lowered positioning results from body lean—and not from sideways flexion of the trunk.

Trunk

Although the trunk should have no rotation or lateral flexion, it must be sufficiently flexed forward, as in the straightaways. Usually this means flexing forward about 60 degrees from the upright position. This flexion helps reduce frontal surface area and resistive drag, keeps the center of gravity positioned toward the back of the skate, and provides a more stable upper-body mass for pushing leverage.

LOWER-BODY POSITION IN TURN MECHANICS

Although a proper upper-body alignment is crucial for the legs to function effectively, it is the legs themselves that ultimately apply power to the ice. Granted, errors in upper-body position can be detrimental to crossover performance, but it is safe to say that equivalent discrepancies in the lower body are still more devastating.

The lower body essentially consists of the hip joint and legs. Each leg has its specific actions in executing turns, and therefore deserves separate discussion.

Hips

Although the legs do most of the work of applying force through push-off in the turns, the hips also play an integral role in effectively transmitting energy to the ice. Quite often, the hips' position will be correct if the upper body's position is. Basically, all the principles that apply to the upper body also apply to the hips: they should

- remain stable with no vertical displacement,
- experience no rotation, and
- be maintained in a line parallel to the direction of centrifugal force.

During the crossover steps, the height of the hip joint is essentially determined by the maximal angle in the knee joints as they go through their steps. In general, this angle should be about the same as it is in the straights: 100 to 110 degrees. A lower angle allows both legs greater sideways push displacement, and it may be necessary for building maximal acceleration through the turn.

In pack skating, the group sometimes experiences congestion in the turn, resulting in a lowering velocity through the first half of the corner. In this situation, it may be appropriate to slightly elevate the knee joint (and, therefore, the height of the hips). Doing so shortens lateral push displacement, but the greater hip height often makes crossover steps safer by lessening the chance of mixing your skates with your competitor's.

When the pack proceeds through the second half of the turn, the skaters who lead the group often accelerate. This causes a "slinky effect" where the skaters at the back are forced to speed up even more if they are to maintain contact with the skater(s) ahead. In this situation, knee bend will once again have to deepen in order to generate the necessary power to accelerate.

Right-Leg Mechanics

During the crossover, the mechanics of the right leg in many ways are simpler than those of the left leg. Virtually all aspects of the push-off are the same as those of the straightaway technique. The primary difference lies in the execution of the recovery once the right leg has finished its lateral push.

Push

The right leg's push begins immediately, once the left leg has finished its sideward push under the body and begins to lift off for stroke recovery. Just as it does during the straight stroke technique, the right leg begins its force initialization and push-off for a turn from a position directly under the body. The push begins as pressure is applied on the inside edge of the blade, and it continues outward until full extension of the knee and hip occurs. The precise amount of lateral displacement depends exclusively on the knee's preextension angle when the push begins.

Direction is undoubtedly the most important aspect of the right leg's push. It is vital that the extension of the right leg travel along an imaginary line of centrifugal force extending out from the center of the turn. For this to occur smoothly, your body must be positioned so that push-off force originates from the middle to the back half of the skate. The lateral push should be an *accelerated* motion. The simultaneous extension of the hip and knee should experience a continuous increase in velocity as the push-off progresses. In this way, the end of the push will demonstrate a definite "snap" of power. The extended push of the right leg is shown in figure 2.12a.

Lift-Off

The skate lift-off in a turn is essentially identical to that of the straightaway. Once the leg has reached maximal extension to the side, the skate is gently lifted off the ice

a

b

2.12 Crossover steps: *(a)* right leg in full extension; *(b)* the skates pass close to each other as the left leg pushes through under the body.

while the blade is maintained in a horizontal position to the surface. The skate should never be more than a few inches off the ice!

Recovery

Once the skate no longer contacts the ice, it must begin its recovery motion to prepare for the next cycle. The recovery action of the right leg primarily combines hip adduction (moving the leg *toward* the midline of the body), knee flexion, and a marginal degree of hip flexion (sufficient to allow clearance of the left skate). These joint motions do not occur in sequence; rather, they combine to bring the right skate around in front of the left leg skate as it begins to push through under the body.

The most important aspect of the right leg's recovery is relating its proximity to the left skate as they pass one another (see figure 2.12b). The back of the right skate's blade should pass very close to the tip of the left skate's blade, without risking collision between the skates. If the right leg passes too far in front of the left leg as it pushed through, it may seriously compromise the direction of push of the left skate. Practice and increased confidence will correct this common error among novice skaters. A coach can most easily observe this problem from the center of the turn.

Set-Down

All three dimensions of space (frontal, horizontal, and vertical) are involved in the position of the set-down. The set-down of the right skate should be a smooth motion, with the entire blade surface contacting the ice at the same instant. To ensure this action, many coaches recommend that the back half of the blade be placed down first. This is a good practice to adopt because it helps ensure that the next push from the right leg will originate from the middle-rear of the skate.

The direction and angle of the skate also are relevant to the set-down. Set down the right skate in a manner that facilitates fluid and coordinated crossover steps: place the skate down in the direction of the turn and angle it slightly to the inside, so as to apply immediate pressure on the inner edge of the blade. See figure 2.13. Overall, the entire sequence from lift-off to set-down should be an uninterrupted and smooth motion.

Left-Leg Mechanics

Perfecting the push of the left leg during crossover steps is usually more difficult than the right leg. The mechanics differ drastically from those of any other aspect of the speedskating stride because the left leg does not extend out to the side of the body, but rather pushes through under the hips in the same direction as the right leg. Since this occurs as the right leg crosses over in front, the left leg will carry all the body weight. This tends to cause instability, and it can easily result in inefficient movement in the hips and a misalignment in the upper body.

2.13 Crossover steps: set-down of the right leg.

Push

The left leg begins its push as soon as the right leg lifts off the ground. To maximize pushing leverage, angle the left skate on the outside edge of the blade. You can accomplish this correctly only by leaning the hip inward into the corner. The actual amount of lean will depend on velocity and the radius of the turn. Naturally, a faster turn speed or a tighter turn will require more lean angle to prevent the center of gravity and most of the body mass from succumbing to the effects of centrifugal force. However, this inward lean should not disturb any of the critical factors of alignment of the upper body. During the entire push and extension of the left leg, the upper body must remain stable and undisturbed.

With the body leaning in toward the center of the turn, the left leg's push begins from a position *slightly to the outside* of the body (i.e., to the inside of the turn). By angling the blade on the outside edge, the push proceeds in a straight line parallel to the centrifugal force. This is probably the most important aspect of the left-leg action. Pushing too far to the rear places excessive pressure on the front half of the skate, significantly reducing the effectiveness of force application and power. It also twists the trunk and shoulder inward, further disturbing the mechanics of both pushing legs.

Like the push from the right leg, the extension of the left leg under and through the hips should occur in an accelerated manner, with push-off forces coming from the center to the rear of the skate. Push the left leg through to full extension to get a distinctive snap of power at the end of the stroke. See figure 2.14 for an illustration of full extension of the left leg.

Recovery

With the left leg, the recovery process begins as soon as the leg reaches full extension. As the skate lifts off the ice, the knee flexes progressively. Although the skate should initially lift off the ice so that the blade is parallel to the surface, the gradual flexion of the knee causes the toe of the skate to begin to point downward toward the ice. As the knee continues to bend, the hip begins to abduct and bring the leg back under and through the body. During this process, the skate may eventually become perpendicular to the ice. The blade tip of the left skate should then pass close to the heel of the right blade as the hip continues to flex. Once clear of the right leg, the left leg is powerfully driven forward, stepping slightly inward, with the knee and skate pointing in the direction of the turn.

Keep in mind that as the left leg goes through this process of recovery and passes behind the other skate, the right leg is already initiating its lateral push to the side. During the entire recovery process, the left skate should stay as low to the ice as possible without risking unnecessary interference or collision with the ice or the opposite leg.

Set-Down

Driving the knee forward through and under the body is necessary to ensure that the skate is positioned correctly once you set it down. Step into the turn slightly, with the skate's blade leaning into the turn, and as close to the inside of the corner as possible. This stepping in maximizes the length of the following left-leg push by increasing the range of motion and displacement of the subsequent stroke. If the skate is not far enough forward, too much pressure is applied on the front half of the blade. To help prevent this misplaced pressure, place the skate down with the back half of the blade contacting the ice first.

2.14   Crossover steps: left leg in full extension.

Equally important, both the knee and toes of the set-down leg should aim in the direction of the turn. This positioning will not only make negotiating tight turns significantly easier, but will also help maintain upper-body alignment throughout the crossover steps. Overall, the set-down process of the left leg should be smooth and fluid, with the independent actions of the joints blending together to create a coordinated, efficient motion.

CROSSOVER ARM SWING

Since the mechanics of the arm swing during the crossover stroke differ considerably from those on the straightaway, they deserve some special attention. During the straight, the purpose of arm motion is to set leg cadence, maintain balance, and supplement push-off forces as the legs extend. In the corners, however, an arm swing serves several additional purposes. In fact, the right and left arms have rather different functions for assisting performance.

In longer metric skating races (3, 5, and 10 kilometer), the crossover arm swing usually involves only the right arm. In the 500 (and sometimes the 1000) meter, both arms are used in the corners. Most skaters also prefer to swing both arms in the first and last corner of a race.

Right-Arm Swing

As in straightaway technique, the forward and backward flexion of the arms coincides with the right and left leg's outward extension, respectively. Overall, the action of the right arm helps resist the outward pulling of centrifugal force in the turns, facilitates proper body position, and enhances push-off forces. The most important aspect of a right-arm swing is undoubtedly the direction of movement with respect to both the fore and aft trajectory of the arm.

Forward Swing

The forward part of the right-arm swing is directed in the same radius, or arc, as the direction of the turn. This is important because it helps ensure that the push mechanics and upper-body alignment are executed correctly. Swinging the arm in a straight-line tangent to the turn instead reduces pushing force and tends to torque the upper body toward the outside, pulling it out of alignment. Swinging the arm excessively across the midline, on the other hand, would tend to cause an equally destructive inward rotation of the trunk and shoulders.

At the top of the swing, the hand should be at about chin height. Following the arc of the turn, the end of the forward swing should bring the hand almost directly in front (but not across the center of gravity or the body's midline). The elbow joint should maintain a slight flexion at the end of the swing, with a joint angle of about 150 to 160 degrees. Time this point to correspond exactly with the maximum range of push displacement of the right leg.

Backswing

The transition to a backswing is made almost immediately after the top of the forward swing. As the right leg reaches full extension, the left leg begins to push under and across the body. Therefore, the right-arm swing should be rhythmic, with no static position or pause at the top of the forward swing.

Much like the arm swing for the straightaway, the hand's movement should pass close to the hip as it moves rearward. Unlike the straight-line swing, however, the arm should not swing outward during the backswing. Rather, it should maintain a trajectory aligned with the arc of the turn. As the arm reaches the top of the backswing, the elbow joint should be perfectly straight, maintaining a compact position, close to the body. The hand should usually reach no higher than the head. Elevating the arm higher than head-height tends to cause the shoulders to rotate outward, resulting in a more rearward-directed left-leg push. Refer back to figures 2.10 through 2.14 for an illustration of arm-swing mechanics.

Left-Arm Swing

When skating the corners, the left arm primarily maintains balance and facilitates a faster crossover cadence. Although the action of the left arm is considerably more subtle than that of the right, proper form can help increase acceleration through the turn by complementing the efforts of the legs.

Forward Swing

Overall, the position of the left arm should be fairly compact. Most of the action occurs at the elbow joint. Hold the upper arm close to the body, reaching a final angle of about 70 to 90 degrees (vertical). The lower arm swings forward at the elbow to a small angle that may approach 45 degrees. At the terminal point of the forward swing, the hand should not cross the midline of the body, and it should extend no higher than chin height. The shoulder should display little or no action during the arm swing and stay as relaxed as possible. Excessive flexion or abduction in the shoulder can disturb upper-body alignment and push efficiency, so it should be heavily discouraged. Because of the regular turnover of the legs throughout the crossover sequence, avoid holding any static position at the top of the forward swing.

Backswing

The backswing of the left arm also takes place primarily at the elbow joint, and it must correspond precisely with the lateral extension of the right leg. The backswing must reach its end point the instant that the opposite leg reaches its full extension. By the end of the swing, you should extend the elbow completely, with the hand reaching no higher than about hip-height. The upper arm may extend back at the shoulder, assuming a final angle of up to horizontal position. Avoid shoulder movement, which can have a detrimental effect on overall mechanics.

SPEEDSKATING PHYSIOLOGY AND BIOMECHANICS

Little research has been done on speedskating exercise, perhaps not all that surprising since speedskating is virtually impossible to reproduce in the laboratory. Field research is difficult to perform due to the nature of the sport and also to variations in temperature, wind, ice, and environmental conditions that make it almost impossible to compile valid, reproducible data. With indoor, climate-controlled skating ovals, it has become possible to control for these variables, but speedskating continues to receive relatively little attention from sport scientists.

Almost all the research that has been done relates to the cold-weather version of the sport: ice speedskating. In Holland, researchers have been interested for years in the physiology of speedskating. Dutch physiologists have also published some research related to in-line speedskating. Interestingly, research in Holland and North America differs considerably in focus. In North America, researchers lean toward investigating such speedskating parameters as strength and anaerobic power. In the Netherlands, however, researchers seem more interested in biomechanics and the physiological variables related to aerobic performance and marathon skating. This focus may be explained by their time-honored tradition in long-distance skating, whereas Americans have historically produced more sprint and short-distance skaters.

Research has uncovered many intriguing facts about speedskating physiology:

• High aerobic power doesn't guarantee success in speedskating. Specific strength, muscle-fiber composition, and the ability to tolerate and remove lactic acid are all cited as very important.

• There are no significant differences in performance indices such as oxygen uptake, ventilation, or heart rate between in-line and ice speedskating (de Boer et al 1987b).

• Although in-line speedskating relies on aerobic processes for most energy production, the level of the anaerobic threshold is equally crucial for performance success.

• Speedskating is unique in that sustained, high-level isometric contractions are a significant and necessary element in the movement performance.

• During the glide phase, the force of the extensor muscles of the hip and knee joints lie between 25 and 35 percent of maximal values (Eckblom, Hermansen, and Saltin 1967).

- Unlike running or cycling, which primarily use the muscles involved in flexion and extension of the hip and knee joints, speedskating involves virtually all the muscles in the lower body.

- Due to the amount of time spent in the deep sitting position, speedskaters are strong at deep-knee angles, whereas other endurance athletes are not (Foster 1993).

- Compared with skaters who have low power outputs, better skaters tend to show a combination of higher work per stroke and lower stroke frequencies (van Ingen Schenau, de Groot, and de Boer 1985).

- During skating, a cruising speed can be maintained that is about twice as high as during running and at about 15 percent lower metabolic costs (van Ingen Schenau, de Groot, and Hollander 1983).

Interesting Research-Supported Facts About Speedskating Biomechanics

- Speedskating is one of the few weight-bearing sports that does not involve any up and down vertical motion of the athlete's center of gravity.

- Speedskating is a sport where technical prowess is a necessity if one is to be able to fully and effectively utilize the physiologic capacities.

- Despite the fact that speedskating is the fastest nonmechanized form of human locomotion, its efficiency has been calculated roughly 12 percent lower than cycling's, primarily because the energy used to maintain the static contraction of the glide phase is not used for external power output (Prampero et al. 1976).

- Ice skaters demonstrate a smaller preextension knee angle (that is, a deeper knee bend) and significantly greater knee-extension velocity than do in-line speedskaters (de Boer et al. 1987b).

- Because of differences in body position, in-line skaters tend to focus the "push" from a position on the skate that is more forward than that of ice skaters (de Boer et al. 1987b).

- Anatomically, successful speedskaters seem to have a relatively shorter upper leg compared with the lower leg (van Ingen Schenau, de Groot, and Hollander 1983).

- Ice speedskaters attain higher velocities at shorter distances by increasing stroke frequency rather than by increasing the amount of work per stroke (van Ingen Schenau, de Groot, and de Boer 1985).

- Analysis of film, electromyography, and force data shows that the glide phase of ice speedskating comprises roughly 50 percent of each stride (de Boer, de Groot, de Koning, Sargeant, and van Ingen Schenau 1987a).

- Despite a deep knee bend, the head and shoulders are actually at the highest height in the 500-meter ice event because of a more upright trunk position (van Ingen Schenau and Bakker 1980).

- Speedskaters are regarded to be generally better-looking than other athletes, to train harder, to have a higher tolerance for pain, and to be more friendly than most sport athletes, in the author's unbiased opinion.

KLAPSCHAATS—THE KLAPSKATE

In the early 1990's, Dutch skate manufacturers Viking and Raps began experimenting with a revolutionary new skate design. Actually, their project was based on an old idea—one borrowed from the original Canadian patent applied for at the end of the 19th century. The klapskate, (also called the clap or slapskate) is based on a design that features a free-floating heel similar in concept to a cross-country ski boot and binding (see figure 2.15). This design was created through the use of a spring-loaded joint between the front part of the blade and boot, leaving the heel to detach at the end of the push-off. This allows the ankle to extend at the end of the push without the blade tip touching the ice.

History of the Klapskate

Although initially met with skepticism about its effectiveness, strength, and durability, the klapskate is now considered the most revolutionary technological development in skates to date. Any initial doubt about the skates' potential was soon extinguished as both men and women repeatedly shattered world marks that should have stood for decades. Many skaters, however, were frustrated over the apparent unwillingness of Dutch manufacturers to provide the new skates to athletes who were not from the Netherlands. Allegations of favoritism, the inability of production to meet the explosive demand, and the relatively slow acceptance of these new skates meant that klapskates appeared sporadically in the 1996-1997 World Cup season. Over the following year, however, other skate manufacturers such as Maple, Finn, Easton, and Marchese began to produce their own version of klapskate technology. Not only was the question of availability almost immediately satisfied, but the competition from other manufacturers meant that skaters had access to the latest developments in blade materials and design.

2.15 The klapskate.

Over the 1997–1998 season, more and more skaters switched to klapskates. World records began to fall like dominos. The klapskate had taken over the world of long-track ice speedskating. One after another record fell, often in rapid succession as skaters in the same competition continually posted faster and faster times. Controversy soon followed, however, as some skaters, coaches, and national governing bodies began to protest the use of klapskates in the 1998

Olympic Games, citing that some countries had access to the technology long before others. Several months before the '98 Olympics, the International Skating Union (ISU) declared that klapskates would be permitted in the games, but that the issue would be reviewed the next congress meeting. The resulting wave of media attention and differing attitudes among coaches, athletes, and officials began to raise mixed feelings about how the klapskate was changing the face of the sport. Skaters who were at the top of the World Cup standings the previous year were now struggling to break the top 10, while lesser-known skaters came out of nowhere and began to shatter world records by several seconds. Above it all, one thing immediately became clear—some skaters were able to adapt very quickly to the new skates because the change in mechanics favored their individual technique and physical attributes. Others were less fortunate as they proved unable to exploit the newfound potential these less-restrictive skates now offered.

How the Skate Works

The klapskate works by allowing the ankle joint to extend at the end of the push-off without the toe of the blade touching the ice. Although a relatively simple concept, this new skate proves considerably superior once the skater has adapted to the necessary modifications in technique. A recent study by Dutch researchers found that skaters using klaps were able to improve personal best times an average of 6.2% (van Ingen Schenau et al. 1996). What follows are some of the advantages of the klapskate:

- The ability to flex the ankle at the end of the stride results in a longer sidewards push displacement without having to squat lower. This also means that the calf muscles can now be freed of their normal suppression and contribute greatly to pushing force.
- The klapskate distributes motion over more muscle groups.
- The use of the calf muscles allows a skater on klaps to more easily overcome ice and wind friction.
- Overall, the push-off mechanics that these skates permit improve propulsive energy.

Skating Technique on Klap Blades

Because klapskates allow for the involvement of the calf muscles during push-off, traditional speedskating technique must be significantly modified to take advantage of the newfound mobility of the ankle joint. Research shows that skaters on traditional skates appear to lose contact with the ice before the push leg reaches full extension. The objective with klapskate technique is therefore to lengthen push displacement, keeping the blade on the ice as long as possible. The value of klapskates can be viewed another way: a skater can achieve the same push displacement as one on traditional skates while displaying a higher (more straight) knee angle.

For the most part, classic speedskating technique works well with the new klap technology. The only aspect which must be modified is the last one-third of the pushing motion. Although not discrete in application, the push can be thought of as taking place in two sequential stages: push acceleration and ankle snap.

Continued

Push Acceleration

The skater should initiate the push in much the same manner as on traditional skates, accelerating the leg laterally by building the majority of power in the first third of the stroke. The push should still originate from the middle to rear of the skate, corresponding to the vertical line of gravity.

Ankle Snap

As the leg reaches full extension, the point is reached where a skater on traditional blades would begin to lose contact with the ice. At this point, the skater must dynamically contract the calf muscles to transmit as much pushing power as possible through the ankle joint, and ultimately to the skate blade. This is accomplished by rolling the focal point of the pushing skate forward from roughly the middle of the blade to the pivot point of the klap hinge (located under the ball of the foot). This plantar flexion of the ankle joint must be powerful and explosive, yet smooth and fluid.

Another major impact of the klapskate is on start technique. Because the blade is free to detach from the heel, the traditional "toe-pick" start is not possible. This start involves lightly embedding the blade tip of the front skate into the ice, with the front skate raised at about a 45-degree angle. Some klap manufacturers have designed blades with release mechanisms that will allow for a traditional start by holding the heel of the blade onto the boot until after the first stride. However, it seems that all skaters, instead, have chosen to use a modified start technique where both skates begin flat on the ice and 45 degrees to each other.

The Future

The debate over whether or not the klapskate, which takes advantage of moving parts, should be allowed in competition will likely continue as some athletes grow frustrated adapting to the new technology. The fact remains, however, that the introduction of the klapskate has significantly lowered every (long-track) speedskating world record. In a sport that is all about speed, it is hard to imagine how skaters could ever very easily readjust to the slower traditional skates.

3

Skating Drills

Speedskating is a technical sport. Learning to skate with a high degree of efficiency comes only with great practice, perseverance, and time. The phasic nature of the speedskating movement pattern, although complex, allows athletes to selectively practice certain elements of the stroke cycle. Learning a complex skill as a whole is a difficult task. When the skill can be broken down into discrete elements, however, learning becomes much easier.

This section comprises some of the drills developed by my former coach, Jocelyn Martin Sicotte. When I was a novice skater, these drills helped me enormously to improve my technical ability. Once I began to coach, I used many of these same drills to help other skaters of all abilities hone their skills. By recruiting and exploiting select aspects of the speedskating movement pattern, each component of the stroke cycle can be practiced independently.

Many experienced skaters are technically proficient. Few, if any, however, are flawless. Almost everything can be improved on in some way. Using the following drills, you can learn or teach calibration of body posture and increase your level of sensory acuity. Even expert athletes can (and should) perform these drills periodically as a technical check.

PRINCIPLES OF LEARNING PROGRESSION

These drills work well because they employ a teaching strategy called *stacking*. The drills are arranged sequentially. They each build on the technical and perceptual skills developed in previous drills, the skill learned in one drill being incorporated into all those following. The stacking format also allows you to focus on one issue of alignment at a time.

Some general principles should be followed as you use this drill progression:

• Regardless of ability, all skaters should begin with the first drill and progress slowly through the sequence.

• Practice each drill until it can be performed naturally without error or hesitation. Once you attain this level of proficiency, progress to the next drill.

• Continue through the drill sequence only until you are unable to execute the drill without error. Whatever exercise at which "failure" occurs must be practiced repeatedly before continuing to the next drill in the sequence.

• When you complete the failure-level drill, go back, review, and practice the last drill that could be performed without flaw. This way, you will finish on a positive note.

• It takes only one trial to determine which drill will become the terminal level of momentary failure. The next time you perform the drills, you may start either from the beginning of the sequence or from the drill *before* the one that was the terminal exercise in the previous practice session.

• Feedback is vital to success. Seek it from an external source (i.e., another person or coach) or another medium (e.g., video). Even skaters with the best perceptual ability need to receive information about their actions.

• All drills, whether they involve static or dynamic movement, require some forward momentum. The drills should not be performed with a great deal of speed, but with enough to sustain a glide of roughly 15 meters (50 feet).

• Address only one issue of misalignment at a time (see figure 3.1). As a general rule, start from the feet and move upward. Since balance and vision are both important for learning, the only exception to this rule is the position of the head. First make sure that the head is upright, with the eyes focused ahead about 15 meters (50 feet).

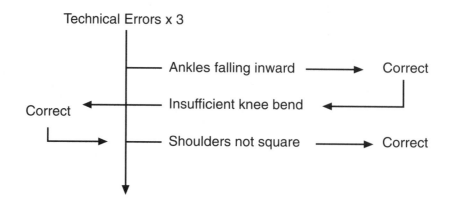

3.1   It is important to correct only one issue of misalignment at a time.

COACH'S CORNER—INSTRUCTIONAL METHOD

Whether you are an experienced coach helping young skaters develop, a novice skater, or merely someone helping a friend learn something new, you can do several important things to enhance the effectiveness of your teaching. Most people feel at least some fear and apprehension when they are learning anything new. Their worrying can result in hesitation, which is detrimental to the entire learning process. As a coach or observer, everything you say and do has an impact on the athletes you are instructing. The following tips and ideas can facilitate the penetration of information and maximize the overall effectiveness of the learning process.

Demonstrating

Some individuals learn best by observing and imitating others. Some people respond better to verbal information about the task. All individuals, however, can benefit from a visual demonstration.

- An effective demonstrator must be able to accurately reproduce the drill precisely as the students are to perform it.
- It is important that skaters view the demonstration from all available angles: front, rear, and side.
- It is essential that all demonstrations be accompanied by a verbal explanation. Students should first observe the demonstration and then listen to the verbal explanation followed by a "redemonstration." Students are then given practice time. Figure 3.2 highlights the preferred instructional method.

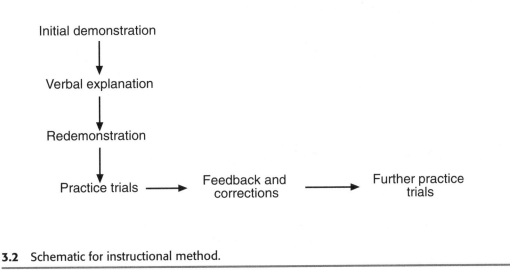

3.2 Schematic for instructional method.

Providing Feedback

Feedback, commonly referred to as *knowledge of results* (KR), is imperative in the learning process. KR must be provided in a manner that makes sense. It must come almost immediately following the task, so that an individual can immediately compare the feedback information with his or her sense of how the performance went. How you communicate KR is crucial to the overall penetration and value of the feedback. Negative verbal feedback can destroy an athlete's confidence, create frustration, and hinder the attainment of goals.

There are three effective methods for providing feedback and correcting misalignment in body position. Whichever one proves most worthy, it is important to add variety to the feedback to force skaters to think more for themselves.

Focus on What the Athlete Is Doing Right

With verbal feedback, a good method is to first outline a strong point and to avoid using the word "no." For example, you might say, "The outward angle of your skate looks great, but you will need to bend your knee more to maximize your push." Never begin with criticism or a remark about what the skater is doing wrong, such as saying, "Your knee bend isn't low enough. If you don't lower your hips, your push will be wasted." Although this criticism gets the point across, it will have a dramatically more negative impact on the skater.

Tell the Skater What to Do Differently

So long as feedback avoids the use of negative terminology, it is permissible to start by explaining what the athlete should do differently to correct the problem. Rather than using words like "error," emphasize how the corrective action can be of great benefit.

Position the Skater

Sometimes any amount of verbal feedback is insufficient to facilitate a change in the movement pattern. A viable option is to simply move the skater's limbs into the desired position. This is most safely done in a static position, but with caution can also be done as the person glides. Be sure to correct this way only when you know the source of the problem, and make sure that you provide corrective information to supplement feedback or visual observation.

As a coach, you must be enthusiastic about what your are teaching, be confident in your abilities, and convey a true sense of caring and compassion toward the skaters. Get excited about the smallest improvements, provide immediate praise after a success, and always end the session on a positive note.

STRAIGHTAWAY DRILLS

For each of the following drills you will find the name of the drill, its objective, key points to watch for, a verbal explanation, difficulties commonly encountered, and, in some cases, advanced progression subdrills. It is important to note that not all the possible difficulties are listed, but only those that represent the most common sources of errors.

The drills in this chapter will help both ice and in-line skaters. Many of these drills were first developed years ago by ice skaters. Because the two disciplines share technical similarities, these drills will develop skills of benefit to athletes of both sport forms. Where differences in application are necessary between ice and in-line skating, the distinctions in execution will be noted. The last section of this chapter outlines special drills I have developed to help in-line skaters make the transition to double-push skating.

Static or Dynamic Drills?

In this learning progression, the first four drills are static while the last three are dynamic. *Static drills* are called that because, other than the forward glide momentum that must be achieved to perform the drill, no movement of the body is required. Body position is maintained in suspended equilibrium throughout the course of the drill. The static drills focus primarily on issues of alignment and basic body position during each of the stride phases. They are therefore critical to master before progressing to the dynamic drills.

Dynamic drills, on the other hand, require active movement of parts of the lower body while gliding. These drills emphasize continual activity and the application of force and physical energy. More correctly, the dynamic drills require this active movement of the lower body while maintaining static alignment in the upper body.

Drill 1: Straight-Line Calibration

Objectives:

Learn to glide in the basic position.

Increase perception of gliding directly on the top of the skate.

What to Watch For:

Feet are shoulder-width apart.

Knees are flexed to about a 100-degree angle (knee-caps should be positioned directly over the toes).

A line down from the center of gravity intersects the middle to back third of the skate.

The trunk is flexed forward about 45 to 60 degrees from a straight-up posture, with the back slightly rounded.

Both hands rest comfortably on the lower back.

The head is up. Eyes look straight ahead.

Body weight is evenly distributed on both legs.

Gliding occurs directly on top of the wheels or blade.

Explanation:

Take a few strides to get up some speed. Assume the basic position, then glide in a straight line directly on top of the wheels or blade. See figure 3.3.

Common Difficulties:

Knees are not bent enough.

Remedy—use knees-to-the-wall drill. That is, with the front wheels against a wall, bend until the kneecaps (patellae) touch the wall.

3.3 Drill #1. Straight-line calibration.

Center of gravity is too far forward, placing too much pressure on the front of the skates. Remedy—sit back more, as if preparing to sit in a chair. Elevate the trunk if warranted.

Advanced Drill Progression:

To improve stability, perform the drill again with the laces untied, or untie the laces one eyelet at a time on subsequent trials.

Note. Unless otherwise stated, all the remaining drills should be performed while maintaining the same correct, basic body position.

Drill 2: Skating Bow

Objectives:

Practice edge control by gliding in the basic position with both ankles collapsed outward.

Get comfortable rolling on the outside edge of the wheels.

What to Watch For:

Maintain all aspects of basic position as outlined in drill 1.

Look for the equal and symmetrical collapse of both ankles.

Ensure that the glide path is straight.

Explanation:

Glide in a straight line, with both fists between the knees. Keep both ankles collapsed outward throughout the glide. Maintain all key points of basic position. See figure 3.4.

Common Difficulties:

Glide path is not straight.

Remedy—ensure that equal weight is carried by each skate. Both skates must be kept parallel, pointing in the direction of travel.

The collapse of the ankles is not symmetrical.

Remedy—this is usually best corrected with additional practice.

Advanced Drill Progression:

Repeat the drill with only one fist between the knees.

Repeat the drill with the knees as close together as possible.

To improve stability, gradually unlace the skates until they are completely untied.

3.4 Drill #2. Skating bow.

Drill 3: Hypo-Glide

Objective:

Learn to glide with the push leg in an almost fully extended position with the body's weight directly over the support leg.

What to Watch For:

Push leg should extend straight to the side with only a slight bend in the knee.

Skate of the push leg should be about two inches ahead of the support leg's skate.

Support leg should bend to about 100 degrees and carry all the weight.

Support leg's skate angles slightly on the outside edge.

The toes and knee of the support leg side are in the same vertical plane as the skater's nose.

Shoulders are even and parallel.

Glide is in a straight line.

Explanation:

Glide in a straight line with the push leg extended out to the side. Make sure all the body's weight is carried on the glide leg. Keep the knee, nose, and toes in the same vertical line. See figure 3.5, a–b.

3.5 Drill #3. Hypo-Glide: *(a)* front view; *(b)* side view.

a

b

Common Difficulties:

You turn in the direction of the extended (push) leg while gliding.

Remedy—move the push leg forward slightly. Ensure that all the body's weight is carried by the support leg.

The shoulders twist.

Remedy—make sure that the upper body is directly over the support leg.

Advanced Drill Progression:

Repeat the drill, but glide while holding the extended push leg a few inches off the ground.

Repeat the drill with the support leg's skate angled increasingly on the outside edge.

Drill 4: Late-Recovery Toe Drag

Objectives:

Practice a static, late-recovery glide with all the weight on the support leg.

Fine-tune the balance necessary for a smooth weight transfer.

What to Watch For:

Support leg should bend to about 100 degrees and carry all the body weight.

Center of gravity is over the middle of the support skate.

3.6 Drill #4. Late-recovery toe drag.

ecovery leg points downward.

ecovery leg's skate rolls with the toe wheel on the ground.

recovery blade should be a few inches above the ice's surface.

g skate glides with the wheels slightly angled to the outside.

ght line.

ght line with the support leg carrying all the weight. Position the knee
leg directly beside or slightly behind the other, pointing down toward
the *wheel* of the recovery leg to roll on the ground; keep the toe of the
bove the surface of the ice. See figure 3.6.

culties:

toward the side of the recovery leg.

ase amount of pressure on the recovery leg. Ensure that the support
entire body weight. Try tucking the recovery leg up close behind the

to maintain balance for the duration of the glide.

drill 3.

vist.

Remedy—keep the hips square. The knee of the recovery leg must be tucked up close
behind the support leg's knee.

Advanced Drill Progression:

In-line—repeat the drill, but glide while holding the recovery leg's skate a few inches off
the ground.

Repeat the drill with the support leg's skate angled increasingly on the outside
edge.

Drill 5: Single-Leg Push

Objectives:

Transfer all the skills learned thus far into dynamic motion.

Fine-tune the perception and mechanics of a dynamic push-off.

What to Watch For:

Support leg is carrying all the body weight.

Knee should flex to 100 degrees throughout the drill.

Hips and shoulders should remain level.

Push leg extends directly to the side until the knee is straight.

Wheels (or the skate blade) of the push leg stay in contact with the road (or ice) at all
times.

The recovery of the push leg is straight inward, in constant contact with the surface.

Support leg glides in a straight line.

Explanation:

To begin, assume the basic position (figure 3.7a). Then push the leg straight out to the side until full extension is reached (figure 3.7b). Keep the upper body directly over the toe of the support leg at all times. To recover the push leg, turn the skate slightly inward, allowing it to glide back toward the center (3.7c). Repeat with the same leg until forward momentum is lost.

3.7 Drill #5. Single-leg push.

Common Difficulties:

You push the leg back slightly, rather than straight to the side.

Remedy—ensure the correct knee bend, sitting back slightly. Push from the middle of the skate. Exaggerate the movement, trying to push to the side and forward slightly.

You rotate the shoulders during push-off or recovery.

Remedy—keep the weight centered over the support leg. The knee, nose, and toe should lie in the same vertical plane during the push. Do not "lean" on the pushing leg.

The skate of the push leg trails behind the support skate during the recovery.

Remedy—bend the support leg more, keeping the center of gravity more toward the rear of the skate.

Advanced Drill Progression:

Repeat this drill, but alternate push legs: that is, push out the left leg, recover, push out the right leg, recover, and so on.

Repeat the drill with the support leg's skate angled increasingly on the outside edge.

Drill 6: Toe Sweeping

Objectives:

Introduce the first step of the recovery action into the movement.

Learn to keep the recovery skate pointing straight ahead at all times.

What to Watch For:

Knee of the support leg remains flexed to 100 degrees throughout the drill.

The push leg extends directly to the side until the knee is straight.

The support leg glides in a straight line.

Wheels or blade must stay flat on the surface throughout the push.

For in-lines—initiate the recovery by allowing the extended push leg to slowly fall back, flex the knee gradually, and allow the skate to roll onto the toe wheel by tilting it forward about 45 degrees.

With the recovery leg bent and the skate rolling on the toe wheel, allow the skate to slowly regroup toward center by following a semicircular path around the back.

For ice—follow the instructions for in-line skaters, but hold the toe of the blade a few inches off the ice during the recovery.

Explanation:

Begin by pushing the leg straight out to the side until full extension is reached (figure 3.8a). To recover the push leg, flex the knee as the skate falls back and rolls onto the toe wheel (3.8b). Allow it to follow a semicircle around the back, returning it to a position directly beside the support skate. Repeat with the same leg until forward momentum is lost.

Common Difficulties:

The upper body does not remain over the support leg or the glide is not straight.

Remedy—decrease the amount of weight carried by the push leg.

3.8 Drill #6. Toe sweeping.

a

b

Balance is insufficient to allow proper execution of the drill.

Remedy—practice the drill in a stationary position, holding onto someone for support.

Advanced Drill Progression:

Repeat this drill but alternate the push legs: push out the left leg, recover, push out the right leg, recover, and so on.

Repeat the drill with the support leg's skate angled increasingly on the outside edge.

For in-lines—modify the recovery so that the skate of the push leg stays a few inches above the ground as it follows the semicircle around the back.

Drill 7: Full Recovery

Objective:

Combine all elements learned to this point, adding a weight transfer into the recovery process.

What to Watch For:

All of the key points outlined in the previous drill.

At the end of the push, lift the skate off the ground, keeping it parallel to the road and pointing straight ahead.

Keep the skate low to the ground, initiate the recovery by turning the toes in first.

The recovery leg should follow a semicircle around the back.

As you approach the end of the recovery, allow the hips to begin to fall toward the regrouping leg. Let the shoulders move parallel to the hips.

3.9 Drill #7. Full recovery.

a

b

c

As the weight transfer continues, set the skate down directly beside and slightly ahead of the support skate.

When set down, the back half of the wheels or blade should contact the surface first.

Explanation:

At the end of the push (figure 3.9a), lift the skate slightly off the ground and allow it to recover around the back (3.9b). As the leg regroups, begin to let the hip fall inward toward the regrouping leg. Set the skate down on the outside edge, slightly ahead of the support skate, stabilizing the motion of the center of gravity (3.9c). Repeat with the same leg until momentum is lost.

Common Difficulties:

Too much weight is on the front half of the support skate; that is, the center of gravity is too far forward.

Remedy—check basic position. Make sure that the recovery skate is set down slightly ahead of the support skate.

Skate of the support leg collapses inward.

Remedy—maintain proper upper-body alignment, keeping the upper body positioned over the support leg.

Balance is insufficient to allow proper execution of the drill.

Remedy—practice the drill in a stationary position, holding onto someone for support.

Advanced Drill Progression:

Repeat this drill but alternate the push legs: push out the left leg, recover, push out the right leg, recover, and so on.

Progress into the full movement pattern, including slight pauses at the end of the push and just before the following extension.

CORNERING DRILLS

Drills aimed at improving the mechanics of cornering ability typically break down the crossover stroke into exercises that involve the left or right leg and that involve both legs. The following group of drills comprises the most common and basic ones used by most coaches and athletes. For the crossover stroke, the most important aspects relate to the direction of push, complete extension of the pushing legs, and the application of push-off force from the midpoint of the skate; the focus here primarily is on actions of the hips and legs. Nevertheless, upper-body posture also plays a key role in proper execution. Misalignments in the upper body are among the most common source of error in cornering, so make sure that all issues of upper-body position are first satisfied.

The drills you find here are effective for both ice and in-line skaters. Any differences specific to executing them on wheels or blades will be highlighted.

Constant Versus Changing Radius

All the cornering drills are best performed in circles. By using circular paths you can practice the technical elements of the drill as well as develop strength and endurance in the turn-specific musculature.

Constant-radius drills involve performing numerous repetitions using a circle that is always the same size. It is not necessarily important to have the circle traced out on the ground, although it certainly does add another dimension to the drill and its objective. In general, the size of the circle can be fairly small (3-meter/10-foot radius) since these drills are usually done at low speeds. Whatever the radius of the circle, the skater should perform each successive revolution as closely as possible to the previous one.

Drills with a changing radius involve performing a drill's actions repeatedly but varying the circle's radius for each successive revolution. There are basically two types of changing radius drills. The first involves skating in an *ever-growing* circle as the number of revolutions increases. This format is definitely the easier to perform because velocity tends to gradually increase as the drill continues. Using a larger circle at higher velocities requires less skill overall and is much easier to control. For this reason, it is recommended that beginners or novice skaters use these types of corner drills.

The second type of changing-radius drill is considerably more difficult, and it involves performing the drill in an *ever-shrinking* turn radius. The difficulty arises because the centrifugal force becomes increasingly more difficult to manage as the skater either increases speed or tightens the circle. Because performing these decreasing radius turns must involve a considerable inward lean, they should be reserved for more advanced skaters who have already mastered the basics of turn mechanics. Figure 3.10 illustrates the differences between these drill types.

Note: These drills assume a counterclockwise (to the left) turn direction.

a) Constant radius drills   b) Decreasing radius drills   c) Increasing radius drills

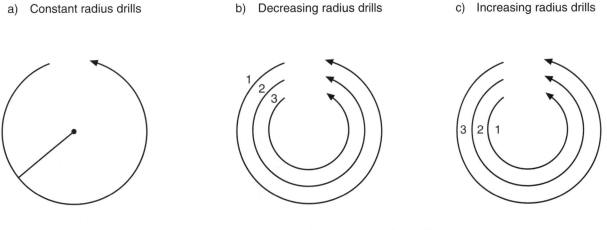

3.10 Corner drills: *(a)* constant radius; *(b)* decreasing radius; *(c)* increasing radius.

Drill 1: Right-Leg Push and Hold

Objectives:

Ensure that extension of the right leg directly counters the force of centrifugal motion.

Practice pushing off from the middle to the rear of the skate.

What to Watch For:

Right leg begins to extend from a knee angled about 100 degrees; it then extends out from the center of the turn until the knee has little or no bend.

Both skates must stay in constant contact with the surface during the push and regrouping of the right leg.

The left leg remains bent to 100 degrees, with the skate aiming in the direction of the turn.

Shoulders are parallel to the hips and in line with the direction of centrifugal force.

The upper body is directly over the left skate.

The push must come off the middle of the right skate.

Both skates are angled so that force is applied only to the left side of the wheels or blade.

Both arms rest comfortably on the lower back.

Explanation:

Keep the left leg bent, with the upper body positioned directly over the top. Push the right leg directly to the side to reach full extension. Glide and balance on the (left) support leg for a count of three with the push leg's skate maintaining continuous contact with the ground. Do not allow the push skate to trail behind during the glide. Regroup the push leg by directing it back inward. Repeat 10 times. See figure 3.11, a–b.

3.11 Corner drill #1. Right-leg push and hold.

a

b

Common Difficulties:

The right leg pushes to the side and back, rather than directly to the side (in line with centrifugal force).

Remedy—keep the knees bent and the hind end lowered to focus weight on the middle to rear of the skate. Exaggerate the extension by pushing forward slightly.

The upper body is not over the left support leg.

Remedy—push the left hip inward slightly to ensure that the left leg carries all the weight.

The shoulders twist to the left.

Remedy—the right skate is likely pushing back rather than straight to the side. Keep the head up, eyes focused ahead, and push the right skate along the line of centrifugal force.

Advanced Drill Progression:

Repeat the drill. When the right leg reaches full extension, lift and hold the skate a few inches off the ground, making sure that the wheels or blade are parallel to the surface.

Swing one or both arms as you extend the right leg.

Drill 2: Left-Leg Push and Hold

Objectives:

Practice pushing the left leg through and under the body in direct opposition to centrifugal force.

Ensure that the left-leg push comes off the midpoint of the skate.

What to Watch For:

The left leg pushes through the body as the right skate crosses over in front.

Once the crossover has taken place, the right leg should be bent about 100 degrees.

Both skates stay in constant contact with the surface, using only the left edges of the wheels or blades.

The left leg pushes straight sideways under the hips, countering the centrifugal force.

The left leg reaches full extension with no bend in the knee, and it is tucked immediately behind the right knee.

There is little or no distance between the two skates, as observed from the center of the turn (the right skate should partially occlude the view of the left).

Both arms rest comfortably on the lower back.

Explanation:

As the right leg crosses in front of the left leg, push the left leg straight to the side through and under the body. Glide and balance on the bent right leg, holding the left leg in full extension for a count of three. Regroup to the starting position and repeat 10 times. See figure 3.12.

Common Difficulties:

The extended left leg trails too far behind the bent (right) support leg.

3.12   Corner drill #2. Left-leg push and hold.

Remedy—assume a deeper right-leg bend, so that the knee of the left leg is snug-up, close behind. Push the extended left leg forward slightly as it passes under the hips.

The shoulders rotate to the right.

Remedy—the left leg is likely pushing back excessively. Ensure that the left leg pushes straight sideways along the imaginary lines of centrifugal force.

Advanced Drill Progression:

Swing one or both arms as you extend the left leg.

Drill 3: On-Surface Crossovers

Objectives:

Combine the actions of the previous two drills.

Practice crossover technique while maintaining continuous contact with the road.

What to Watch For:

With the right leg extended, the upper body should be fully supported by the left leg.

The heel of the right skate should pass close to the toe of the left one as it recovers in front.

The left leg's push begins as the right skate begins to cross in front.

The toe of the left skate should pass close to the heel of the right.

Both skates should stay in contact with the surface at all times.

Both legs should push directly to the side.

Explanation:

Start by pushing the right leg into full extension to the side (figure 3.13, a and b). Hold it in a fully extended position for three seconds. Push the left leg through as the right leg crosses in front (3.13c). Hold it for three seconds. Regroup the left skate as the right leg now begins to push again. Make sure the skates pass close together and stay in contact with the surface at all times.

3.13 Corner drill #3. On-surface crossovers.

a

b

c

Common Difficulties:

One or both legs push too far back.

Remedy—If the shoulders are rotating inward (to the left), correct the shoulder alignment by ensuring that they remain parallel to the hips and in line with the center of the turn.

The push appears to be coming off the front of the skate.

Remedy—shift the center of gravity toward the rear of the skate by increasing the knee bend and/or lowering the hind end and/or decreasing trunk flexion.

Advanced Drill Progressions:

Swing one or both arms with the action of the legs.

Tempo-Increase Drill: For the first five cycles, push and hold for three seconds. Decrease the count to two seconds for the next five. Execute the last five with a one-second count.

DOUBLE-PUSH DRILLS

The double-push technique is a radically different method of in-line speedskating (see chapter 1) that is considerably more complex than the classically oriented technique adapted from ice speedskating. Learning the double-push can be a frustrating experience. Most novice skaters have not yet developed the basic level of technical proficiency necessary to learn such an intricate movement pattern. Experienced skaters have an equally difficult time because they must break habits of movement that have, for most, become almost second nature.

Even more than classic technique, the double-push cannot be taught as a whole. Few skaters will be able to simply pick up the technique from watching others. Those who can usually undergo a time-intensive process of repeated observation, imitation, trial, and self-correction. Since the double-push technique is relatively new to the in-line community, few coaches or athletes truly understand how it works. Until now, most skaters have had to fend for themselves to learn this technique.

The following drills have had great success in helping athletes teach their bodies to move in ways that initially feel foreign and incorrect. Learning the double-push is almost like learning how to skate all over again. If you are an experienced skater, you must virtually forget everything you learned about the technical aspects of the sport, open up the mind, and allow the body to move freely and without inhibition.

Follow this particular learning progression meticulously to achieve success. As with the earlier drill sequences for classic technique, attempt a subsequent drill in this series only after you can perform the drills up to that point perfectly.

Please note that there are no "common difficulties" addressed in this double-push drills section because the technique is *so* new and because there are too many possible errors to mention.

Drill Series 1: Edge Control

This drill series consists of three subdrills that progressively teach the skater edge control. Each subdrill introduces a novel aspect. First achieve competence in one drill part before continuing to the next one in the sequence.

Subdrill A: Outside-Edge Glide

Objective:

Increase competence in rolling on the outside of the wheels.

What to Watch For:

Glide in the basic position.

Both ankles should collapse outward equally and symmetrically.

Follow a straight-line glide path.

Explanation:

Glide in a straight line with both ankles collapsed outward. Maintain key points of basic position. See figure 3.14.

3.14 Edge control subdrill A: Outside-edge glide.

Subdrill B: Platform-Width Change

Objective:

Maintain an outward ankle collapse while changing the width between the two skates.

What to Watch For:

Glide in the basic position.

Collapse both ankles outward equally and symmetrically.

Follow a straight glide path.

Explanation:

Glide with both ankles collapsed outward throughout the course of the drill. Starting with the skates together (figure 3.15a), push both skates apart to a width of about 24 inches (3.15b); then pull the skates back together (3.15c). Repeat several times.

3.15 Edge control subdrill B: Platform-width change.

a

b

c

Subdrill C: Platform-Width Change With Edge Manipulation

Objectives:

Repeat subdrill B, but incorporate edge dynamics into the push (widening) and pull (narrowing).

Increase the pulling leverage by using the outside edge of the wheels as the skates come together.

What to Watch For:

Glide in a straight-line path.

Ankles should collapse inward to use the inner edge of wheels while widening the push.

Ankles should remain collapsed inward until the farthest point of widening, then roll outward.

Maintain an outward collapse as you pull the skates together, using the outside edges for leverage.

a

b

c

3.16 Edge control subdrill C: Platform-width change with edge manipulation.

Explanation:

Glide in a straight line. Starting with the skates together (figure 3.16a), collapse the ankles inward and use the inner edges of the wheels to push the feet apart (3.16b). When you reach this point, roll the ankles to the outside, using the outer edges to pull the skates back together (3.16c).

Drill Series 2: Scissors Exercises

Scissors drills are so named because they involve the coordinated action of both legs. More specifically, both legs deviate from the body's midline concurrently and then return toward the center (midline) of the body. Further, each cycle of the drill alternates so that both the right and left skates take a turn in front of the other. Before attempting the drills in this series, it is crucial to attain perfection in each of the subdrills of the previous edge-control exercises.

Subdrill A: Introductory Scissors Drill

Objective:

Introduce the first level of scissors activity, with each leg taking a turn in front of the other.

What to Watch For:

Glide in a straight-line path.

As the legs actively pull together, one skate moves in front of the other so that the rear skate moves almost *directly* behind the one in front.

Both skates then move apart again. On the subsequent pulling toward the midline, the skate that was behind now takes position in front.

At the widest point, the skates should be no more than 24 inches apart.

There should be no lateral or vertical deviation in the hips (center of gravity), that is, no weight transfer; and the legs should move independently, with no displacement in the orientation of the pelvis.

a   b

c

d

e

Explanation:

Begin with the skates together (figure 3.17a). Push both skates apart to a distance of roughly 24 inches (3.17b). Pull both legs together, so that one skate moves directly in front of the other (3.17c). Push the legs apart again (3.17d). On the subsequent cycle, draw the other skate in front as the legs pull together (3.17e). Repeat several times. At this point, do not worry about what the edges are doing.

Subdrill B: Scissors Drill With Outside Edge Control

Objective:

Rolling the ankles to the outside, maintain the wheels on the outer edges throughout the entire drill.

What to Watch For:

This drill should incorporate all the points listed for subdrill A.

The ankles must roll to the outside to start the drill.

At the widest point, the skates should be no more than 18 inches apart.

There should be no lateral or vertical deviation in the hips (center of gravity); the legs should move independently, with no displacement in the orientation of the pelvis.

Explanation:

Repeat the drill as outlined for scissors subdrill A. The only change to make involves rolling the ankles to the outside for the entire drill. See figure 3.18, a–e.

a

3.18 Scissors subdrill B. Scissors drill with outside edge control.

b

c

d

e

Subdrill C: Scissors Drill With Edge Manipulation

Objective:

Incorporate edge motion, adding it to the previous scissors drill by rolling the ankles inside for the push and outside for the pull.

What to Watch For:

This drill should incorporate all the points listed for subdrill A.

The ankles should roll inward to use the inside edge of the wheels as the skates move apart.

Roll the ankles outward upon full displacement (no more than 18 inches), using the outside edges to pull the skates back together in front of one another.

Accentuate the points where the ankles roll from outside to inside (widening), and inside to outside (pulling).

There should be no lateral or vertical deviation in the hips (center of gravity); the legs should move independently, with no displacement in the orientation of the pelvis.

Explanation:

Repeat the drill as outlined for scissors subdrills A and B. Begin in the basic position as usual (figure 3.19a). The only change to make involves rolling the ankles inward as the legs move apart (3.19b), and then outward as they pull together (3.19c and 3.19d). Roll the ankles inward again at the beginning of the next push (3.19e). Repeat several times.

a

b

3.19   Scissors subdrill C. Scissors drill with edge manipulation.

c

d

e

Drill Series 3:
Double-Push Exercises With Weight Transfer

Once a high level of proficiency has been reached for all previous drills, the next objective is to incorporate a shift in body weight into the scissors exercises. Because this movement is dramatically different from classic technique, this is the point where the majority of skaters begin to have trouble.

Subdrill A: Scissors Drill With Weight Transfer

Objectives:

Introduce a shift in the center of gravity (weight transfer) to the execution of the scissor motion.

Incorporating proper edge dynamics, begin to differentiate between the push and pulling/support legs.

What to Watch For:

Begin by designating one leg as the push leg, the other as the support leg.

As the skates widen, the body weight moves away from the pushing skate. The body weight and support leg should move together.

The push-leg skate should use the inside edge of the wheels, the support leg skate should use the outside wheel edge.

With the legs/skates at their widest point, almost full body weight should be carried by the support leg.

Maintain the support leg skate on the outside edge as it pulls inward to take position in front.

Both skates remain on the ground at all times.

3.20 Weight transfer subdrill A. Scissors drill with weight transfer.

d

e

Explanation:
Perform the scissors drill as outlined in the previous drill. Once forward momentum is achieved (figure 3.20a), the skates widen, and the body weight moves *away* from the skate of the *push leg*; in other words, shift the body weight *toward* and *over* the *support leg* (3.20b and d). The support leg and body weight should move together as a unit. The push leg should use the inside wheel edge while the support leg should be positioned over the outside wheel edge. Once the widest point is reached, the support leg should pull toward the body's midline (using the outside wheel edges) while the push leg falls in behind (3.20c and e). The support leg in front will now become the push leg as the skate rolls from the outside to the inside of the wheels as it pushes. As this occurs, the rear leg becomes the new support leg as the body weight again *moves away from the push*. The support skate now uses the outside wheel edge as the leg moves with the body weight. With the body weight still moving away from the push, the support leg pulls inward using the inside wheel edges. The push leg now falls in behind.

Subdrill B: Weight Transfer Drill With Recovery Toe Sweep

Objectives:

Introduce a modified recovery to the previous drill.

Ensure that the majority of body weight is over the support leg as it pulls toward the midline.

What to Watch For:

Begin by executing the drill sequence in the same manner as the previous exercise.

Once the pushing skate reaches full extension, ensure that almost full body weight is over the support leg.

As the support leg pulls inward using the outside wheel edge, gradually flex the knee of the push leg so that the skate rolls on the toe wheel.

As in the previous drill, the pulling support leg should take position in front of the recovery leg.

Explanation:

Once forward momentum is achieved (figure 3.21a), repeat the last scissors drill. When the push leg reaches full extension (3.21b), roll the skate onto the toe wheel and regroup it behind as the support leg pulls inward (3.21c and e). Ensure that the support leg performs its action on the outside wheel edge of the skate. With the push leg recovered behind the support leg, begin the next stride by moving the body weight away from the front push leg. The recovery leg becomes the support leg as soon as all wheels contact the ground (3.21d). Ensure that the support skate is immediately placed down on the outside wheel edge. Repeat the sequence several times.

3.21 Weight transfer subdrill B. Weight transfer drill with recovery toe sweep.

c

d

e

Subdrill C: Double-Push Arm Swing

Objectives:

Incorporate proper arm-swing mechanics into the double-push movement pattern.

What to Watch For:

Double-push arm-swing mechanics are similar to those described in chapters 1 and 2.

Always swing the arms away from the direction of push.

Hold the arms in a static position as the support leg pulls inward and the recovery leg sweeps behind on the toe wheel.

Explanation:

Repeat the exercise as in subdrill B, but include a two-arm swing into the motion.

First, achieve forward momentum (figure 3.22a). As the leg pushes to the side, swing both arms across the body away from the direction of push (3.22b).

Hold the arms in this position as the support leg pulls inward and the push leg recovers behind on the toe wheel (3.22c). As the front leg begins to push and the recovery skate moves with the body weight, swing the arms back across the body (3.22d). Again, hold the arms in this static position during the pulling/recovery action (3.22e). Repeat several times.

3.22 Weight transfer subdrill C. Double-push arm swing.

c

d

e

Subdrill D: Slow, Exaggerated Double-Push Skating

Objective:

Transform the skills learned to this point into slow and exaggerated double-push skating.

Explanation:

Implement all the key points as outlined in the preceding drill, but add the following modifications. Rather than rolling the push leg onto the toe wheel to recover behind the support leg, lift the skate off the road when you reach full extension (figure 3.23a). To do this, it is imperative that all the body weight is over the support leg. Once the push leg lifts off, pull the support leg inward toward the midline as in 3.23b (while it still supports the entire body weight). Continue the pull so that the leg crosses under and across the body as the free (push) leg continues to recover behind (3.23c). At the onset of pushing force, the body weight begins to move away from the direction of push (3.23d). As this occurs, "throw" the free leg out to the side in the direction of weight transfer, setting it down on the outside edge (3.23e). During this process, the center of gravity should move together with the set-down leg, falling away from the pushing side. Once the recovery skate touches the ground, it then becomes the weight-bearing support leg. Perform the drill very slowly, and gradually accentuate all aspects of the movement.

3.23 Weight transfer subdrill D. Slow, exaggerated double-push skating.

b

c

d

e

Advanced In-Line Techniques

Speedskating requires proficiency in many technical elements beyond the actual movement pattern. These secondary skills and methods involve coping with race dynamics and a host of factors inherent in the sport itself. This chapter outlines the more important of these techniques and skills that drive competitive success.

In-line racing is a pack sport. It can involve an enormous variety of course settings, race conditions, and other factors that influence a race's outcome. In-line racing demands a great deal more versatility of its participants than does ice speedskating. A solo endeavor whose chief measure of success is the time clock, long-track ice speedskating requires no less commitment or dedication on the part of its athletes. Long-track ice racing does not require the pack awareness, however, or the mobility, technique, and tactics so crucial to in-line racing.

In-line racing is unique in terms of technical components. In fact, the sport has much more in common with bicycle racing than it does with any other type of speedskating. Mastering the skills and techniques in this chapter will not by itself assure that an individual can dominate the competition. Without such consistent proficiency, however, success would be virtually impossible.

RACE STARTS

There are basically two types of outdoor race starts, and they differ dramatically from one another in form, purpose, and execution. The first (less important to this discussion) is the solo time-trial start used for the 300-meter sprint race. This event occurs almost exclusively in the national selection trials and in such international events as the World Championships and Pan American Games. Relatively few individuals will ever use this start, and those who do have likely been taught by a well-trained coach. Therefore, this start method needs only brief discussion here.

Sprint Start

The 300-meter solo time-trial sprint is unique because the race is not a "gunned" start in which a skater must react to a starter's pistol. Rather, the skater may begin whenever he or she is ready. The timing device is initiated once the skater "breaks" the electronic beam on the start line. In this start method, a skater explosively launches off the line with maximal power, reaching peak velocity as rapidly as possible. The theory behind the sprint start is that the skater should have as much momentum as possible before breaking the beam and starting the timing device. Using a conventional type of start position for this race is a poor option, since the timer is activated the instant the skater moves the front skate across the beam. To take full advantage of the start format, the sprint start involves using the rear leg to first cross the line and initiate the timing. This allows the skater to already be in motion the instant the clock starts.

4.1 The 300-meter sprint start.

Step 1

The skater assumes the initial position with the skates in a T shape, each skate at a 45-degree angle to the direction of travel. The stronger leg, placed in front to be used as the push-off skate, has the last wheel touching the middle wheel of the rearward skate. In this way, the skate of the power leg is slightly more forward and closer to the starting line.

Step 2

Keeping the skates together, the knees are deeply flexed as the hind end sits back. During this lowering of the center of gravity, the arms are positioned straight out in front of the body to maintain stability. In this position, body weight is evenly distributed over both skates, with no motion occurring in the feet or legs. This low, static position is held about one or two seconds until the skater feels stable. (Figure 4.1a.)

Step 3

From the seated position, the next movement involves the rearward leg extending back in the same direction as the line of the orientation of the front skate. To perform this, all the body weight must be carried by the front leg, which remains in a deeply flexed position. This is immensely important, since the skate of the front, power leg must not roll during the step-back. (Figure 4.1b.)

b

c

d

e

Step 4

The rear leg remains in this extended position with all the body weight over the front, power leg. The skater rocks back to transfer all of the mass onto the rear leg. Accomplishing this transfer involves extending the front leg smoothly and completely, lowering the hips slightly, and allowing the entire upper body to travel horizontally until the free (rear) leg supports all of the weight. As the body weight is transferred onto the rear leg, it progressively bends at the knee to a 100-degree angle. The arms should follow the upper body, drawing into and over the rear leg. The entire movement of body weight must be smooth, and the transfer often moves in a slight arc, with the body weight being lowered and then raised as full support is carried by the rear leg. Once the hips have moved back and all the body weight is positioned over the rear leg, the transition to the next step is quite abrupt, with little time spent on the rear leg. (Figure 4.1c.)

Step 5

From the position achieved in Step 4, the skater now reverses the rocking motion and trajectory of the center of gravity. The rear leg powerfully extends to thrust the hips and body weight back toward the front, power leg. As the rear leg progressively straightens, the front knee flexes to accommodate the body's weight (figure 4.1d). The front, power leg allows the momentum to be carried forward as it simultaneously pushes from its original 45-degree angle to launch the body across the start. The hips are explosively thrust up and forward by the power leg, as the rear leg flexes at the knee and hip to drive through and under the body in preparation for the first stride. In this way, momentum is fully exploited, with the rear, free leg breaking the beam first. (Figure 4.1e.)

Mass Starts

Most in-line races use a mass start, in which all participants begin simultaneously from one starting line. The largest events may have well over a thousand participants (see figure 4.2). Whereas the elite skaters at the front usually get away cleanly and without incident, those remaining in the field have to deal with the mayhem that can result from so many skates moving about in seeming chaos. For inexperienced skaters, the start of a race can be intimidating, and sometimes even a dangerous experience. What makes the situation frightening is that not all skaters are pushing in the same direction at the same time. Some skaters push to the left, others to the right, and all seem to be frantic to avoid colliding.

The best remedy for fear and apprehension is to increase one's level of confidence. Confidence can be increased relatively easily with some modifications to body position which increase stability and decrease the risk of entanglement. The following list of recommendations should lessen stress and make mass starts safer and more effective.

- Position yourself in the start field according to your ability. This is only common sense. If you are an advanced skater, make sure you are at or close to the front. Do not get stuck behind several rows of skaters who are slower than you. If you are a novice or intermediate skater, make sure you are somewhere in the middle of the field. Nothing is more frightening than being slow off the start and having numerous skaters squeezing past you on both sides.

- Stay low. Keeping your center of gravity low helps to increase overall stability and decrease the chance of falling if you tangle skates with another competitor.

4.2 Large events like the North Shore Marathon (Duluth, Minnesota) draw over 2,000 skaters.

- Shorten your push displacement. Until you move clear of other skaters, it is a good idea to shorten the distance that you push to the side. This may mean you will not completely straighten the knee of your pushing leg at the maximal point of sideways extension.

- Take quicker strides. A faster stroke frequency goes hand in hand with a shorter push. Striding more often also means that you do not have to push as hard, and it gives you better fine control over your power output and speed.

- Be as solid as possible. You should aim to decrease the amount of lateral travel in your center of gravity. During a normal skating stride, the center of gravity "falls" or shifts from side to side with each push. But this horizontal moving of the center of gravity decreases stability at certain points in the stride cycle. Therefore, try to keep your hips in the same vertical plane without excessive sideward movement.

- Keep your head up, with your eyes focused only a few meters ahead. This will help you keep your feet (as well as those of others around you) in the field of peripheral vision.

- Gradually lengthen the push displacement, reaching full knee extension during the push once you're clear of heavy traffic.

- Use your arms to help maintain space around you. Until the field spreads out, use a two-arm swing to increase balance and stability—and to keep other skaters from encroaching into your personal space.

BASICS OF DRAFTING

Drafting refers to the practice of closely following one or more skater(s) in an attempt to lower the area of your body exposed directly to the air, therefore lowering the amount of drag and the overall effects of air resistance. Chapter 13 will shed light on the tactical elements of the practice of drafting. Here the purpose is to explain and illustrate the more basic technical elements of drafting and how to take advantage of it.

Learning to draft requires much practice and great perseverance. New skaters sometimes fear tangling skates by getting too close, an apprehension that can impede learning. Effective drafting requires confidence and adaptability, because no two skaters skate exactly alike. Some skaters are as steady as an arrow and as predictable as a drum beat; they are easy to follow. Others have fluctuations in speed, stride tempo, and the range of lateral movement in their stride, making them more difficult to follow. Add to this the confusion of a pack of skaters, and the result can be a very stressful environment.

Versatility is the key to success in drafting. Spending the time to develop and hone your drafting skills will pay big dividends on race day. Without doubt, drafting is the most important and fundamental secondary technical skill for any in-line racer to learn. It can be thought of as the basic technical unit for all pack-style speedskating, providing much of the foundation for the implementation of tactical maneuvers. See figure 4.3.

Drafting is what allows in-line races to be fast and what allows skaters to fully implement and exploit race tactics. It provides a means for skaters to conserve energy in the shelter of others, and allows weaker skaters to hang in with the main pack. Without drafting, put simply, in-line races would be dull and boring. Drafting is so intimately tied to the sport that it defines the true essence of in-line racing. Skaters

4.3 Drafting should be done as closely as possible without contacting the skater in front.

who lack the skill to draft efficiently and confidently suffer a severe disadvantage. To fully understand the importance of drafting, we will first examine some of the basic principles of aerodynamics.

Aerodynamics 101

Aerodynamics is a science that seeks to understand what happens to air as it encounters an object. In the case of a moving object, aerodynamic research focuses more specifically on how much resistance, or drag, the object in question creates as it splices through the tiny molecules that make up air. Whether the object is an automobile or a human on wheels, the laws of airflow hold uniformly true. Much as golfers strive for ways to drive a golf ball farther, skaters look for ways to maximize speed and efficiency on skates.

When a moving object collides with air molecules, it must force them out of the way if it is to continue. As the object proceeds, the air moves around the object and converges at some point behind (see figure 4.4). The act of moving the air aside creates resistance to movement. In aerodynamics, *drag* is a quantifiable but "unit-less" term used as a measure of this resistance. The two most important factors in determining the amount of drag an object creates are its frontal surface area and its velocity.

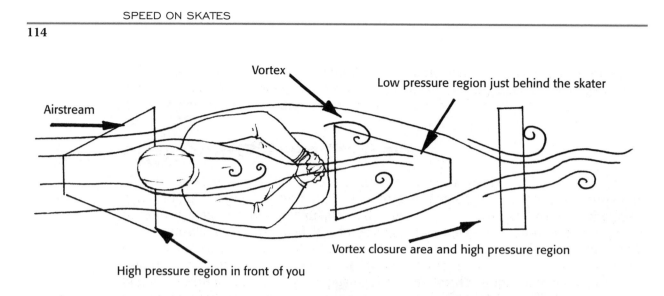

Vortex

Low pressure region just behind the skater

Airstream

Vortex closure area and high pressure region

High pressure region in front of you

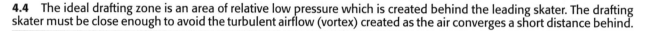

4.4 The ideal drafting zone is an area of relative low pressure which is created behind the leading skater. The drafting skater must be close enough to avoid the turbulent airflow (vortex) created as the air converges a short distance behind.

Frontal Surface Area

Frontal surface area can be thought of as the amount of square space that the air "sees" as an object moves through space. The greater the area, the more resistance to movement and the greater the drag force. Many of us unknowingly conducted our own experiments in aerodynamics when, as children, we held our hands outside the car window. Even at low speeds, we could feel the resistance increase dramatically as the hand moved from a horizontal to vertical position. The implication for a speedskater exposed to the air is quite obvious. The optimal position to reduce the effects of air resistance and reduce drag is one that is *low and compact*.

Velocity

What makes velocity, the other key factor in determining the amount of air resistance, interesting is the exponential relation between speed and drag. That is, resistance (R) increases in proportion to the square of velocity (V): $R = V^2$. Consider a situation where a skater travels at 15 miles per hour. When this same individual travels at twice the speed (i.e., 30 miles per hour) with the same body position and under the same conditions, the measurable drag is not simply double. Rather, the drag increases fourfold. This relation between velocity and drag force is described in figure 4.5.

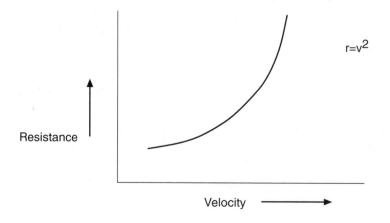

4.5 The relationship between drag and velocity is exponential (resistance = velocity²).

Resistance

Velocity

The *exponential increase in drag force* as the velocity increases has enormous implications for a skater. It explains why acceleration becomes increasingly difficult at higher speeds. More important for skaters, the relation further demonstrates how important drafting becomes for conserving energy during a race.

Energy Savings

It is difficult to precisely quantify the effects of drafting in an actual field setting under race conditions. The direction and force of the wind, the size of the skater you follow, how closely you draft the skater in front, and the velocity of motion all factor in to dictate how much drafting can help. A conservative energy savings estimate is about 25 percent. In strong head winds with a protective wall of skaters in front to act as a shield, these savings could easily approach 50 percent or more.

Distancing

One of the most common questions asked about drafting is "How close should I follow?" Without doubt, the most commonly observed execution error among developing skaters is to allow too much distance to open up between the lead and drafting skaters. See figure 4.6. An area of relative negative pressure is created behind a fast-moving object. This zone does not extend indefinitely, but closes up after the air moves around the object and forms a turbulent vortex. Therefore, a skater must follow closely enough to avoid the interrupted, "dirty" air. In general, one should draft as closely as possible without interfering with the lead skater's stride. When following another skater, the distance should be small enough to touch one's chin to the hands of the skater in front. Following some individuals, this is nearly impossible: skaters who have a big circular recovery or kick back excessively require leaving a little more space to avoid contact. The goal, however, remains the same: that is, get as close as possible without risking unnecessary contact.

4.6 The benefit of drafting is minimized when the distance between skaters is excessive.

Maintaining this close proximity when drafting is a difficult skill to master. Subtle pace changes at the front of the pack tend to become magnified toward the rear as everyone makes the adjustment. As the leader accelerates, the pack strings out as successive skaters respond to the increase in pace. When the group slows, the skaters toward the back experience the equivalent of a traffic jam. This yo-yo or slinky effect can leave the skaters at the back either sprinting to stay in contact with the pack, or encroaching on the back of the skaters ahead. Either reaction wastes valuable energy that will most certainly be needed later in the race. Even the best skaters will have some trouble dealing with this annoying but unavoidable situation. The only way to maintain your draft during pace changes is to understand a little about pack dynamics.

One key to maintaining adequate distance between you and the skaters in front of and behind you is to always be aware of what is happening at the front of the pack. Being able to anticipate the "slinky" is valuable. When the *pace slows* at the front, one should *be prepared to close up* on the skater directly in front. Inattention is a recipe for disaster—and a common cause of accidents. If the pack begins to compress, stop skating and let momentum close up the distance in front. It may even be advisable to gently place a hand on the lower back of the skater in front to maintain a safe distance. When doing this, it is a good practice to use the back of the hand to avoid the possibility of dragging the front skater down in the event of a fall. As one approaches the skater in front, slowly bend the arm to absorb any remaining momentum. If the pack continues to slow and your speed is still greater than those in front (as is often the case), avoid pushing the skater in front. If you must push the front skater ahead slightly, ensure that the push is gradual and in a straight line. Never push in an up, down, or sideward direction.

Inevitably, the pack *accelerates* and those toward the rear will be left to *catch up,* each successive skater striving to stay in the draft of the skater in front. Being able to anticipate this can help save energy. Although it is usually best to draft as closely as possible, there are times when falling back a bit is preferable. As the skaters at the front begin to accelerate, allow a small amount of space (perhaps twice the normal drafting distance) to open up between you and the skater immediately in front. This provides more space to accelerate when the skater in front begins his or her surge. If you stay immediately behind the skater in front, it will be difficult to start skating again until after the lead skater begins to pull away. By allowing a small gap to open, you can anticipate this effect and begin to accelerate an instant sooner. This will allow a more gradual acceleration, save energy, and decrease the time it takes to get back into good drafting position.

Synchronicity

The other crucial skill to develop for effective drafting is maintaining synchronicity with the skater(s) in front. This means trying to exactly mimic the timing of the front skater's stride. The instant he pushes with the left leg, for example, you do the same. If she has more lateral movement in her stride than you normally do, then you try to match it. To get maximum benefit from the air pocket the previous skater creates, you should be a virtual mirror image of the person, acting as one body. See figure 4.7. Closely following a skater with a movement pattern similar to your own is easy to do. Some skaters have such a different style, however, that following it requires considerable deviation from your own comfortable style. This is often the case when you follow a skater who uses a big push but a slow leg turnover (cadence). In this situation, the best option is to change position in the pack.

4.7 Experienced skaters fully exploit the benefits of drafting by skating in perfect synchronicity.

Many situations, such as a corner, an obstacle in the road, or a sudden change in pace, can break the rhythm of the pack. These occurrences result in a series of broken draft positions, with skaters striving to get back into harmony. Those skaters who can speedily return to a good draft position after an interruption will have a definite edge. A big part of improving your drafting technique is getting back in a draft position quickly. Once you are comfortable with basic draft position in a straight line, practice getting in the draft position as rapidly as possible.

Sometimes, for whatever reason, one gets completely out of phase with the skater in front: while the skater in front is pushing to the right, you are pushing to the left. There are basically three ways to get back in sync. The first, and easiest, way is to simply take smaller, faster strides until you are back on the same stride cycle. This method takes several seconds, however, and can waste energy. The second way is pushing off the same leg twice to bring you back in sync. Because it keeps the feet moving, it is easier, but this method does require a certain coordination. The third method involves taking a split-second rest until the skater in front takes a push while you glide. As this happens, simply start up your own stride at the same instant. Although simple in theory, this is a less desirable choice; the brief pause can interrupt a continuous rhythm and allow a small gap to open. The best choice is to practice until you are comfortable with each of these methods. Experience and personal preference will then help you determine which method is appropriate in each specific situation.

PACK AWARENESS AND MOBILITY SKILLS

Whether you're an elite, intermediate, or novice skater, pack awareness is one of the most important skills to develop. Athletes in all pack sports must develop a keen alertness for the surrounding environment and be able to draw inferences from everything that is happening nearby. Since most skaters race without the benefit of a team, a skater must rely on his own intellect to acquire necessary sensory information. Professional skaters will point to the importance of being acutely aware of what's going on within the pack. Team skaters communicate constantly to inform their compatriots of who is doing what, warning them of dangerous movement, and notifying each other the instant a breakaway occurs. The skaters who race without the benefit of a team must rely solely on individual perceptions and awareness. For these individuals, being acutely aware of internal dynamics is no less important a skill to master. All skaters can benefit in performance by actively developing their perceptual skills.

4.8 Periodically scanning the surroundings is an important aspect of pack awareness.

Knowing when to lead, how to position yourself in the pack to maintain striking distance, and being able to recognize optimal pack position are all integral components of successful mobility. There is a great deal more to being a good in-line racer than having a superhuman capacity for oxygen, 28-inch quads, or a pain tolerance that would frustrate the devil. In-line speedskating requires the ability to cope with pack dynamics, draft effectively, and continuously monitor internal movement within the pack.

Scanning the Surroundings

A skater must constantly process all visual and auditory input. This means keeping both eyes and ears focused on the competition. When at or near the front of the pack, awareness takes the form of continually checking over the shoulder to see what is happening behind you. See figure 4.8. All skaters should get in the habit of doing a shoulder-check after every half-dozen strides, using peripheral vision to scan the area immediately to the side and behind. Make it a habit to scan both sides on an ongoing basis. Although it is easier to keep an eye on the action from the back of the pack, nonetheless it requires active attention.

Reacting to Movement

At most times it is important to stay close enough to the front of the pack to be within reaching distance and to be able to react to progressive movements in the group. Maintaining *reaching distance* means being in a position to respond to any and all breakaways or counterattacks if desired. Sandwiched between two lines of skaters at the back of the pack would be an obvious example of being outside this reaching area. It sometimes takes considerable energy and aggression to maintain a close distance from the front of the pack, but it is still more draining to be too close to the back. One of the best ways to avoid the continual cycling of position within the pack is to never get close to the rear of the group. Once you are at the tail of the pack, it is difficult to move up to the front, especially near the end of the race or if the group is large.

Interpretation

Another important aspect of awareness involves being able to interpret everything that is happening in the race. One must be able to recognize dangerous movement and to use observations to predict what may be about to happen. This interpretive skill develops over time, coming only with experience. Not only must skaters be able to identify the internal dynamics that may lead to a strategic move, but also to recognize which skaters look strong and which ones appear to be hanging on by a thread. These skills help you avoid undesirable situations. For example, remaining behind someone who is weak and may not be able to follow a break is a poor idea. When an important breakaway occurs, the skater in front might delay the chase to the point where latching on to the flyer is impossible. There's nothing quite like practice for honing these important skills, and a group or race environment is obviously the best place for rehearsing.

Sharing the Lead

Many pack sports share points of etiquette. One of these has to do with *taking a pull* at the front of the pack. The unwritten rule is that all skaters of a cooperative pack must take a turn doing some work at the front. In a pack of 20 skaters, naturally, not everybody will be expected to take a turn at the lead. This rule therefore applies more to small packs or breakaway groups where all skaters in that unit are working together toward a common goal. Nobody likes a "wheel-sucker" who hides from the wind by sitting comfortably at the back of the group, only to sprint out and pass when he's 100 meters from the finish to take the win. Some individuals do well using this strategy, but they get little respect from others. There are definitely times to pull and times to hide (see the section on competition). However, at some point during the race, all members of a co-op pack should do their fair share of the work.

In races with one or more teams mixed among individual entrants, it is understood that the team skaters will usually do the lion's share of the work at the front. It is nevertheless a point of etiquette, one borrowed from bike racing. For example, in one New England race, which only eight elite racers entered, five of the skaters were from the same team. However, none of these team skaters was willing to take the lead or push the pace. So the non-teammates (unattached skaters) controlled the race and subsequently tired themselves out. In the last half-mile, three members of the team took off and finished 1-2-3. Sure, the results were impressive, but no team should take pride in racing that way. Many skaters will do anything to win, and though such tactics are not contrary to the rules of racing, most other participants will feel contempt toward those who use them. This demonstrates the fine line between race tactics and what some may deem unethical actions.

Protecting Your Spot

In pack sports such as in-line racing, some positions in the pack are definitely more desirable than others. This is particularly true nearing the end of the race. A chaotic recycling pattern emerges, as all the skaters attempt to occupy the best position toward the front. Although much of this competition for the front relates to team strategy, even solo skaters try to protect their desired positions within the pack. From an aerial perspective, a pack looks like a fluid entity, constantly changing as the skaters surge toward the front in an attempt to find a good, stable draft position. Skaters at the back are continually moving up the side looking for openings to occupy.

Keeping the Door Shut

Protecting the space in front from would-be intruders is a demanding task at best. One way to protect your location is to limit the amount of space between you and the skater directly in front. Keeping the gap small is the best way to make your spot look unattractive. Experienced in-line racers will target the spots of competitors who look tired, rather than those who look comparatively strong. To a skater looking to move into the pace line, a large draft space makes for easy pickings. If you ensure that there is little space in front of you, most skaters will be deterred from choosing to occupy that position.

Guarding

Aside from keeping the draft space small, one of the best defenses against fellow competitors is using the technique of *guarding.* Guarding involves using the arm to form a physical barrier between you and the skater in front. This technique works best if you sit in a slightly more upright position. See figure 4.9. You then not only appear to be larger and a more menacing opponent, but the gap appears to be smaller, making the position seem less desirable. To guard, place the hand near or lightly on the hip of the skater in front. Doing this politely informs a threatening skater that the

4.9 Guarding is an effective way to deter would-be intruders from entering the pack in front of you.

spot is simply unavailable. To *counter* guarding, a rival competitor must look for another spot, barge in regardless of the blockade, or wait and use surprise as a tactic. Although this guarding technique is certainly not foolproof, it will deter most skaters from eyeing your spot with envy.

ECHELONING

Echeloning is a technique that facilitates the speed and performance of a cooperative group. In-line racers more than likely adapted this technique from the team time-trial used in bicycle racing. Echeloning involves a continual change in lead so that each member of the pack skates a short interval at the front while others in the group rest while drafting. The amount of time an individual stays at the front of the pack breaking the wind is usually quite short. Typically, each skater spends equal time leading as all the others, although in some cases a dominant skater will take a longer pull than the others. For echeloning to be maximally effective, all of the group's members must be of similar caliber. Otherwise, weaker skaters will burn out quickly, stronger skaters will not fully use their available energy, and the overall efficiency of the unit will decrease.

Because echeloning is used by skaters with a common goal, it is implemented only in certain situations. In 1995, for example, at the 100-kilometer marathon in New York City, a group of six skaters broke away from the main pack about 20 kilometers into the race. Naturally, each member of this small pack wanted the same thing: to maintain or extend the group's lead over the main pack. In this situation, echeloning was the most effective method for accomplishing this goal. Echeloning can define the essence of symbiotic cooperation, as rival skaters work together toward a common goal.

Changing Lead Off the Front

The most common method of echeloning is changing the lead off the front. This means that the leading skater takes a turn breaking the wind for the others (figure 4.10a), then pulls off to the side (4.10b), and moves into the last position of the pack. The skater who pulls off then exposes the next one in line, who becomes the new leader until she pulls off to the side (4.10c). Thus the group cycles itself in an almost circular fashion. Usually, the group will recycle clockwise. That is, the lead skater will pull off to the right. This does not have to be the case, however. What is important is that each skater pulls off to the same side following the stint at the front of the pack.

a

4.10 Echeloning. Changing lead off the front is an efficient way for cooperative groups to function.

b

c

Although the pattern of cycling is always uniform, the group must decide how quickly to change the lead. The course, environmental conditions, and, most importantly, the size of the group and its intensity of speed usually determine the pace of changes. In large packs the lead changes quickly, whereas in smaller packs (i.e., three or four skaters) each member may stay at the front significantly longer. Where the cycling of the pack is rapid, the lead skater will pull off and slowly regress to the rear. The new lead skater will pull over *almost immediately* after the former leader falls behind slightly as seen in figure 4.10. Although each skater is exposed to the wind, each actually leads for only several seconds before moving into position at the end of the pace line.

In small groups, by contrast, each skater may spend as many as 60 seconds at the front. As a general rule, the lead skater should pull over to relinquish the lead just before beginning to tire and slow the pace of the group. Once in relative shelter at the back of the pack, a skater can rest up for the next turn at the front. In this way echeloning almost resembles interval training, in which short, higher intensity bursts are interspersed with periods of relative rest and recovery.

Changing Lead From the Back

Although less common, sometimes a pack will echelon by changing the lead from the back of the group. That is, a skater will pull off from the *last* position, move up the side, and slide into the lead position. Because moving up the side can be very fatiguing, the cycling of the pack from the back is always fairly rapid. Once the rear skater pulls out and moves along the side, the skater now at the back follows almost immediately after, falling into the draft of the skater in front. Because of the more rapid nature of this recycling, the skater who moves into the front position is the leader for only a few seconds. While the remainder of the pack cycles off the back and moves to the front, skaters can rest until they once again find themselves in the last position.

Two reasons make this method of echeloning less desirable. For starters, pulling off the back and accelerating to move up to the front of the pack is physically demanding, especially at higher speeds. Second, having the fast-moving skater pull in front to take the lead of the pack tends to spread out the group as the skater who was once in front accelerates to close up the small gap and get in a good drafting position. Each successive skater in the pack then must speed up to stay close to the skater in front, causing a slinky effect. On the plus side, this method ensures that the group's pace is kept fast. In many races, a pack often displays a sort of randomized echeloning from the back, with skaters moving up to be in the more desirable front positions or to support a teammate who may be leading the group.

RESTING DURING A RACE

Experienced skaters know exactly how and when to take a breather during a race. Even a few seconds of rest can be enough to remove some lactic acid from the legs, temporarily revitalize one's energy, and relieve the strain on aching back muscles.

There are two good, basic ways to rest during a race. The first is placing the hands on the legs just above the knees and using the upper body to facilitate leg action (figure 4.11a). During gliding, this technique can help reduce the strength that the leg muscles require for supporting body weight, or it can enhance push-off forces during sideward extension of the leg.

a

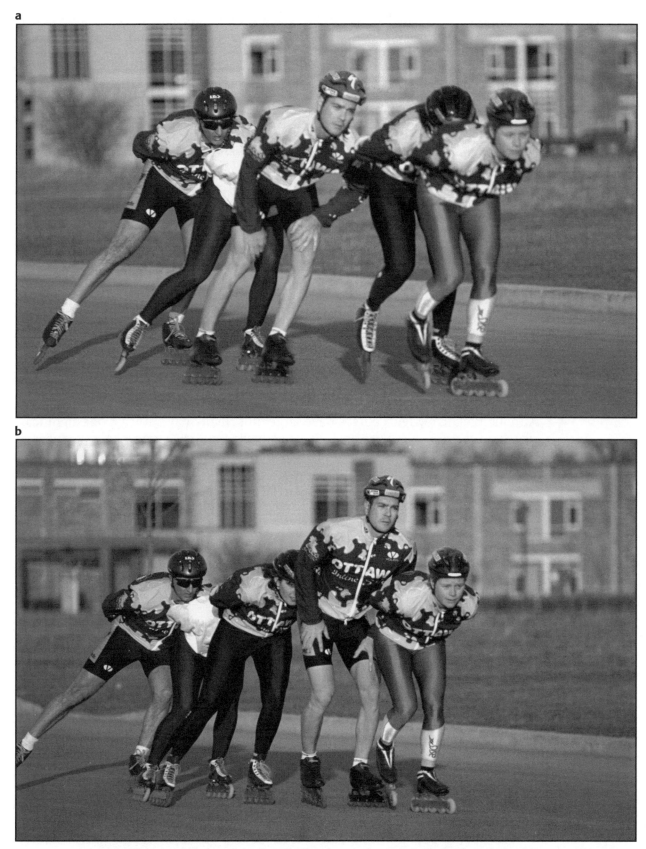

b

4.11 Two common resting techniques: *(a)* using the hands to help support the body and supplement pushing force gives the legs a much-needed break; *(b)* standing up momentarily provides valuable rest for the lower back.

To use this method while gliding, place both hands just above the knees. With the elbows slightly bent, the arms try to actively extend against the legs, which reduces the amount of intramuscular tension in the working muscles and thereby helps increase blood flow. To use it while skating, again place both hands on the legs with the elbows bent. When the one leg pushes to the side, the arm on that leg also should extend, to reduce the amount of force that the quadriceps muscles must generate to produce propulsion. The hand on the other leg simply helps support the knee bend. The skater strides normally, with the hands staying in contact with the legs at all times. The time and practice it takes to be able to feel the support that the arms add is well spent.

The second resting technique involves "standing up" momentarily, during either a downhill or slow time in the race (figure 4.11b). This so-called standing means straightening the knees and raising the trunk. Even a few seconds of up-time can make a big difference. Not only does this position momentarily give the lower-back muscles time to relax, but also the brief release of tension in muscles of the lower body helps improve blood flow to remove lactic acid. Keep in mind that competitors may be watching for skaters to take such a rest so they can then launch an attack on the group. Always pay attention to other competitors when you take such a break, and be prepared to quickly return to skating motion at the slightest hint of pack activity.

SKATING THE HILLS

Although relatively few courses have large hills, many have at least one significant rise in elevation. Skating the hills effectively requires some slight changes in technique, which mostly depend on the length and grade of the hill. Even short and small hills, however, require some modification to technique.

Uphills

Skating up a hill considerably changes the mechanics of efficient motion. As the incline reduces speed, it alters the biomechanical characteristics of push execution in several ways. Here are five key areas of skating technique that deserve special attention in going up hills.

Direction of Push

When skating uphill, the direction of push should be more rearward. Pushing directly to the side, which is good on a flat road, does not counteract the effect of gravity, and therefore does not generate much forward propulsion. It is difficult to specify the exact direction of push because it depends on the incline of the hill. Suffice it to say that a steep hill will require a skater to push back more than a gentler one.

Forward Shift in Body Weight

In addition to directing the push more rearward for skating uphill, you should shift the body weight more forward on the skates. On flat ground, a deep-seated body position will position the center of gravity roughly over the middle of the skate. When skating up a hill, both the knees and trunk should be bent slightly less. These changes in basic body position will carry the center of gravity forward more. This being said, the skater should still avoid excessive flicking of the toes at the end of the push.

Shorter, Faster Strides

In combination with the more upright body position, a skater should use a faster stride cadence to climb a hill. The decreased angle in the knees will result in a shorter push displacement, further facilitating a higher stroke frequency.

Shortened Recovery Stroke

As you might expect, the upward incline will drastically increase the level of deceleration between strides. Tied in with the increase in stroke frequency is a progressive shortening of the recovery phase as a hill steepens. Rather than circling the recovery leg around the back when weight transfer occurs, the leg should regroup in a more direct fashion. The lack of glide on very steep hills means that there is little or no weight transfer at all.

Arm Use

On most hills, both arms should swing in coordination with the legs' activity. A two-arm swing is preferable, not only because it supplements the force output, but also because it helps keep the stride frequency high and regular.

Uphill Skating Tactics

When skating up a relatively long hill, the incline can be divided up into three sections. Each of these reflects slight differences in objectives and technique. When practicing hill-climbing technique, all inclines should be executed in this manner. The three phases of hill climbing are attack, maintenance of tempo, and acceleration.

Attack

It is advisable to attack the beginning of each hill. This means accelerating as the hill approaches, increasing stroke cadence, and aggressively ascending the initial slope of the incline. The purpose of this tactic is to delay the point at which significant deceleration occurs and force the other skaters in the group to match your speed. Since speeds are fairly low on most hills and the benefit of drafting is minimal, it is best to pull out from the group to begin the hill climb. This will also enable you to avoid getting stuck behind skaters whose lower speed or progressive fatigue can interfere with your approach to the hill.

Maintain Tempo

As the hill progresses and you begin to lose speed, your goal is to find a comfortable rhythm that you are confident you can maintain to the top. Therefore, your objective for the hill's middle third is to maintain a steady speed, leg tempo, and skating rhythm. The quicker you can get into a comfortable "groove," the better you will be able to negotiate the incline. Time spent training on inclines will help you determine what type of stroke cadence and level of effort is appropriate. It is essential that the intensity of your effort be low enough to resist fatigue and avoid a major drop-off in speed midway up the hill. The goal is to ascend the hill at the highest rate possible while saving some energy for the final third of the climb. Chasing skaters who start out faster than you would prefer is a risky practice. These skaters often fade in the second half of the hill, so stick to your game plan and you will likely catch them before the end.

Acceleration

During the last third of the incline, you should gradually accelerate up to and over the crest of the hill. As this is the point where most skaters "bonk" (run out of steam), being able to accelerate and pull ahead of the group has a major psychological impact on rival skaters. Because of this, the last third of a hill is an opportune time to launch a solo attack. It is vital to be able to reserve the energy for this tactic by not ascending the hill too quickly. Since other skaters may also employ this type of maneuver, you should always be ready to follow the lead of others who try to break away.

Downhills

Skating down an incline also requires significant, but more subtle, changes in technique. Going on a steep downhill, it is usually preferable to simply glide. However, you can best negotiate many downhills by continuing to skate. Consider these modifications to technique when you descend an incline.

Direction of Push

Unlike uphill skating, the direction of push for descending an incline is completely *sideways*. Try to accentuate this direction by pushing sideward but also slightly forward. A deeply seated body position should be emphasized, using push displacement to full advantage. In addition to the direction of push, it is important to extend the push leg with near-maximal velocity. The added speed down the hill will require a "faster" push to apply propulsion effectively.

Stroke Frequency

When skating down a hill, stroke frequency can be significantly slower than on a flat road. Since the momentum from gravity helps maintain speed down the hill, glide time should be optimized. Increasing the time to execute the recovery of the pushing leg is one simple way to fully take advantage of gravity's effect. Most skaters will be able to determine the most effective stride cadence instinctively by observing the precise instant when velocity begins to decrease during the glide. The next push should be performed before excessive deceleration occurs.

Gliding

For gliding down a hill in a pack, it is recommended to place one hand on a knee to increase stability and to reduce the legs' energy cost for supporting the body's weight. The *back* of the other hand is placed on the lower back of the skater ahead. (Using the palm of the hand only increases the likelihood of clutching the skater's clothing if balance is lost.) Gliding down a hill can provide valuable rest time.

SKATING IN THE RAIN

Few skaters opt to train in wet weather. The reality is that at some time most of us will experience the perils of skating in the rain (figure 4.12). Races will usually be canceled if rain is falling at start time. Once the gun goes off, however, almost all races will continue, regardless of what falls from the sky.

Skating on wet pavement requires some major changes in technique. It is nearly impossible to apply push-off force without slippage. The truth is that even the most accomplished wet-weather skaters who know how to best deal with this situation

4.12 Skating in the rain poses a unique challenge for in-line racers.

will have problems. Wheel selection, for example, can significantly affect traction with the road. But implementing slight changes in skating mechanics offers a more decisive advantage than any selection of hardware.

Apply Push-Off Force Gradually

When you skate on a dry road, traction is rarely, if ever, an issue. The forceful extension of the pushing leg should therefore accelerate throughout the entire range of sideways motion and then display a distinct snap of power at the end of the push. When you skate on a wet road, you must change so that your push-off force is applied evenly as the leg extends to the side. Since most of the push-off force develops in the first one-third of the extension, slippage will occur almost immediately as the leg begins to extend. Modifying the push so that the leg develops force more gradually will undoubtedly reduce the amount of power generated, but is worth it in terms of reduced wheel slippage.

Stay on Top of the Wheels

Try to maintain the wheels nearly vertically when you skate on a wet road. Normally, the wheels progressively angle toward the inside edge as the push extends to the side, and when traction is not an issue, this is the most effective way to apply force to the road. In wet conditions, the wheels tend to slip more if they are on the inside edge, especially if they are worn down. Therefore you should try to keep the wheels vertically aligned through most of the push.

Shorten Push Displacement and Increase Stride Tempo

Overall, it is advisable to shorten push displacement and increase stride tempo for skating in the rain. Doing so helps reduce the chance of slipping when the leg is fully extended, while the increase in stride tempo helps maintain a high power output by applying force more regularly.

Don't Waste Energy

Skating in the rain is considerably more fatiguing than skating in dry weather. More muscular effort is required to maintain balance and stability and avoid wheel slippage on a wet road. Though changes in the mechanics can increase your traction, they often do so at the expense of efficiency. To offset this loss, conserve all your available energy by reducing needless, extraneous movements in the pack.

FINISHING SPRINT

Even if you're not in the lead pack of skaters, having a strong finishing sprint is a definite asset for improving personal performance. Skaters with good finishing-sprint technique can move up several placings in the last few hundred meters. Conversely, skaters who lack proficiency in this area can lose just as many positions. A description of the three important aspects of a solid finishing sprint follows.

Setting Up

Regardless of your relative position in the pack, it is important to set up for the sprint to the finish. This means leaving yourself in optimal position when the first move toward the finish occurs. The exact specifics depend on the course and the size of the group you are in. For example, consider a road course with a tight turn at 300 meters from the finish. In this instance, it would be important to be at or toward the front of the group going into the corner. Positions would likely change very little in the last straightaway, so it is safe to assume that the final corner would be a key catalyst in the sprint to the finish.

Knowledge of the course helps you determine where the final break might occur. Skating over the entire course before the event is not always a practical solution, but reviewing the final mile definitely is.

Learning to determine the best time to surge toward the front of the pack near the finish requires experience. Exploit your strengths whenever you can. A skater who has a good top-end speed and fares well in a big field sprint should wait as long as possible before initiating the sprint to the finish. Quite the opposite, a skater who lacks such top-end speed but who can sustain a high intensity for a longer distance should try to initiate the pack sprint earlier. Sometimes this means being the one to first take off and pull the pack apart. Other times, one can simply wait until someone else breaks from the pack, and then draft this skater until she or he begins to tire. When skating without teammates, it is often impossible to control and manipulate the finishing stage of a race to suit one's preference. However, to maximize your finishing placement, do whatever you can to exploit specific strengths.

Sprint Technique

Several modifications to skating technique can help during the finishing sprint. Concentrate primarily on using a higher stride frequency (as opposed to pushing harder each stroke), especially in the last few-dozen meters. Although the best skaters combine more work per stroke as well as higher stroke frequency, it is primarily an increase in stride frequency that generates greater speed in a sprint (van Ingen Schenau, de Groot, and de Boer 1985).

When you are skating on fresh legs, you can apply more force on each push to accelerate and reach top speed. In the last moments of a race, however, the legs are usually fatiguing rapidly, making it almost impossible to elevate the force levels of the already-straining leg muscles. It is for this reason that skaters should consciously elevate stride cadence in a sprint. (Figure 4.13.)

A second modification to technique in the finishing sprint relates to knee bend. Although deeper knee flexion requires more muscular effort to execute push-off, it has two main benefits. A deeper knee bend will lower the center of gravity, thereby increasing overall stability. And the sideward push displacement will be increased, elevating the range over which the extensor muscles can generate propulsion and maximize speed and acceleration.

Third, both arms should swing forcefully to complement coordination and power output and to keep leg tempo high. Surprisingly, many skaters seem to forget to swing their arms until the last few meters.

4.13 For the lead pack, the majority of races end in a field sprint.

Hawking the Line

In some instances, a competitor may be sprinting in direct competition to reach the finish line. A technique known as *hawking the line* is commonly used by top skaters to ensure that the battle is won. International rules state that the victor is the one whose skate first crosses the line, so long as at least one wheel remains in contact with the road. In close sprints, a hawk is used to extend one skate ahead of the body. A skater who may be slightly behind the rival competitor may actually be able to defeat the opponent by using a hawking technique. Extreme balance and flexibility are required to safely perform a hawk at high speeds, however, and it therefore should be attempted only by experienced skaters.

Jabbing

The first, and more basic, hawking technique is *jabbing*, a technique that involves thrusting one leg straight forward with the wheels either completely flat (preferable) or balancing on the heel wheel. See figure 4.14. To perform the jab hawk, a skater must have all of the body weight on the rear, support leg. With the body weight sitting back slightly, the jutting leg is thrust as far forward as possible, while keeping at least one wheel on the road, and the knee is in full extension. Although jabbing itself is not difficult to perform, at higher speeds it can result in a momentary loss of balance. To succeed with this technique, timing is critical. The leg must be thrust forward at the precise instant if it is to be of value.

Anthony White

4.14 The jabbing technique.

Lunge

The lunge technique is considerably more difficult to execute, and only the best skaters will be able to perform this technique at sprint speed. The most difficult lunge involves projecting the front skate forward on the rear wheel while the rear skate balances on the toe wheel, somewhat like performing the splits. An easier version of the lunge involves keeping the front thrusting skate flat, while the skate of the rear leg balances on its toe wheel. Overall, the lunge is superior to the jab because it allows a skater to extend one skate significantly more forward, and a skater using this technique can expect to beat a competitor who is using the jab. Performing a lunge at high speeds, however, requires exceptional strength, flexibility, and stability. See figure 4.15.

4.15 The lunge technique: in pro racing, sometimes the difference between two positions is a matter of inches.

Jeff Dowling

PART II

Training

Improving Speed and Endurance

The human body is a complex mix of interrelated systems that function together to allow a person to perform near-miraculous physical feats. Exercise physiology, a science that serves to understand the mechanisms responsible for how our bodies adapt to physical stress—and subsequently improve over time—focuses on ways to improve all aspects of performance and physical potential. Through research and technology, modern exercise physiologists have developed methods for determining the precise frequency, intensity, time, and type of activity to optimally stimulate positive changes and adaptations. This information can be used to enhance the energy systems primarily responsible for facilitating peak performance in sports involving speed and endurance. The body has three energy systems and each is relevant to the sport of speedskating. This chapter highlights those systems and discusses their practical applications to training. It also describes the relation between heart rate and certain physiological indices and the practice of using exercise heart rate as a training tool.

PRINCIPLES OF TRAINING

A basic understanding of the general principles of training and the physiological processes that govern performance adaptation will help you in your quest to train for speedskating. This section will provide the conceptual framework for much of the training content that follows in this and other chapters.

Principle of Overload

Physical training involves exposing the body and its systems to a stimulus of sufficient intensity, duration, and frequency to produce a noticeable or measurable improvement in performance capability. To force the body to continually adapt, the level of *overload* it experiences must be greater than the normal functional demand on it. There are four components that can be manipulated to target specific physiologic effects. These components, collectively known by the acronym FITT, are varied primarily according to the precise physical adaptation an athlete seeks. Overload derives from these components:

- Frequency (F)
- Intensity (I)
- Duration/Time (T)
- Type of exercise (T)

Principle of Progression

According to the principle of *progression*, to sustain continued change and adaptation, it becomes necessary to gradually increase the *degree* of overload imposed on the body. The progression principle thus ties into the concept of training thresholds, since the level of overload required to force the body to adapt continually changes as the individual grows stronger. An individual exposed to a given level of overload will eventually reach a plateau in physical performance and adaptation. As one becomes fitter, therefore, it becomes necessary to continually increase the absolute amount of overload to observe further increments in performance capacity.

Principle of Overcompensation

The relationship between a training stimulus and the resulting adaptation is described by the principle of *overcompensation*. In essence, this principle demonstrates how a biological system deviates from a balanced state as the applied stimulus results in a process of breakdown and momentary fatigue. With recovery occurring between training sessions, the system bounces back and grows stronger, eventually surpassing its previous level of potential capacity. This concept therefore is a cornerstone in physiologic theory of training, the foundation of virtually all methodology related to performance enhancement. See figure 5.1.

Principle of Specificity

To achieve maximal effectiveness, the mode of training must approximate, as closely as possible, the *specific* activity for which one is training. In other words, applying this principle to speedskating, there is no better form of training than skating itself.

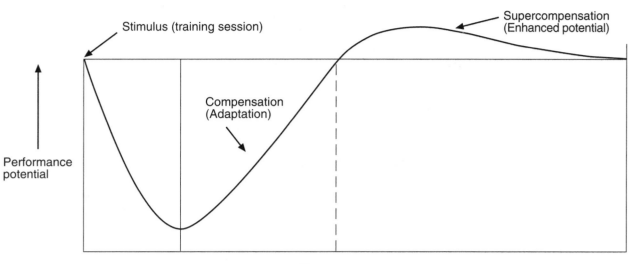

Stimulus (training session)

Supercompensation
(Enhanced potential)

Compensation
(Adaptation)

Performance
potential

Time

5.1 The principle of overcompensation. Performance improvement is achieved through successive alternating waves of stress and recovery. Following the application of a training stimulus (stress), the body adapts (recovery) and grows stronger (supercompensates).

For example, if the goal is to improve performance in a 10-kilometer in-line race, then the best training is to practice skating 10 kilometers (k) at race speeds. This would not only make training very dull, however, but would also be very physically fatiguing on the body. Fortunately, the specificity principle states that training should be specific to two main factors, which emphasize the need in training for the variables to closely approximate all aspects of the sport or event one is training for.

Specific Movement Pattern

The first specificity factor relates to the *pattern of muscular activity* observed in the specific sport form—training should be highly specific to how a muscle is worked. For our purposes as speedskaters, for changes at the muscular level to be transferable to actual performance, training must be developed so that it closely resembles the movement pattern of speedskating with respect to the type of muscle contraction, movement velocity, and joint angle.

Main Energy System Used in the Sport

To further maximize performance, training must focus on eliciting its primary effect on the particular energy system most heavily relied on during competition. This is particularly important for speedskating, since there is considerable variation in energy system demand/contribution between ice and in-line skating, and between various metric ice distances.

THREE ENERGY SYSTEMS

The body has three energy-providing systems at its disposal. Each has a specific pathway along which adenosine triphosphate (ATP), the basic cellular compound of energy, is created and utilized. Which system is the key provider of energy depends essentially on the intensity and duration of the exercise being performed.

140

The workings of energy systems are actually intricate and complex. Here we simply provide enough information to give you a foundation to understand some of the concepts and terminology under discussion. Each pathway is described separately, and then we describe how these systems function together.

Anaerobic Alactic System

The anaerobic alactic system (ATP-CP) provides an extremely rapid and powerful source of energy, without depending on oxygen transport and consumption. The chemical reactions involved are simple, and the fuel sources, adenosine triphosphate (ATP) and creatine phosphate (CP), are stored directly in the muscles, so the system can rapidly produce energy. While ATP is the basic energy unit that acts as a high-energy "battery pack," CP can be thought of as a molecular "battery charger" because of its vital role in resynthesizing ATP within this system. Because only ATP and CP are used in the anaerobic alactic system, the fuel substance glycogen is not consumed. As a result, this energy pathway produces no lactic acid (it is alactic).

The downside of the ATP-CP system is that is has a very limited capacity. In fact, if this energy pathway were the only one at our disposal, we could sprint with maximal intensity for only six to ten seconds before fuel depletion would terminate activity. Before this system can prime again, three minutes of complete rest time are required to fully restock the muscles with CP (see figure 5.2). Moreover, CP cannot be restocked during exercise. This substance can be reproduced only during the recovery phase while the aerobic system is running 100 percent.

Fuel depletion is the only cause of momentary failure in the ATP-CP system. In speedskating, this system is important for sprint events such as the 300 meter and 500 meter, and contributes progressively less with increasing race distance.

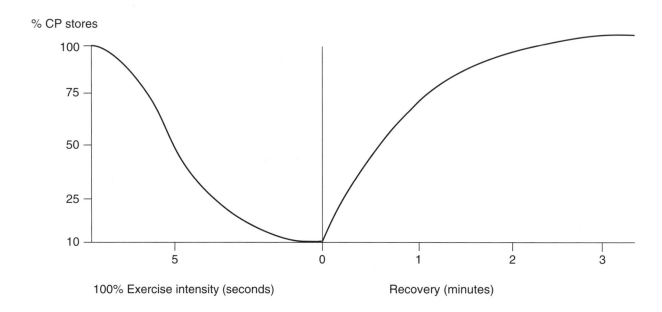

% CP stores

100% Exercise intensity (seconds)   Recovery (minutes)

5.2 The time-course of creatine phosphate (CP) use and resynthesis. At an exercise intensity of 100 percent, CP stores are depleted after about 6–10 seconds. When the aerobic system is running in high gear, its repletion occurs at an exponential rate.

Reprinted by permission from J.D. MacDougall and D. Sale, Department of Kinesiology, McMaster University, Hamilton, Ontario

Anaerobic Lactic System

This system, also termed the *lactic acid system*, is the main energy source for efforts lasting from 20 to 60 seconds. The primary fuel source for the anaerobic lactic system is glycogen. This substance, stored in both the liver and the muscles themselves, breaks down in the absence of oxygen to produce energy-yielding ATP molecules. Because of the complex nature of this system, the production of energy is comparatively slower.

With glycogen being consumed within this energy pathway, lactic acid is produced as a by-product. The intensity and, therefore, duration of the exercise largely determine the rate at which glycogen is used. This, in turn, determines the rate at which lactic acid is produced. Figure 5.3 illustrates the function of the anaerobic lactic system. Although the body has several means of eliminating and reusing lactic acid, it has limits. Once the rate of lactate production exceeds the body's removal capabilities, lactate begins to accumulate in the muscles and appears in the bloodstream shortly after. Lactic acid itself, in fact, is the primary limiting factor in performance. Since fatigue is induced by *high* lactic-acid levels, rather than by a depletion of fuel, this restriction (known as *end-product inhibition*) provides an athlete with the all-too-familiar burning sensation in the active muscles.

To recognize the importance this energy pathway has for the speedskater, one must look at the duration and intensity of the event. For the shorter metric ice races (such as the 500- and 1,000-meter sprints and the 1,500 meter), the lactic acid system is heavily used. However, even for considerably longer races which involve random fluctuations of high intensity effort (such as an in-line race or ice marathon), the anaerobic lactic system is vitally important. The fact that the speedskating movement pattern reduces muscle blood flow and forces muscles more readily toward anaerobic energy production further highlights the importance of this energy system for speedskating (van Ingen Schenau, de Groot, and Hollander 1983).

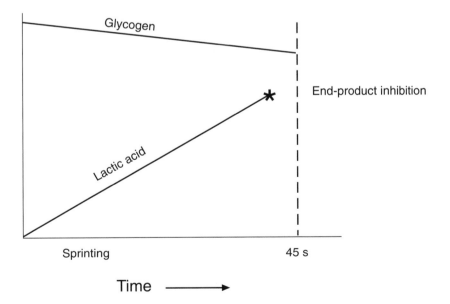

5.3 With a high exercise intensity such as a 45-second sprint, the degradation of glycogen is so rapid that large amounts of lactic acid are produced. Because the high lactic acid levels interfere with muscular function, such a limitation is referred to as end-product inhibition.

Data from MacDougall and Sale lecture notes.

There are no good methods for directly measuring and quantifying the energy yield of the anaerobic energy systems. In the laboratory, the most common simple test for indirectly measuring an individual's anaerobic (lactic) capacity is the Wingate exhaustive bicycle test. A subject is instructed to pedal as many revolutions as possible in a maximal 30-second bout while the power output is measured in 5-second intervals. The maximal 5-second power is assumed to correlate with the capacity of the ATP-CP system, while the 30-second average power output is used to infer the capacity of an athlete's anaerobic system.

Anaerobic Threshold

Among athletes in virtually all endurance sports such as speedskating, the anaerobic threshold (AT) is a major topic of discussion. Yet few athletes can actually define the term or its true impact on performance. Very simply, the anaerobic threshold (also known as the *lactate threshold*) refers to that intensity of exercise at which the production of lactic acid begins to exceed its rate of removal. See figure 5.4.

The precise timing of the AT usually corresponds with a shift toward anaerobic processes. Because it is possible for lactate production to exceed its re-uptake while aerobic processes still dominate, the term *lactate threshold* is more accurate. However, since most athletes seem to be more familiar with the term *anaerobic threshold*, it will be used exclusively for the duration of this book.

Although no universally applicable level of lactic acid can be associated with the AT, many sport scientists agree that the AT corresponds to a fairly predictable blood lactate concentration of four (millimoles). Many of them accept that through intensive training, it is possible to postpone the accumulation of lactic acid until higher intensity levels (i.e., raise the intensity level at which the AT occurs). Even between individuals of similar conditioning or performance level (or both), there exists significant discrepancy in the intensity at which this point occurs.

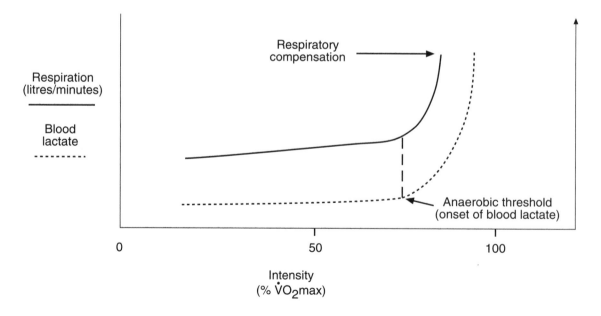

5.4 The anaerobic threshold. With increasing exercise intensity, the production of lactic acid eventually exceeds its rate of removal. This point, termed the anaerobic, or lactate, threshold is associated with an abrupt increase in both ventilation (respiratory compensation) and blood lactate concentration.

Reprinted by permission from J.D. MacDougall and D. Sale, Department of Kinesiology, McMaster University, Hamilton, Ontario.

Most often, athletes who have a high ability to use oxygen also have a high AT, but the relative importance of these two performance variables seems to depend heavily on the nature of the competitive event. Research seems to indicate that the power output corresponding to the AT is often a more representative indicator of performance capability than is an athlete's ability to use high levels of oxygen, particularly for endurance-type sports (e.g., in-line racing) that fluctuate in intensity (Åstrand and Rodahl 1986). In short events, where intensity levels exceed those that aerobic processes alone can support (such as the 1,500-meter), it may be that a high maximal aerobic power is more advantageous. In truth, the factors that determine endurance performance are far too complex to be explained by rationalizing only between these two physiological indices.

Aerobic (Oxygen) System

The aerobic energy system is the dominant one for producing ATP in prolonged exercise. This pathway, most closely associated with endurance-type activity, relies on the presence of oxygen for breaking down protein, fat, and carbohydrate nutrients to produce energy. Because these substances are available in large quantities, the aerobic system has a huge capacity for producing ATP. In terms of exercise duration, the aerobic system becomes the dominant contributor for energy in activities lasting longer than about two to three minutes. As exercise time increases, the aerobic system dominates more and more, while the anaerobic pathways contribute increasingly less energy.

The aerobic energy system is undoubtedly the most important for the in-line skater, as well as for metric skaters competing in distance events (5K and 10K). The power and capacity of this system, referred to as *oxygen uptake* or *oxygen consumption*, reflect the overall efficiency of this energy pathway. For many sports of prolonged duration, there exists a strong correlation between *maximal oxygen consumption* ($\dot{V}O_2$max) and performance capability. However, sport scientists have concluded that this relation is relatively weak for the sport of speedskating. That is, a well-developed aerobic system, and therefore a high $\dot{V}O_2$max, can greatly facilitate performance but not automatically guarantee success. A host of other technical and physiologically related factors prove equally important for certifying such performance success. Eric Heiden, likely the standard reference among speedskaters, had a $\dot{V}O_2$max of only about 63.8 ml/kg/min—high, but not extraordinary.

Concept Of Oxygen Consumption

Oxygen consumption ($\dot{V}O_2$) refers to oxygen being used within the cells of the body to carry on aerobic energy processes. This index, also known as *aerobic power*, is a volume measure of the total oxygen being used by the body at any particular time. Within limits, the amount of oxygen depends on the actual demand. That is, up to a certain point oxygen consumption rises in linear fashion as the workload of activity increases.

Probably the most recognizable format of this concept is the abbreviation $\dot{V}O_2$max. Like the anaerobic threshold, $\dot{V}O_2$max is a topic of heavy discussion among athletes, and it is also a source of great confusion and misinformation. Clinically, $\dot{V}O_2$max can be defined as the point during incremental exercise at which bodily oxygen consumption either ceases to rise further or begins to decline, even as the intensity of work continues to increase (figure 5.5). Oxygen consumption is considered to be the most useful indicator of an individual's ability to perform sustained heavy muscular exercise, and it reflects the power and efficiency of the aerobic system.

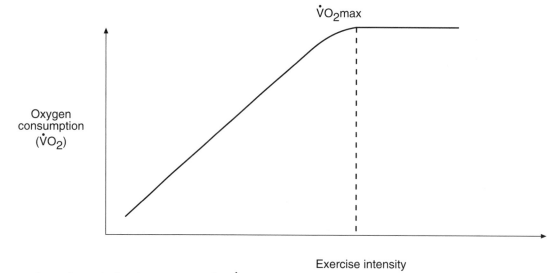

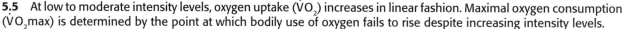

5.5 At low to moderate intensity levels, oxygen uptake ($\dot{V}O_2$) increases in linear fashion. Maximal oxygen consumption ($\dot{V}O_2$max) is determined by the point at which bodily use of oxygen fails to rise despite increasing intensity levels.

Athletes who use a large proportion of their body mass, such as cross-country skiers, typically record the highest $\dot{V}O_2$max values. Conversely, athletes who use only limited muscle mass usually record substantially lower values. Speedskaters typically record $\dot{V}O_2$max values similar to middle- and long-distance runners (Foster 1993). The average sedentary adult male or female has mean $\dot{V}O_2$max values of about 45 and 35, respectively. Elite speedskaters, in contrast, usually record values between 62 and 75 for males or between 50 and 52 for females. By comparison, cross-country skiers have recorded values as high as in the 90s.

BALANCE AND INTERPLAY OF THE ENERGY SYSTEMS

Although the three energy systems are often described as relatively separate and independent means of producing energy, almost all activities require that these energy pathways interact in a complicated way to transform bound-chemical energy into the mechanical energy used to facilitate muscle function. As discussed, the actual role each system plays and its contribution to total energy production essentially depends on the intensity and duration of an activity. See figure 5.6. In other words, the availability of oxygen in the muscle cells largely determines the extent to which energy production proceeds aerobically or anaerobically.

In table 5.1 we see that for a two-minute, high-intensity effort, such as an elite 1,500-meter ice race, the anaerobic systems yield about 50 percent of the energy, while the aerobic energy pathway supplies the remaining 50 percent. Table 5.2 shows the relative contributions of the three energy systems for a work time of 20 minutes, representative of a good 10K in-line race, the aerobic system dominating heavily.

Take some caution in interpreting these values, because they represent continuous activity performed at a steady state (pace). In-line racing and marathon ice skating are somewhat similar to road cycling in that race tempo often changes. Virtually all races have occasional, randomly interspersed sprints and attempts to break away from the main pack of skaters. Because of these high-intensity efforts, the anaerobic energy pathway is much more important than the values in the tables may indicate. It is safe to conclude, however, that the aerobic energy pathway is mainly

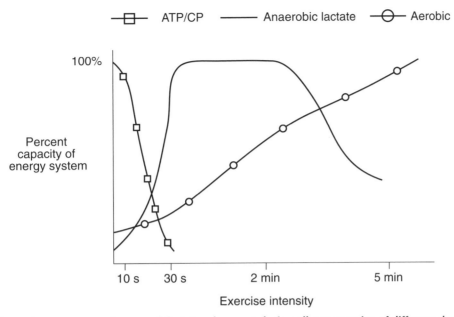

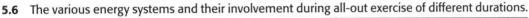

5.6 The various energy systems and their involvement during all-out exercise of different durations.

Reprinted, by permission, from J.D. MacDougall and D. Sale, Department of Kinesiology, McMaster University, Hamilton, Ontario.

responsible for energy yield in events exceeding three to four minutes. Still, the lactic acid system must be trained to allow the body to tolerate the high lactic-acid levels reached during the repeated high-intensity bouts. In simplified terms, then, both in-line and long-distance ice racing rely mainly on aerobic processes for the bulk of energy production, but also require a well-developed anaerobic system for achieving competitive success.

Table 5.1

Energy System Contribution With Steady-State Exercise Time

	EXERCISE TIME, MAXIMAL EFFORT						
Process	**10 s**	**2 min**	**10 min**	**20 min**	**30 min**	**60 min**	**120 min**
Anaerobic	85%	50%	10–15%	8%	5%	2%	1%
Aerobic	15%	50%	85–90%	92%	95%	98%	99%

Note: Based on data from Åstrand and Rodahl 1986 and MacDougall and Sale lecture notes.

Table 5.2

Percentage of Energy Contribution for a 20-Minute Steady-State Work Time

Work time	**Anaerobic alactic**	**Anaerobic lactic**	**Aerobic**
20 min	1%	7%	92%

Note: Data from MacDougall and Sale, 1993.

Intensity of Training

When you begin exercise at even low to moderate intensity, the anaerobic system is activated immediately, while the supply of oxygen within the cells is adjusted to meet the actual demand. Even once the aerobic system is up to speed and oxygen is adequately present to allow aerobic energy production, the anaerobic system remains active and produces lactic acid. The body can deal with this substance in moderate amounts, and can even transform it usefully. As exercise intensity rises slowly, the aerobic system has time to adapt to the gradual demand for energy. Although the anaerobic system is still active, most muscular energy will come through aerobic supplies until the production of lactic acid exceeds its re-uptake and removal (i.e., anaerobic threshold). At that point, the proportion of energy yielded by the anaerobic lactic pathway increases greatly, even as the aerobic system continues to work.

When an exercise is suddenly intensified (for example, in a breakaway during an in-line race), the sluggish aerobic system cannot respond quickly enough to meet the sudden incremental demand for energy. The actual intensity of the surge will determine exactly what happens next. If the intensity is so great that the aerobic system can simply not respond quickly enough to the sudden demand for energy (as is usually the case), then all further energy must be provided anaerobically. In this case, the anaerobic system kicks into high gear to accommodate the more rapid need for energy. This is the primary reason why the anaerobic system is so important for in-line racing.

During a short high-intensity effort, glycogen rapidly degrades. If the intensity exceeds the level of the anaerobic threshold, lactic acid will begin to build up rapidly in the muscles. Such an intensity cannot be sustained for long because lactic acid has a detrimental effect on muscular function. If the intensity once again subsides below the AT, the lactic acid will gradually be removed.

HEART RATE TRAINING

For some time physiologists, coaches, and athletes have known the value of monitoring heart rate during exercise to improve the quality and effectiveness of training. With the development and widespread availability of the modern telemetric monitor, heart rate monitoring has become a focal point for many athletes. From the weekend warrior to the elite athlete, many more athletes in endurance sports are using heart monitors. For many, the heart monitor is more a fun and trendy gadget than it is a performance-enhancing tool. Many individuals apparently do not know how to use their monitors for the best benefit. Careful monitoring of heart rate offers these benefits to athletes:

- Instant and continuous feedback information about the intensity of effort
- A valuable index of recovery between and after exercise bouts
- A valuable diagnostic for charting progress and checking fitness
- An indicator of fatigue (through charting resting heart rates), leading to the early detection of overtraining or illness

Since there are several good publications available specifically on heart rate monitoring, this section will only outline some theory behind heart rate monitoring and briefly describe how to effectively implement such monitoring in training for speedskating.

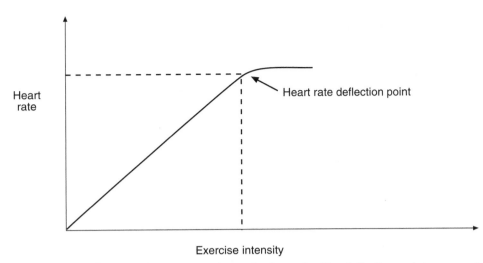

5.7 The relationship between heart rate and exercise intensity. The deflection point represents the highest intensity or heart rate which can be sustained without the rapid accumulation of lactic acid.

Physical Activity and Heart Rate

Heart rate monitoring is one of the most commonly used and easily understood standards for measuring the intensity and effort of physical exercise. There is a linear relationship between the intensity of exercise and the observed response in the heart rate, as can be seen in figure 5.7. What makes this interesting is that the one-to-one relation observable at low- to moderate-exercise intensities does not hold true once the activity level becomes intense. That is, there occurs a distinct point at which intensity and heart rate no longer increase in parallel.

The actual point at which heart rate and intensity fail to increase in linear fashion is often termed the heart-rate deflection point (Janssen 1987). Physiologically, this point represents an important transitional event. Essentially, it signifies when the athlete shifts from aerobic to anaerobic energy supply. What this means is that this point represents the maximal heart rate—and, therefore, intensity—that can be sustained for extended periods without experiencing lactate-induced exhaustion. So the heart-rate deflection point represents the level of the anaerobic threshold.

Monitoring the heart rate is one of the most notable and simplest ways to quantify the effects of endurance training. As the efficiency of the cardiovascular system improves, so too does the heart rate response at both rest and vigorous exercise. A change in heart rate following regular endurance training is often the first indication of improved physiologic capacity. In fact, following a sedentary period the heart rate response can change from even a few weeks of moderate-level activity.

Maximal Heart Rate

The highest rate at which the heart can beat is called the *maximal heart rate* (HRmax). An individual's age is the factor that most influences the value of HRmax. Simply put, this relation is expressed by a simple formula: HRmax = 220 – age. On average, maximal heart rate therefore decreases approximately one beat per minute for each year of advancing age.

Maximal heart rate is not affected by the conditioning process or improved adaptations in physiologic capacity. Nor can maximal heart rate be increased by endurance training. In fact, highly trained athletes may even experience a decrease in maximal heart-rate capability (MacDougall and Sale 1993).

Resting Heart Rate

Because the heart rate is very sensitive to improvements in endurance fitness, the most effective way to measure improvements in cardiovascular fitness is to monitor the resting heart rate. Endurance training improves heart and lung efficiency, thus attenuating the neural input to the heart and resulting in markedly lower readings. The average untrained individual has a resting heart rate of about 72 beats per minute.

Well-trained individuals may have resting heart rates between 40 and 50 beats per minute. Values in the low 30s have even been observed in elite in-line skaters. Although there is some evidence that resting heart rate may be genetically disposed, the influence of training has a far more profound effect. These factors affect the resting heart rate.

Time of Day

True resting heart rate must be recorded in the morning after a good night's sleep *before rising from bed*. Heart rate rises throughout the day, in general, and it may later reach 10 to 15 beats higher than the resting, morning value.

Fatigue

Resting heart rate observed in the morning can be affected by fatigue. An intense workout on the previous day will likely result in a slightly elevated resting heart rate when it is measured the next morning. Because of this, the morning heart rate is a sensitive indicator of overtraining, and it can also tell us much about the body's recovery process. Illness, anxiety, drugs, and alcohol can all affect resting heart rate. Figure 5.8a is an example of a heart-rate-tracking sheet of an athlete. Short-term fluctuations indicate temporary changes in fatigue and recovery, while the long-term gradual decrease indicates positive adaptations in the cardiovascular system. (See figure 5.8b.)

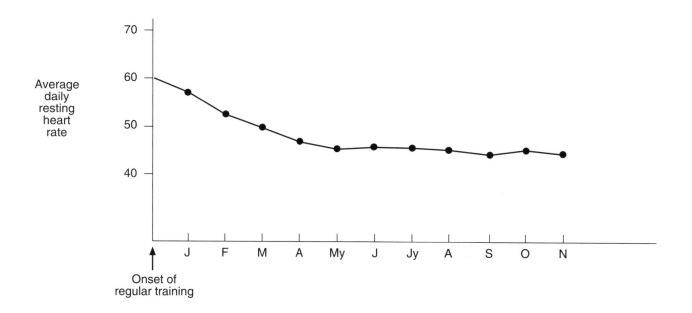

5.8a Examples of heart rate tracking are (*a*) long-term: average resting heart rate over a one year period; b) short-term: fluctuations can be the result of alternating waves of fatigue, recovery , and illness.

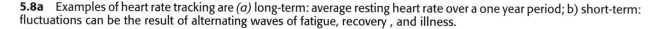

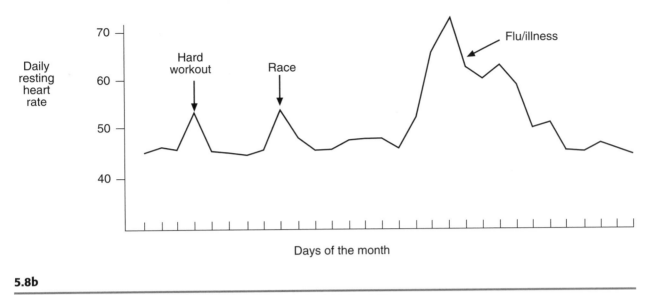

5.8b

Reprinted, by permission, from P. Janssen, 1987, *Training lactate pulse rate.* (Oy Litto, Finland: Polar Electro), 27.

Fitness Status

Although resting heart rate is susceptible to even small improvements in performance capacity, highly trained athletes may not see any significant decrease in their resting values over time. In fact, aerobic power ($\dot{V}O_2$max) also fluctuates little throughout the year, even among athletes who stay only slightly active in the off-season. Since resting heart rate usually reflects aerobic potential, it also may not change noticeably throughout the annual training design. Nevertheless, well-trained athletes should still monitor resting heart rate for its ability in detecting subtle changes in recovery that may lead to poor adaptation and overtraining.

Oxygen Uptake and Heart Rate

If you wish to use a heart rate monitor for training, understanding certain facts about oxygen consumption is beneficial. Many training books use $\dot{V}O_2$ as an expression of intensity and suggested effort. Heart rate and oxygen uptake relate in a one-to-one ratio. That is, they both rise in a linear fashion. Since $\dot{V}O_2$ is related to both the energy system being taxed and the fuel substrate usage, the heart rate becomes a vital means of monitoring training to reach optimal athletic potential. The strong relationship is why heart rate is useful for zoning in on the specific energy system. Without monitoring the exercise heart rate, there is no absolute way to know if you are training at the desired intensity.

The intensity of effort is usually expressed in one of two ways:

1. As a percentage of maximal heart rate (HRmax).
2. As a percentage of $\dot{V}O_2$max (percent $\dot{V}O_2$max).

Many coaches are careless about specifying which format they are alluding to. Table 5.3 shows the relationship between these two indices and demonstrates how different these two modes of expression really are.

Table 5.3

Differences Between Two Commonly Employed Intensity Measures

% Maximal heart rate	% Maximal oxygen consumption
70	50
75	65
80	70
85	80
90	85

Note: Data from MacDougall and Sale, 1993.

Although heart rate typically follows several well-documented principles and patterns, various factors, including age, gender, physical conditioning, disease, and genetic endowment can alter these trends. Heart rate training is not a precise science, but nonetheless is accurate enough to be incredibly valuable.

DETERMINING THE ANAEROBIC THRESHOLD

Expensive and complex laboratory equipment is required to precisely determine the level of the anaerobic threshold. Many university and sport-science centers have the facilities to perform such a test, but they may charge a considerable fee. Testing to determine the AT is almost always done in conjunction with a test of maximal aerobic power ($\dot{V}O_2$max). The heart rate response to incremental exercise is observed throughout each progressive workload of the test. Once the test has been completed, the technicians can use the data to prescribe intensity training zones based on the heart rate that corresponds with the level of the AT.

The mode of exercise testing used to determine both $\dot{V}O_2$max and AT should be appropriate and sport-specific. For speedskaters, physiologic testing should be done on a bicycle ergometer (as opposed to a running treadmill). This is because the observed reactions of heart rate, oxygen uptake, and the level of the AT during speedskating are more like cycling than running.

Sport scientists have concluded that data from laboratory tests have limited transferability to speedskating performance because the slope of the HR/$\dot{V}O_2$ relation is significantly different between testing modes (Snyder et al. 1993). That is, the heart rate response, measured oxygen uptake, and the anaerobic threshold that are observed during a laboratory test cannot accurately determine heart-rate training zones for speedskating training. With competitive speedskaters, it is more practical to obtain such data from an actual skating test than to rely on information from a laboratory procedure. See figure 5.9.

Modified Conconi Test

Italian physiologist Francesco Conconi was perhaps the first to effectively utilize the relation between heart rate and workload to help cyclist Francesco Moser break the world's one-hour solo-cycling record in 1984. To understand the aim of Conconi's test, recall that at low- to moderate-work levels, heart rate and exercise intensity

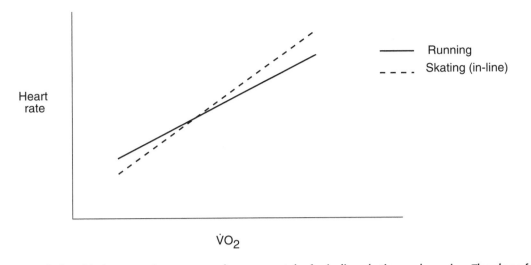

5.9 Relationship between heart rate and oxygen uptake for in-line skating and running. The slope for in-line skating is significantly greater than that for running and cycling. For example, for a given intensity ($\dot{V}O_2$), heart rate values are higher for skating.

Reprinted, by permission, from A.G. Snyder, K.P. O'Hagan, P.S. Clifford, H.D. Hoffman, and C. Foster, 1993, "Exercise response to inline skating: comparisons to running and cycling," *International Journal of Sports Medicine* 14: 38-42.

increase together, forming a straight line. The point where heart rate fails to rise in this linear fashion despite further increases in intensity represents the anaerobic threshold. The Conconi test strives to determine this threshold. If the heart rate corresponding to the AT is known, it is then possible to develop different heart rate zones to be used for training.

Not all researchers agree with the usefulness of Conconi's method, because it is often difficult to obtain a clear point where the heart rate ceases its linear rise with increasing workloads. Nevertheless, the test can be useful for charting the changes in exercise heart rate that occur with training. At the very least, the data can be used to formulate generalized heart-rate training zones.

The purpose of the test is to collect heart rate data for gradually increasing workloads and to plot the results on a graph. Heart rate (pulse rate) values are recorded on the vertical axis, and intensity-workload on the horizontal axis. Intensity is expressed on the graph with minutes, as workload is increased each minute. The test description you can read here uses the protocol recommended for cyclists. That is, a cyclist is used to pace the skater, using a bicycle equipped with a cyclo-computer that indicates both revolutions per minute and power-output, preferably in watts. The cyclist dictates the pace by following predetermined increments in workload.

Test Requirements

Performing the Conconi test requires certain facilities, personnel, and equipment. These are what you must have:

- A smooth 400-meter track or equivalent
- A heart rate monitor with sufficient memory to record the heart rate data
- A friend on a bicycle who is able to maintain a steady pace and is fit enough to perform the required workloads
- A sheet of predetermined workloads (in watts) to determine pacing velocity
- Graph paper or a personal computer with a suitable program
- A day with negligible wind

Test Execution

Here is a detailed breakdown of how to perform the test for in-line skating. It includes directions both for the skater and cyclist.

- Warm up for 10 minutes, followed by some light stretching, before you perform the test.
- Skate on the inside lane of the track; the cyclist paces you by riding to the outside and very slightly behind. *Do not draft* the cyclist.
- The workload to begin the test will depend on the ability of the skater. An initial workload of between 100 and 150 watts is usually appropriate (corresponding to an initial heart rate of about 60 percent of predicted maximum).
- The cyclist increases the workload by 10 to 15 watts every minute while the skater keeps pace. Therefore, the workload increments should occur roughly every lap.
- Heart rate is recorded every minute.
- The skater maintains stroke mechanics and cadence throughout the test.
- The test ends when the skater either reaches predicted maximal heart rate or can no longer sustain the current workload.

Plotting the Data Points

Once the data from the test has been compiled, record the heart rate values and corresponding workloads on the graph (figure 5.10). If the test is valid, the point where the heart rate fails to increase linearly should be clearly visible. Hopefully, the individual heart rate points will form a nice straight line. If the data points are close

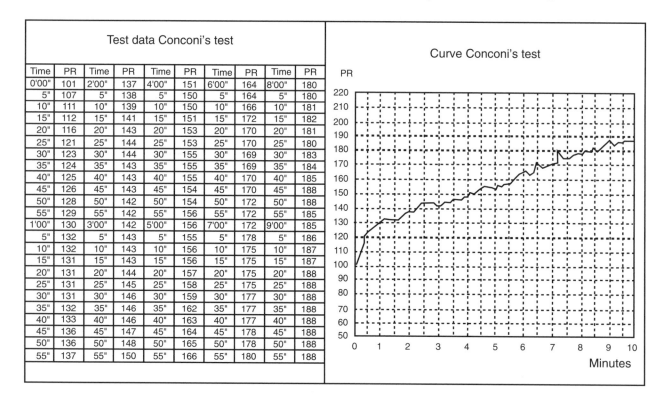

Time	PR	Time	PR	Time	PR	Time	PR	Time	PR
0'00"	101	2'00"	137	4'00"	151	6'00"	164	8'00"	180
5"	107	5"	138	5"	150	5"	164	5"	180
10"	111	10"	139	10"	150	10"	166	10"	181
15"	112	15"	141	15"	151	15"	172	15"	182
20"	116	20"	143	20"	153	20"	170	20"	181
25"	121	25"	144	25"	153	25"	170	25"	180
30"	123	30"	144	30"	155	30"	169	30"	183
35"	124	35"	143	35"	155	35"	169	35"	184
40"	125	40"	143	40"	155	40"	170	40"	185
45"	126	45"	143	45"	154	45"	170	45"	188
50"	128	50"	142	50"	154	50"	172	50"	188
55"	129	55"	142	55"	156	55"	172	55"	185
1'00"	130	3'00"	142	5'00"	156	7'00"	172	9'00"	185
5"	132	5"	143	5"	155	5"	178	5"	186
10"	132	10"	143	10"	156	10"	175	10"	187
15"	131	15"	143	15"	156	15"	175	15"	187
20"	131	20"	144	20"	157	20"	175	20"	188
25"	131	25"	145	25"	158	25"	175	25"	188
30"	131	30"	146	30"	159	30"	177	30"	188
35"	132	35"	146	35"	162	35"	177	35"	188
40"	133	40"	146	40"	163	40"	177	40"	188
45"	136	45"	147	45"	164	45"	178	45"	188
50"	136	50"	148	50"	165	50"	178	50"	188
55"	137	55"	150	55"	166	55"	180	55"	188

5.10 Sample Conconi test data. PR = pulse rate.

Reprinted, by permission, from P. Janssen, 1987, Training lactate pulse rate. (Oy Litto, Finland: Polar Electro), 93.

together but do not form a perfectly straight line as in figure 5.10, a line can be drawn to intersect, or come closest to, the greatest number of data points. If there is little correlation between the data points so that no relation is obvious, the test must be considered invalid. Either perform a retest to obtain better values or use the results as a baseline measure for comparing with future tests. Retests must try to replicate all external conditions of the original test.

CALCULATING HEART-RATE TRAINING ZONES

Once the deflection heart rate (representing the level of the anaerobic threshold) has been accurately determined from either a Conconi or laboratory test, it is then possible to calculate various heart-rate training zones (see next section, where they are described) to use for specific training. The anaerobic threshold represents the highest intensity and heart rate that can be sustained for about an hour, information that is immediately useful for long-distance races. Because the AT represents the point at which energy processes shift toward anaerobic metabolism, with it heart rate ranges can be developed to exploit each energy system. That is, the heart rate itself can guide your developing certain performance attributes and specific physiologic effects.

Step 1

Calculate your maximal heart rate by one of two methods: the predicted method or the direct method.

Predicted method—This fairly accurate method uses established norms to predict the maximal heart rate.

$$\text{Predicted HRmax} = 220 - \text{age.}$$

For a 30-year-old, the calculation would be $220 - 30 = 190$ (maximal heart rate). However, there is some significant variability between individuals an d between sport forms. For fit individuals accustomed to strenuous exercise, the second, direct method is preferable.

Direct Method—To be useful, this test must be performed during skating, rather than during another activity such as running or cycling. Ensure you are well rested and thoroughly warmed-up before attempting this test. First warm up for 10 to 15 minutes and then do some light stretching.

Next, perform a three-minute maximal skating interval, using the highest possible steady pace you can sustain in this time. In the last 30 seconds, your efforts should be maximal; *sprint* for the last 10 seconds. Your heart rate at the end of the three minutes should closely reflect the maximal heart rate specific to skating.

Step 2

Determine what percentage of the maximal heart rate is representing the anaerobic threshold. To do this, divide the maximal heart rate (HRmax) into the heart rate that corresponds to the level of the AT (HR_{AT}). Here is an example:

$$\text{HRmax} = 190; \text{HR}_{AT} = 162; 162/190 \times 100 = 85.2 \text{ percent}$$

Therefore, the anaerobic threshold occurs at 85.2 percent of maximal heart rate. To compare your level to research statistics, consider the following: in untrained individuals, the AT typically occurs at about a level of 70 to 75 percent of maximal heart rate, but in well-trained athletes, the AT occurs much higher, at heart rate values of roughly 85 to 90 percent of maximum.

Step 3

Substitute test data to determine personal heart rate zones. It must be noted that the Conconi test is a crude method for determining the AT compared with a laboratory test. So you should regard heart rate zones based on such test data with caution. Use training zones based on Conconi results only as guidelines.

USING TRAINING ZONES

The heart rate zones described here are based on the five-tier model presented by Janssen (1987). See table 5.4. Two of these zones incorporate heart rate readings below the level corresponding to the anaerobic threshold, whereas the remaining three are at or above threshold.

On days following strenuous workouts, it is generally recommended that you either take a day of complete rest or perform only an easy recovery workout. The recovery heart rate here is not truly a zone, but an additional recommended maximal level of intensity for such a training session. These workouts are not aimed at improving condition, but rather at facilitating the overall recovery process.

Zone 1

This zone constitutes heart rate levels well below the level that corresponds to the AT. It primarily comprises easy aerobic conditioning days for developing and maintaining baseline aerobic fitness during the off-season or for recovery time in between hard exercise bouts.

Table 5.4

The Five Heart-Rate Training Zones and Anaerobic Threshold

Zone	Heart Rate (in beats per minute)
Recovery heart rate	126
Zone 1: well below AT (used for recovery workouts)	<146
Zone 2: at or slightly below AT	146–156
Anaerobic threshold heart rate	156
Zone 3: at or slightly above AT	156–166
Zone 4: well above AT	166–176
Zone 5: very much above AT	>176

Note: These values are intended to be samples for prescribing heart rate ranges for each zone. In this example, the anaerobic threshold corresponds to a heart rate of 156 beats per minute. Adapted, by permission, from P. Janssen, 1987, Training lactate pulse rate. (Oy Litto, Finland: Polar Electro), 58.

Zone 2

The heart rate values in this training zone lie at or slightly below the AT level. Since research indicates that the most effective heart rate for improving aerobic fitness is near the level of the AT, this zone is beneficial for in-season, steady-state training of extended duration.

Zone 3

This training zone includes heart rate values at or slightly above the AT level, and it aims at training of moderate duration, steady-state, or of variable intensity. The goal of training in this zone is to allow the gradual buildup of blood lactic acid. Most novice and intermediate in-line racers will elevate heart rate to this zone for a 10-kilometer race.

Zone 4

Heart rates well above the level of the AT belong in zone 4. Because these heart rate values are so intense, such training is almost exclusively interval in structure. It involves an increased proportion of anaerobic energy production, and it results in the rapid buildup of blood lactate. This heart rate zone typifies the values observed in most elite in-line racers for a 10-kilometer distance.

Zone 5

This zone involves heart rate values very much above the level of the AT, so skaters use this range exclusively for short, high-intensity interval repetitions when the goal is to elevate the heart rate to near maximal. Lactic acid production will also be very high. Such training fatigues the body, and is usually only implemented by advanced competitive racers.

VALUE OF HEART RATE IN RACING AND TRAINING

For the most part, an in-line race of 10K will result in heart rate readings constantly above the level of the AT (zone 4). When the intensity exceeds the level of the AT and energy production is highly anaerobic, the heart rate will slowly rise, even when skating at a steady pace. Given the fluctuating nature of such short races, monitoring heart rate is admittedly questionable. The random pace means that the heart rate readings rarely level off to reach a steady state. When an important breakaway occurs, its duration is never known, so it would make little sense to measure exertion by virtue of heart rate alone. Therefore, if you monitor heart rate during a short in-line race, the readout should be considered strictly informational. For experienced skaters, perceived exertion level should be taken into account along with heart rate to help dictate pace.

With longer in-line races of an hour or more, monitoring heart rate is more useful. Certainly, changes in pace will result in values above the level of the AT, and slower moments will cause the heart rate to drop significantly below this level. The *average* heart rate, however, should lie around the AT level. Exceeding this limit for an extended time may not have immediate consequences, but if the heart rate does not come back down to the AT level, the accumulated lactic acid will result in early muscle fatigue.

For ice speedskaters, using a heart monitor during races of 1,500 meters or less is needless. These distances are so highly anaerobic that heart rate readings would continually increase throughout the race. Skaters will benefit more from heart rate readings in long-distance metric events (5K and 10K) when they can adjust intensity within the desired range. For simplicity, most ice skaters choose to use lap times to gauge intensity, rather than rely on heart rate readings. For marathon ice speedskating, too, observing exercise heart rate during the event is advantageous (for the same reasons that such a practice is more valuable to the long-distance in-liner).

Monitoring the heart rate for a speedskater primarily contributes to the effectiveness and quality of training. Implementing the heart-rate training zones, based on knowing the AT heart rate, allows a skater to stay on target and zero in more specifically on the energy system being taxed. These zones have particular relevance to interval training, which will be discussed in the next chapter.

6

Skating Intervals

For years, athletes and sport scientists have debated whether continuous or interval training better prepares an athlete for the strenuous demands of endurance competitions. Proponents of each method have been adamant in their opinions—but the answer ultimately lies in the precise nature of the event. To evaluate training for a particular athlete, you must analyze the physiologic requirements of the sport activity. This chapter has two main purposes, theoretical and practical. First, it will explain some of the key theories and concepts involving the two mainstay types of training, interval and continuous, and weigh the respective benefits that each form can offer for a speedskater. Second, it will outline the various forms of interval structure and configuration, and show you how to apply them to target specific physical attributes and energy-providing pathways.

CONTINUOUS TRAINING OR INTERVALS?

Interval training is a source of misunderstanding for many skaters, and its structure can become so confusing that the purpose of the training session can be lost in the overall complexity and design of the workout. Although most skaters use some form of interval training, many do not truly understand why they employ it. A brief comparative analysis of the continuous and interval types of training should lay the groundwork for you to better understand workout designs.

Continuous Training

Continuous training refers to exercise done at a relatively steady, submaximal intensity for an uninterrupted and prolonged period. This form of training has its greatest impact on the body's ability to transport oxygen to the working muscles. Sport scientists have long contested whether the continuous mode of training is most effective for elevating maximal aerobic function ($\dot{V}O_2$max) and the level of the anaerobic threshold. Since it is well understood that a high $\dot{V}O_2$max helps athletes achieve success in continuous sports (which depend heavily on aerobic processes for energy production), athletes in most endurance sports have usually relied primarily on continuous training.

Four key variables influence the outcome of continuous-type training:

Frequency

Duration

Type of exercise

Intensity

The first two variables relate to the volume of work performed. According to the American College of Sport Medicine (ACSM 1990), an athlete needs at least three or four workouts per week (*frequency*) to invoke favorable adaptation in aerobic fitness through continuous training. For a training session to sufficiently stimulate improvements in performance indices, the ACSM further concludes that the training must be sustained for a minimum of 15 to 20 minutes in *duration*.

The third important variable related to continuous training is the *type of exercise*. Since continuous training primarily affects the development of the oxygen transport and delivery mechanisms (i.e., central performance factors), a variety of cross-training activities can be used. Any true *aerobic activity* (one that is rhythmic, continuous, and involves the use of large muscle groups) is appropriate, because most gains in central fitness can transfer to other sport forms that also rely heavily on aerobic performance.

Last, the *intensity* of the training session must meet certain requirements. In fact, intensity is considered the most important factor in virtually all types of physical training. The ACSM (1990) states that a continuous exercise session must achieve between 50 and 85 percent of $\dot{V}O_2$max (60 to 90 percent of maximal heart rate) to sufficiently tax the oxygen-transport capability. During incremental exercise, the stress on the heart begins to plateau before the intensity of the anaerobic threshold is reached. So further increases in exercise intensity would not result in more adaptive stress to the heart, despite additional increases in the fatigue-influencing heart rate. In this respect, continuous training helps to increase the heart's stroke volume, or the amount of oxygen-rich blood that can be pumped each time the heart beats. Because maximal stroke volume peaks fairly early as intensity levels rise, continuous training allows the maximal number of heartbeats at full pumping capacity without resulting in heightened blood-lactate levels. Table 6.1 summarizes ACSM requirements for improving aerobic fitness.

Interval Training

Interval training describes a training method that alternates relatively short bouts of heavy exercise with predetermined periods of rest. With interval training, the primary benefit is that you can greatly increase the total, accumulated exercise time

Table 6.1

Summary of ACSM Recommendations

Frequency	Intensity	Type	Time
3–4 times per week	60–90% HRmax	Continuous, large muscle mass	15-20 min minimum

Data from American College of Sports Medicine, 1990. The recommended quantity and quality of exercise for developing and maintaining cardiorespiratory and muscular fitness in healthy adults, *Medicine and Science in Sports and Exercise*, 265-274.

beyond what you could perform during a single continuous-exercise bout at the same intensity. A reasonably conditioned athlete, for example, can skate at a constant intensity of 100 percent $\dot{V}O_2$max for about 10 minutes before lactate-induced exhaustion would terminate the effort. Using the same intensity (100 percent $\dot{V}O_2$max) for repeated periods of three minutes *interspersed with equal rest*, the skater can exercise for about an hour before experiencing the same level of fatigue. Thus, by using the intermittent-exercise (interval) method, a skater can increase the exercise time done at 100 percent $\dot{V}O_2$max from 10 minutes to a total of 30 minutes.

Whereas continuous training exerts its effect on central aerobic factors, interval training has its primary impact on the energy-providing systems and the peripheral adaptations of a local level. That is, the more intense nature of interval training results in positive performance effects on the structural and biochemical properties of the muscles themselves. Interval training can also help the body tolerate high levels of lactic acid and expedite its speedy removal and re-uptake by other body tissues. Since interval training usually stresses the anaerobic energy pathways responsible for high-intensity, short-duration efforts, it is commonly referred to as *speed training*.

Significantly, the adaptations, or positive changes, you achieve through interval training are highly specific to the training activity you employ. This means that for an interval session to optimally benefit speedskating performance, the workout must use skating intervals. Identical interval training on a bicycle, for example, can produce similar adaptations to the *energy-providing system*, but improvements at the *muscular level* will not transfer well to actual skating performance.

Which is Best?

Answering the question of which type of training is better for a speedskater prompts some evasion or at least a compromise. Both methods should be used! The two types of training exert different stimuli on the body, and together they produce adaptations that contribute to increased ability and improved performance. Interval- and continuous-training methods complement each other in preparing for competitive demands. But you must combine them carefully to ensure a balanced training regimen. It should now be evident that the role and importance of interval training can only be ascertained by considering the actual intensity and energy demands of an event.

TRAINING TO MATCH THE REQUIREMENTS OF AN EVENT

The practical structure of interval training allows a high degree of manipulation by the athlete. You can alter the duration and intensity of exercise bouts, the recovery time between work sessions, and the total volume of work performed. The partitioning of these elements, referred to as the *work-to-recovery ratio*, essentially dictates the specific physiologic effect on the body and what main energy system will be exploited. Through these variables, interval training can encompass enormous variety, allowing you to tailor all aspects of the workout to best suit the demands of competition you face.

Before getting too excited, consider how much and how accurately the interval training method actually reflects the physiologic demands of the specific event. Most in-line races are 10K, with an intermediate performance time of some 20 to 22 minutes. And most in-line racers will compete at a level significantly above the AT (see chapter 5), where random changes in pace can cause lactic acid to accumulate rapidly. For this reason, in-line racers must practice at intensities both similar to and higher than race pace. Such training can help increase the level of the AT, as well as the tolerance and removal of blood lactate. Such a single high-intensity exercise bout would certainly tax the body in this manner, but the volume of work that could be performed would still be low. The best way to overcome this deficiency is to employ interval-training methods that provide recovery periods in between heavy work bouts.

For ice skaters, particularly those who specialize in sprint and middle-distance events, interval training is the only way to reflect the speed and intensity of specific competition. For these athletes, it is a more complicated matter to determine the ratio of work to recovery and the energy system that should be stressed most heavily. Still, interval training is undoubtedly the primary focus for all ice speedskaters as they prepare for the intense demands of competition.

It should now be evident that no matter what the event one is training for, the relevant factor is that the role and importance of the interval session reflect the main energy system and intensity you will rely on in competition. An interval session for a 1,500-meter ice specialist would therefore be markedly different from one for an in-line racer who competes in distances from 10 to 20 kilometers.

Intensity is the primary factor used to differentiate between types of interval training. In turn, intensity affects the work and recovery times, as well as the number of repetitions in the interval sessions. Short events of high intensity create high concentrations of lactic acid; skaters in them rely most heavily on the anaerobic pathway for energy production. To train for such comparatively short distances, a session must therefore maximally stimulate positive adaptations in the more powerful anaerobic system through its interval composition. In addition to significant anaerobic contribution, however, longer events (such as a 10K in-line race) rely heavily on the aerobic system for energy production. Therefore, for longer events in-line athletes should use intervals that also aim at taxing the metabolic pathway that involves oxygen.

Elevating the Anaerobic Threshold

Despite debate, coaches and scientists have long believed that the most effective method for raising the level of the anaerobic threshold is to use long-duration continuous training in which heart rate values hover near the level associated with the AT. For example, if a skater has an AT that occurs at 80 percent of maximal heart rate, the optimal subanaerobic training intensity for long duration exercise would be 79 percent of HRmax. An intensity just below the AT allows the individual to maximize exercise time while remaining below the level at which blood lactate would begin to accumulate and eventually limit exercise duration. In this case, fuel supply would be the main limiting factor. This does not mean that the skater's intensity and heart rate corresponding to the level of the AT should never be exceeded during a continuous workout session. It is possible, and even advisable, to temporarily exceed threshold intensity for a short time before lactate reaches detrimental levels. Intensity can fluctuate slightly above and below the level of the AT—provided that sufficient time is also spent below threshold to remove built-up lactic acid. Such variable continuous workouts are called *fartleks*.

Manipulating Work and Recovery Time

Interval training is considered the most effective method for conditioning the body to go fast. Through the collaboration of coaches and research scientists, we now have at our disposal accurate guidelines for formatting intervals in specific ways. To best prepare an athlete for competition, interval training can be structured precisely to stimulate adaptations in energy-providing systems, improve the tolerance and removal of metabolic waste products, and enhance overall muscular function. Coaches and athletes can do this by manipulating the volume and recovery variables that constitute the interval session. Being aware of the relative importance of each energy system in the event for which one is training is the first step in designing personalized interval-training sessions. These factors constitute volume and recovery variables:

Volume of Work Performed
- Duration of each repetition (work time)
- Number of repetitions within the set
- Number of sets of the entire session

Recovery Time
- Recovery time between repetitions
- Recovery time between sets

Work Time

Work time is intimately tied to the intensity of the exercise bout and is therefore important for determining the actual effect of the training session. Many intervals, particularly those targeting the anaerobic system, should be skated with maximal intensity for the given time. This is obvious for short intervals (e.g., a 30-second work bout). For an interval repetition of three minutes in duration, however, there are two approaches. First, the repetition can be skated with high intensity to maintain a constant speed for the entire duration without fatigue and subsequent slowing. Starting out too hard and fading in the final minute of such an interval drastically reduces the effectiveness of the exercise. After such an overly arduous start, all subsequent repetitions will suffer because of excessively high lactate accumulation. This type of approach, used in conjunction with a longer recovery period, is employed when the goal of the interval session is to tax the anaerobic energy system and improve the tolerance and removal of lactic acid.

The second approach would be to skate the three-minute work bout at a lower, moderate intensity. Because lactic acid will not accumulate to the same degree, the recovery period between repetitions would be significantly less, for example, 90 seconds instead of 3 minutes. This partitioning of work to rest time would serve to exploit the larger-capacity aerobic system. These two examples demonstrate how intensity, in combination with recovery time, is often the key factor for determining the overall effect of the training session.

Number of Repetitions Within the Set

The number of repetitions within a single set will depend on the time of year, the fitness of the individual, and the specific focus of the interval session. Naturally, novice skaters and those beginning interval training in the early preseason will start with a few repetitions. For intervals directed at improving the power output of the aerobic system, what is crucial is that the skater performs each of the desired number of repetitions with the same target intensity. Once fatigue begins to reduce the attainment of the target intensity for any given repetition, the set is normally terminated. The training session can then be concluded, or adequate recovery should be taken before completing more repetitions in a second set. However, with some interval sessions (e.g., those aimed at the anaerobic system), it is to be expected that the gradual accumulation of lactic acid will result in progressively slower skating. This means that in order to maintain the same target intensity, the skater must work harder each successive repetition. Because of this, such interval sessions can be termed progressive-fatigue workouts.

Regardless of ability, all skaters must follow the principle of *progression*. This means either gradually introducing a higher number of repetitions or slowly increasing the intensity of the intervals as conditioning improves. The number of repetitions should be increased first, followed by elevated intensity levels. As a general rule, shorter, more intense intervals will involve more repeats than intervals of longer duration.

Number of Sets

The number of sets also reflects the conditioning level and stage of progression the skater is experiencing at a specific time of year. For most skaters, one set is appropriate for early in the training season. The number of sets should gradually increase as the season progresses and the skater's fitness level improves. Shorter intervals, aimed purely at the anaerobic energy pathways, tend to involve more sets than longer intervals, directed at improving lactic acid removal or developing the aerobic system.

Recovery Time Between Repetitions

How much recovery time you take between exercise bouts will depend on the work time or intensity of the repetition and what energy system you are training. Intervals aimed at specific energy paths and using a specific goal typically implement a predictable ratio of time between work and recovery. Some individuals prefer to use recovery heart rate as an index for determining roughly how much recovery time to take before the next repetition. A heart rate of 120 beats per minute is often used in this way to signify that sufficient recovery has taken place before the next repetition is performed. Although this method is practical for certain interval-training methods, its accuracy in representing optimal recovery across the full range of interval application is widely debatable.

Although the terms *rest* and *recovery* are often used interchangeably, it is preferable to talk of "recovery" when discussing the period of time between repetitions or sets. Rest is a more static term, which implies that the skater can merely sit around between repetitions. Conversely, recovery implies more activity on the part of the skater, and it describes the actual process that occurs during this period. Therefore, "recovery" rather than "rest" is used throughout this chapter.

Recovery Time Between Sets

Set recovery refers to the time between the last repetition of one set and the first repetition of the following set. The purpose of set recovery is to allow sufficient time for lactic acid to be removed and for the energy systems to recharge so that further repetitions can be performed with the desired intensity. For example, consider an interval session that involves three-minute work bouts, repeated four times with a recovery period of three minutes. With each subsequent repetition, lactic acid in the blood increases; that is, its concentration will be higher at the start of each new interval than it was at the start of the previous one. Because of the short recovery time, blood lactate does not return to the levels it had before the repetition, but continues to increase throughout successive intervals (see figure 6.1). For this reason, the skater must take set recovery in order to perform subsequent repetitions. More time is taken between sets than between repetitions.

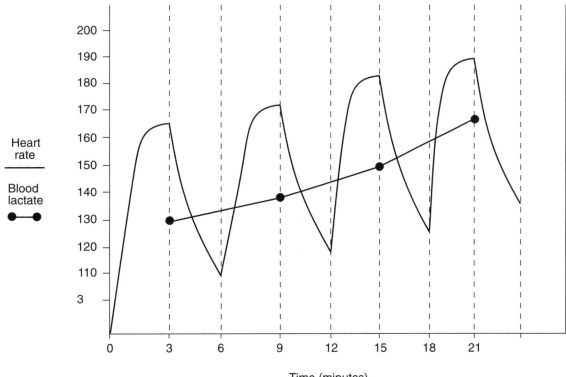

Time (minutes)

6.1 Heart rate and blood lactate profiles for an interval session using a three-minute work time and a three-minute recovery time. Although heart rate rises and falls between work and recovery, post-repetition blood lactate values continue to rise for each subsequent repetition.

PRINCIPLES OF INTERVAL TRAINING

It is important to apply the principles of overload, progression, and specificity to interval training. Quite simply, this means conducting all interval sessions with skating as the training medium, as well as gradually increasing both the volume and intensity of the sessions over time to ensure continued change and performance adaptation. These principles aside, there are several other interval-specific guidelines that are important to follow.

Warm-Up

Most interval-training methods are intense, which increases the risk of acute trauma or injury to the muscles, ligaments, and tendons. To lessen risk, all skaters should warm up sufficiently before performing an interval session. Many athletes use the first repetition as the warm-up to the session, an unwise practice that is strongly discouraged. Among other things, a good warm-up increases the muscles' temperature, activates the aerobic system, and stimulates the neural pathways to the muscles. A proper warm-up for an intense interval session should include the following:

1. Ten minutes of light skating, significantly below the level of the anaerobic threshold (HR zone 1–2).
2. General and specific stretching, with particular focus on the muscles of the legs, hips, and back.
3. Three to four accelerations, 100 meters in length and separated by about two minutes. Each acceleration should be progressively more intense: for example,
   - repetition 1—accelerate to 70 percent of maximum speed,
   - repetition 2—accelerate to 80 percent of maximum speed,
   - repetition 3—accelerate to 90 percent of maximum speed, and
   - repetition 4—accelerate to top speed.
4. Three to five minutes of very easy skating to "shake out" the legs.
5. Another stretch, this time for only a few minutes. Concentrate on the legs.

Seasonal Development

In developing the three metabolic pathways for producing energy, pay special attention to the most important principle for optimal functioning of each system: the order in which they are developed. Interval training is an integral tool for developing each energy pathway, and all training sessions must be structured accordingly.

It is best to phase intervals into the training regimen only after a skater has developed a solid aerobic base through endurance training. Many coaches agree that an individual should first spend at least six to eight weeks of base training, and MacDougall and Sale (1981) even recommend about three months of prior endurance training. The point here is that endurance training always comes first. Ignoring this guideline (noncompliance) can result in early-season burnout, overtraining, mental deterioration, or a loss of motivation early in the competitive year.

A foundation of solid endurance, or aerobic fitness, will function as a reservoir to support higher-intensity training. Even though the composition of an interval workout may heavily stress the anaerobic pathway, the activation of the aerobic system helps remove lactic acid and recharge the anaerobic system during the

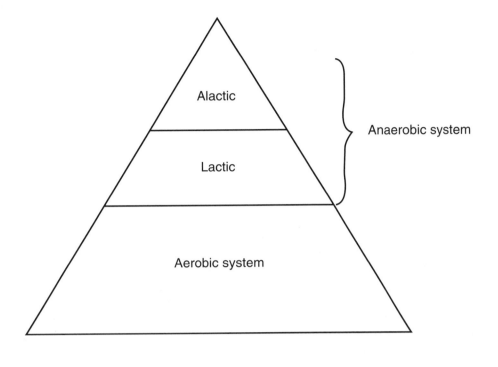

6.2 The pyramid principle.

recovery period. Overall, a well-developed aerobic system will allow a skater to perform more sets and repetitions before experiencing exercise-induced fatigue.

As the season progresses and a skater grows adaptively stronger, shorter and more intense intervals aimed specifically at anaerobic lactic fitness can be executed. This extremely important stacking of energy-system training is commonly termed the *pyramid principle*. According to this principle, energy systems, and therefore interval-training methodology, should be sequentially focused to build the pyramid from the bottom up. That is, aerobic fitness must be the primary goal before pursuing higher intensity training.

Once interval training is phased into the training regimen, the composition of the workouts should promote adaptations in the anaerobic lactic system. After investing sufficient time in this area, you can shift attention to intervals that improve the power and capacity of the ATP/CP system. The pyramid (figure 6.2) thereby highlights that each energy system acts as a stabilizing foundation for the one(s) above. If one level is not adequately developed, the higher level(s) will ultimately crumble.

Frequency of Interval Training

Because interval training is very physically demanding on the body, the sessions should be initially implemented only once a week. As exercise tolerance improves through the season, intense interval training can occur twice a week. Elite and seasoned speedskaters may use interval training three or even four times over a 10-day cycle, but most skaters are better off limiting this training method to twice weekly.

Because of the intense nature of interval training, be sure to allow sufficient recovery before performing the next interval session. Interval skating relies heavily on the anaerobic energy system, rapidly depleting stores of the fuel-source glycogen. For this reason, it is strongly advised that a minimum of 48 hours pass before the next highly intense workout to ensure that glycogen stores have been sufficiently replenished.

Follow a hard interval session with a day of either complete rest or very low-intensity, continuous training. Equally important to refilling glycogen stores is allotting time to rebuild muscle tissue that may have broken down as a result of high-intensity interval training. Muscle soreness following such a workout is a definite indication of such acute trauma, but it does not always appear until several days after the hard workout.

Active Recovery

An important principle related to interval training is the concept of *active recovery*. The recovery period between repetitions or sets should not be one of complete rest and inactivity, when the athlete sits or stands around. Rather, staying moderately active during the recovery period helps maintain muscle blood flow, keeps the aerobic system active, and facilitates the removal of lactic acid. Physiologists are at odds as to what intensity is optimal for assisting recovery. It is difficult to ascribe heart rate values to recovery activity because the heart rate will remain elevated most of the time between repetitions. It is therefore more appropriate to use the percentage of $\dot{V}O_2$max in this respect. Most experts agree that light postexercise activity (of about 30 to 40 percent $\dot{V}O_2$max) best accelerates the process of lactate removal (MacDougall and Sale 1993). In practical terms, this implies a very light perceived effort, similar to warm-up pace (heart rate zone 1).

Active recovery especially benefits in-line racers in their training. Since most in-line races alternate periods of relatively low effort and high intensity, there is never time to take a complete rest, lower the heart rate, or allow for nearly complete removal of lactic acid. Therefore, a significant aspect of following the principle of active recovery during interval training is to represent such race conditions more realistically.

APPLYING INTERVALS FOR TRAINING EACH ENERGY SYSTEM

You can manipulate the work time, duration of the recovery interval, and total volume of activity performed during the interval session in countless ways to target the usage and relative contributions of the three energy systems. This next section describes how to adjust these variables to target each specific energy-providing system. Table 6.2 summarizes these points.

Interval Training for the Aerobic System

The longest and least intense of all skating repetitions involved in interval training are for the aerobic system. Aerobic repetitions therefore are the first interval mode that a skater should implement in the early preseason. Intervals to improve the efficiency of the aerobic system need not be high in intensity, and the exercise time can range from about three to ten minutes or longer. Although your exercise heart rate will slowly rise and reach its steady state after about two to three minutes, these repetitions do not need to be maximal in intensity. The heart rate target for such

Table 6.2

Summary of the Factors Related to Interval Structure for Each Energy System

Interval type	Work time	Rest time	Work-rest ratio	# Reps	# Sets	Intensity	HR zone
Aerobic	3 min	3 min	1:1	4–6	1–3	Moderate	3
Anaerobic lactic							
Lactate tolerance	30–60 s	30–60 s	1:1–1:2	4–6	1–4	High	4–5
Lactate removal	120 s	4 min	1:2	6–8	1–2	High	5
Anaerobic alactic (ATP/CP)							
Peak power	10 s	100–120 s	1:10–1:12	6–10	2–3	Maximal	NA
Peak capacity	30 s	120 s	1:4	4–6	2–3	Near-maximal	NA
Breakaway intervals	60 s	60–120 s	1:1–1:2	8–10	1–2	High	4–5

Note: For short intervals (<2 minutes), the heart rate response does not have time to level off. Therefore, the zones included for these intervals are for guidance only.

interval training would be equivalent to zone 3, just above the level of the AT. By the end of the exercise bout, heart rate values may come within 10 to 15 beats of maximal, but an athlete should not feel exhausted at the end of the interval. If intensity is too high, anaerobic processes will produce excessive lactic acid levels, and will limit the number of repetitions that can be performed. Such long, moderate-intensity intervals (in excess of three minutes) are commonly called *endurance intervals*.

Studies show that repeating exercise bouts of three-minute duration interspersed with an equal amount of rest is effective for improving aerobic fitness (MacDougall and Sale 1981). When intensity is moderately high for such training (90 percent of $\dot{V}O_2$max), a work time of three minutes brings heart rate to near maximal value, allows aerobic processes to reach steady state, and deprives the muscles of oxygen for the longest total duration without excessive lactate production. For endurance intervals lasting three to five minutes, an equal amount of recovery is recommended (i.e., a work-to-recovery ratio of one to one). When the interval is longer (six to ten minutes), recovery time can vary from a one-to-one ratio up to three-to-one. Although the number of repetitions will depend on a skater's fitness and progress into the season, either one set of four to five repetitions or two sets of three repetitions with five minutes of set recovery is a good starting point.

It is important to allow the body to become gradually accustomed to the increased levels of intensity when you first phase in this type of interval training. As work time increases, the intensity level of the bout typically decreases. An example of a longer endurance interval using a work-to-recovery ratio of two to one would be four repetitions of six minutes in duration, spaced by three minutes of active recovery. Refer to figure 6.3 to illustrate how different training schemes affect the aerobic system, as well as the ATP-CP and LA systems.

Interval Training

	Scheme	Systems affected		
		ATP-CP	LA	O_2
Duration	3 minutes			
Intensity	100% $\dot{V}O_2$max	○	○	◯
Work-to-rest ratio	(1:1)			
Duration	10-15 seconds			
Intensity	100-110% $\dot{V}O_2$max	◯	○	◯
Work-to-rest ratio	(1:5)			
Duration	10-15 seconds			
Intensity	Maximal effort	◯	○	○
Work-to-rest ratio	(1:10)			
Duration	30-60 seconds			
Intensity	Maximal effort	○	◯	○
Work-to-rest ratio	(1:4-5)			

6.3 The relative degree of energy system contribution using four different interval training schemes. For each scheme, work time, intensity, and work/rest ratio are noted.

Reprinted, by permission, from J.D. MacDougall and D. Sale, Department of Kinesiology, McMaster University, Hamilton, Ontario.

Interval Training for the Lactic Acid System

Lactic acid is a normal by-product of the anaerobic breakdown of glycogen. Once lactate is produced, it is either neutralized by buffering agents in the blood, taken up by other cells and converted into useful substances, or used to fuel aerobic reactive processes. Interval training for the lactic acid system has essentially two specific purposes. One function is to help build up the body's tolerance to the substance. The second purpose, training, can help develop the mechanisms responsible for the rapid reuse and removal rate of lactic acid. Work and recovery times can be varied accordingly to work toward either of these two important goals.

Recovery Intervals for Developing Lactic Acid Tolerance

In speedskating, blood flow through the leg muscles is significantly restricted, causing lactic acid to accumulate and limit the amount of oxygen-rich blood that reaches the muscle tissue. Therefore, building up tolerance to lactic acid or being able to cope with its high concentration is obviously a worthwhile goal of training.

To facilitate the body's tolerance for lactic acid, interval work bouts should be relatively short and intense, using short rest periods. The goal is to gradually increase the level of lactic acid in the muscles and blood through successive high-intensity efforts. Interval repetitions of 30 to 60 seconds at high intensity should accomplish this job very well. Allot adequate recovery time to allow sufficient lactate to be removed so that the next interval can be performed with equally high intensity. The short recovery period serves to limit the removal of blood lactate.

A suitable work-to-recovery ratio for a 30- to 60-second bout is on the order of one to one or one to two. This corresponds to a recovery period equal to or double the work period. Keeping the lactic acid levels high forces you to skate repeated bouts while the level of lactic acid grows progressively higher, making each successive interval more and more difficult. Because high lactic acid concentrations are associated with a painful burning sensation in the muscles, the number of repetitions that can be done in a single set is usually limited. Most often, five or six repetitions can be performed before lactate levels are so high that recovery is necessary. Although the target intensity should remain constant, it is expected that each successive repetition will be performed progressively more slowly for this type of interval training. At the end of the last repetition, ample set recovery (about 5 to 10 minutes) is required if the skater opts to perform another set. This type of exercise is one of the most physically and mentally demanding forms of interval training.

Sustained Speed Intervals for Lactic Acid Removal

For metric ice skaters who maintain a steady tempo throughout the race, tolerance for high lactic acid levels is likely more important than highly efficient removal mechanisms. For in-line racers, lactic acid tolerance is definitely important. However, wheel athletes also require a heightened ability to remove lactic acid quickly. The stop-and-go nature of most races requires the skater to recover as quickly as possible from a surge in pace and to remove as much lactic acid as possible before the next tempo increase. Interval training for the anaerobic lactic system can be adjusted slightly so as to best develop this critical performance necessity.

Studies of 1,500-meter ice skaters who complete the distance in just under two minutes (120 seconds) show that the intensity and work time result in the highest-observed blood lactate measurement of any metric distance (Foster, Thompson, and Snyder 1993). Therefore, a suitable interval's work time for bringing lactic acid concentration to maximum is a hard, steady effort of roughly two minutes. Heart rate should rapidly climb throughout the interval and reach within five beats of maximal by the end of the bout. Although the work time is not sufficient to allow heart rate to level off, such intervals are assumed to be performed in heart rate zone 5.

Since the goal in this format is to enhance the ability to remove lactate, the protocol involves recovery periods that allow most, but not all, of the lactic acid to be removed before the next repetition (refer back to figure 6.1). This gives the anaerobic system time to recharge, so that each repetition can be performed without progressive fatigue. An active recovery time of about four minutes, representing a work-to-recovery ratio of one to two is ideal. The increased recovery time for this interval format allows a higher number of repetitions to be performed within a single set. The recommended number of repetitions is from six to eight. If a second set is to be performed, take a set recovery of about six to eight minutes before beginning the next series of repetitions.

Breakaway Intervals: A Compromise

I like to refer to the following format as *breakaway interval training* because this method attempts to represent the dynamics of in-line racing. This method uses work bouts of 60 seconds, skated at about 85 to 90 percent of maximal effort. For these intervals, the work-to-recovery ratio is one to one or one to two. The primary distinction of breakaway intervals is that the recovery is not simply active, but what could be called *tempo recovery*. In tempo recovery, skating is performed at a pace roughly equivalent to the slowest pace experienced during a race; that is, it should be moderately fast and of an intensity just below the level of the anaerobic threshold. Breakaway intervals are probably the toughest ones that can be done because they cause lactic acid to accumulate quite rapidly to high levels. Meanwhile, the absence of any true recovery period provides little opportunity for its clearance.

Here is a practical example of a breakaway interval session. Start with one minute of moderate-intensity skating just below race pace. After one minute, skate a hard 60-second bout. For the first 10 to 15 seconds, efforts should be maximal to accelerate to near-top speed. Once top speed is reached, ease off and slowly reduce speed to about race pace for the remaining time (45 to 50 seconds). Once the work bout ends, take 60 seconds of tempo recovery at a pace slightly below AT level. You can usually execute this alternation between work time and tempo recovery up to 10 repetitions or until lactate-induced fatigue terminates the set. This creates a rigorous workout, keeping the heart rate within zones 4 and 5 throughout. Therefore, you should only attempt this format after several weeks of moderate-intensity interval training.

Interval Training for the Anaerobic Alactic System

Recall that the anaerobic alactic pathway provides immediate energy for short high-intensity efforts lasting up to about 10 seconds (see chapter 5). The system has a very low overall capacity, because the creatine phosphate (CP) molecule stored in the muscles is present in very limited amounts. During exercise, the energy released from splitting the CP helps to produce new adenosine triphosphate (ATP) molecules. Once the CP stores have been completely depleted, ATP can no longer be created through this pathway. During a recovery period, the energy released from the metabolic breakdown and usage of ATP helps resynthesize new CP in the muscles. Remember, however, that such production can only proceed while an athlete is resting almost fully and the aerobic system is running at high capacity.

It is valuable to be aware of the time course through which the energy-substrate CP is replenished. It takes three minutes of almost complete rest for CP stores to be fully recharged, but only 30 seconds for them to become half full. In other words, CP replacement occurs quickly at first and tapers off as stores approach full status. Because the stores of CP are roughly 90 percent full after two minutes, it is not usually necessary to provide three full minutes of recovery. Somewhat like training for the anaerobic lactic system, the work and recovery times for training the ATP/CP system can vary, depending on the precise stimulus you provide and the effect you wish.

Training for Peak Power

To use skating intervals for developing the peak power of the ATP/CP system, short and maximal repetitions of ten seconds are effective, using a work-to-recovery ratio of one to ten or one to twelve. An appropriate recovery time would therefore be about two minutes. Because the rate of CP recovery slows down in later trials, you should increase the recovery time for the second half of the repetitions. For instance, the first three repetitions of a set of six should be spaced by two minutes of recovery. For the last three intervals, however, this recovery period should increase to three minutes. For anaerobic alactic system interval training, the number of repetitions in a single set would usually be six to ten, followed by five to ten minutes of recovery before the next set. Please note that because this energy system is best recharged when resting fully, anaerobic alactic training is the only interval training type where nearly complete inactivity between sets or repetitions is advisable.

Training the Capacity of the System

For most speedskaters, the most important aspect of the anaerobic alactic system is its overall capacity to produce energy. With this in mind, interval methods should use maximal work efforts of about 30 seconds, and a recovery period of roughly two minutes (i.e., a work-to-recovery ratio of one to four). Recovery time for the second half of the set should again increase to three minutes.

The theory behind anaerobic alactic capacity training is that if the system is completely depleted and recovery time then allows CP stores to almost fully recharge, the concentration of CP in the muscles following the work bout will be higher than what it had been prior to the exercise. Several studies indicate it is possible to increase CP concentration in the muscles by training this energy pathway in such a manner. Higher initial stores of muscle CP will not directly allow a skater to sprint faster, but they can allow top speed to be maintained *longer*.

Because these intervals are longer than if you directed intervals toward developing the peak power of the system, lactic acid will begin to accumulate to significant levels by about the fourth interval. The accumulation, in general, limits repetitions to four to six, with 10 minutes of set recovery. This time will allow some of the lactate to dissipate before the next set.

Composite Workouts

With a virtually unlimited number of possibilities, interval training offers the skater an enormous variety of training options. When designing an interval workout, there is no reason why the session cannot incorporate more than one type of goal-oriented interval. In fact, there is a growing belief among coaches and sport scientists that the most effective way to achieve performance improvement is to employ a variety of training methods, thereby eliminating the monotony and predictability of training by pursuing a more diverse range of specific physical stimuli. Table 6.3 highlights an

Table 6.3

Sample Composite Workout

Interval type	Work time	Recovery between reps	# Reps	Intensity	# Sets	Recovery between sets
Anaerobic intervals						
Lactate removal (sustained speed) Time: 17 min	2 min	3 min	3	HR Zone 4–5	1	5 min
Aerobic intervals Time: 28 min	4 min	1 min	5	HR Zone 3	1	5 min
Anaerobic intervals Lactate tolerance Time: 15 min	45 s	30 s	4	HR Zone 5	2	6 min
Total workout time: 60 min						

example of such a training session. In this one-hour workout, intervals for both the aerobic and anaerobic energy systems are combined.

Although continuous and interval training should be used in tandem to elevate performance potential, regardless of the specific distance for which one is training, speedskating relies more heavily on the use of interval-training methodology. This is particularly true for training during the competitive season, which will be discussed in more detail in the next chapters.

7

Building Strength and Muscular Endurance

Many coaches believe that other than skating itself, resistance training is the most important method for achieving heightened levels of performance success. And undoubtedly, strength and muscular endurance are important for a speedskater, whatever the distance one trains for.

To evaluate how much resistance training can benefit an athlete of a particular sport, you must first look in detail at the muscular requirements of that activity. The sport of speedskating has some unique aspects in this regard. Generally speaking, speedskating requires the ability to perform in a rather awkward biomechanical position. That is, maintaining the semisquat posture of a speedskater requires significant lower-body strength. Without this strength, a skater cannot maintain the necessary position for extended periods of time. Insufficient strength will result in the early onset of fatigue and a progressive deterioration in the biomechanical advantage of the "sitting low" position. There is no better way, furthermore, to enhance one's ability to sit deep and push hard than to spend some quality time in the weight room.

Speedskating also requires that the muscles of the lower body contract repeatedly to produce force and generate forward motion. The endurance of the specific muscles is therefore an important issue relating to the goals of resistance training. Exactly how much importance is attached to strength versus muscular endurance depends on the discipline and specific event for which you are training.

Almost as much misinformation (a major stumbling block!) as accurate information exists about resistance training. Designing an effective weight-training program is not a complicated task. What is most important is that the makeup and constitution of the program reflect the sport's pattern of muscular activity and the overall training results you seek.

After introducing some of the key concepts and theory related to resistance training exercise, this chapter aims to help readers design and implement an effective program of weight-training exercise that uses sound principles and practices. Second, it provides description and illustrations of effective resistance-training exercises *specific* to speedskating.

IMPORTANCE OF STRENGTH FOR SPEEDSKATERS

To evaluate the value of strength to a speedskater, it is necessary to examine how much improved strength levels can directly contribute to increases in athletic performance. High levels of strength can be a dominant factor, can share usefulness with other physical performance indices, or can be only a minor factor. Because a speedskater performs in such an unusual position from a biomechanical perspective, it should be immediately clear that increases in strength and power, especially at small knee angles, are beneficial to sport-specific performance. Strength alone will not lead to the winner's podium, but it can definitely enhance the quest for personal improvement.

The low, semisquat position a speedskater assumes interferes with blood flow through the working muscles, and is believed to be a major limiting factor in speedskating performance because it induces early fatigue. This reduced blood flow allows the accumulation of lactic acid and other substances that interfere with the contraction of muscle fibers. Training to reduce the onset or to offset this detrimental factor can have obvious advantages. Research has demonstrated that muscle blood flow during isometric contraction is related to the amount of relative force developed within the muscle. In fact, such occlusion begins to be significantly realized when the level of muscular force exceeds a fairly predictable level of an individual's maximal voluntary contractile strength (MVC).

The glide phase in speedskating involves the isometric contraction of many prime-mover and stabilizer muscles. In general, such isometric contractions require relatively low levels of energy. However, even low-level isometric contractions, on the order of 15 percent of MVC, are believed to reduce blood flow through the muscles enough to have a negative impact (Kahn and Monod 1989). Eckblom, Hermansen, and Saltin (1967) determined that the force of the hip and knee joint extensor muscles during the glide lies between 25 and 35 percent of maximal value. This reduced blood flow results in an increase in local muscle-lactate concentration and a lack of oxygen, which can lead to the early onset of fatigue. Furthermore, it can prematurely direct energy metabolism toward anaerobic pathways (van Ingen Schenau, de Groot, and Hollander 1983). Logically enough, these effects become more pronounced as either contraction (glide) time is increased or the amount of tension within the muscles is elevated.

Increasing the level of lower-body strength can have significant advantages: for instance, such gains can increase the absolute level at which blood restrictions become significant. To illustrate this point, consider the following example. A skater has an arbitrary leg-strength index (MVC) of 100 units. At a force level of about 40 units (40 percent of MVC), blood flow will become significantly restricted. Metabolic waste products will begin to accumulate to the detriment of muscular activity and efficient energy production. Through regular strength training, however, the skater increases maximal leg strength to 200 units. Since muscle blood flow tends to occur at a fairly fixed percentage of maximal isometric strength, this individual now can exert 80 units of force before experiencing the same level of muscle blood-flow restriction.

As another illustration of this same point, let's use the same skater, with maximal strength doubled through resistance training (see figure 7.1). For the skater to sustain a given level of performance now requires a decreased percentage of maximal force. In fact, the required force output falls from 50 percent to 25 percent of maximal strength, which points to improved muscular efficiency and a heightened level of absolute endurance.

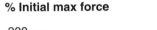

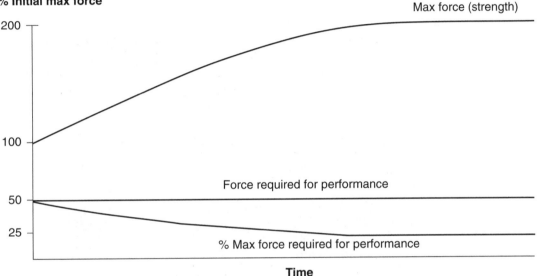

7.1 Effect of increased strength on endurance performance. As maximum strength increases with training, the force output required for top performance (expressed as a percentage of maximum strength) decreases. In this example, maximum force doubled; therefore, the required force output fell from 50% to 25% of maximum strength. Endurance should be improved.

Reprint, by permission, from D.G. Sale, 1991, Testing strength and power. In *Physiological Testing of the High-Performance Athlete*, 2nd ed., edited by J.D. MacDougall, H.A. Wenger, and H.J. Green (Champaign, IL: Human Kinetics), 24.

PATTERN OF MUSCULAR INVOLVEMENT DURING SPEEDSKATING

Speedskating uses muscles in quite an unusual way. Understanding how the lower-body muscles function during skating will help athletes grasp the rationale behind exercise prescription.

Glide Phase

The glide phase of classic speedskating is static in nature. So the muscles of the hip, upper leg, and lower leg engage in relatively high-level isometric contractions. The deep knee bend used during the glide represents a classic catch-22 situation. Because the amount of force a muscle can develop depends on its length and the angle of pull at its tendon, a low (pre-extension) knee angle puts the quadriceps muscles in a progressively inefficient position to develop force as the knee bend deepens. However, this same low position offers significant biomechanical advantages because it increases push-off displacement, elevates the storage of kinetic energy, and ensures that knee extension occurs through the range of motion where maximal force potential can be reached. Thus, speedskaters must develop strength at the low knee angles where most athletes are weak. Skating activity in itself can improve strength levels in the knee area, but only to a point. Even strenuous training can only load the muscles to a certain level. Resistance training is the only real way to strain the leg muscles past the highest tension that skating activity can impose. Since most of the pushing force develops in the first third of the push extension, improving strength within this range of motion is worthwhile. These facts have two implications for weight training. Both relate to specificity of training.

First, resistance exercises must focus on the development of both isometric and dynamic strength. Since it is known that gains in one type of strength do not transfer well to performance in another, a skater who employs solely dynamic strength exercises will experience little or no improvement in isometric strength. Therefore, speedskaters should use exercises emphasizing isometric strength at angles assimilating those of the glide phase (100 to 110 degrees) to supplement the more traditional exercises that are dynamic in nature.

Second, resistance training must also reflect the timing of the muscular events that occur during actual skating. We know that during the static glide phase, contractions of the lower-body muscles are isometric, with no change in the muscles' length or joint angle. The duration of the glide phase dictates how long the time that the muscles engage in such activity—as well as the duration that muscle blood flow is restricted. The implication is that all resistance exercises targeting the muscles of the glide phase should closely reflect this time frame. Therefore, weight exercises that focus on strengthening muscles for the glide should involve an isometric phase equal to or longer than the actual glide time during skating. Thus, isometric strength is probably more important for distance specialists who display significantly longer glide times than sprinters.

Push-Off

During the push-off extension phase, the prime movers that are involved in static contraction during the glide phase must generate forward propulsion by producing a powerful and accelerated push to the side. As the pushing leg extends, smaller (but no less important) stabilizer muscles must be active to keep the hip and pelvic areas motionless. These muscle requirements have two important implications for weight training prescription:

Most strength exercises should be *freestanding* in nature to improve the strength and coordination of both prime-mover and stabilizer muscles. Free-weight exercises involving *multijoint* action are best for such development.

Secondly, a resistance-training program should focus on exercises that employ the explosive action you see during skating push-off. The extension of the hip and knee should be a smooth and coordinated motion that exhibits a definitive acceleration and snap of power at the end of push-off. Athletes usually perform weight-training exercises for general fitness and conditioning in a slow, controlled manner to ensure maximal involvement of muscle fibers. However, for training specificity, the resistance exercises speedskaters use must deviate from this rhythm.

They should instead approximate the contraction velocity at which the muscles shorten during push-off. All lower-body exercises that develop dynamic pushing power, therefore, should be executed in an explosive fashion, as in the actual push-off.

Weight Transfer

The weight transfer represents a series of important transitional events involving the regrouping of the push while the body's weight and center of gravity are positioned entirely over the support leg. During its regrouping, the recovery leg is relieved of the majority of the stress it experiences during glide and push-off, restoring near-normal blood flow through the working muscles. What this process means for strength training is that resistance exercises should attempt to match the *sequential order* of the mechanical events. In other words, the timing of the concentric (shortening), isometric, and eccentric (lengthening) phases of muscle dynamics, as well as the brief rest period, should closely replicate the pattern of muscular usage that occurs during skating. To accomplish this, skaters can use a lifting rhythm and pause between repetitions to mimic the timing of muscular events during skating. The result will be that specific adaptations to the muscles maximally transfer to speedskating performance.

Lifting rhythm, also commonly referred to as tempo, is one of the best ways to improve the specificity of resistance training. For example, lifting the weights as explosively as possible on the "up" portion of the movement closely imitates the high muscle contraction velocity reached during actual speedskating. Since eccentric contractions have little importance in speedskating, resistance exercises need not over-emphasize this phase of the movement.

MUSCULAR STRENGTH

Strength can be defined as the peak force developed during a maximal voluntary contraction under a given set of standardized conditions. For testing purposes and practical application, strength is usually measured in pounds (lb) or metric kilograms (kg; 1 kg = 2.2 lb). The amount of force that a muscle can produce depends on at least five variables: the angle of the joint, movement pattern, type of contraction, speed of contraction, and muscle size or body mass.

Angle of the Joint

A muscle's ability to produce force depends on the momentary angle of the joint at which it acts. This relationship between joint angle and force-generating capacity is commonly referred to as the *strength curve*. Not only does each muscle have its own fairly characteristic strength curve, but the strength curves for a given muscle may vary significantly from one individual to another. Figure 7.2 illustrates a typical strength curve for the quadriceps muscles.

In this example, maximal force (strength) occurs at around 118 degrees. The ability of the quadriceps muscle group to produce force varies as the joint moves through its functional range of motion. In speedskating, the knee moves through a range of motion from about 110 degrees of flexion (glide phase's joint angle) to 180 degrees (full or nearly full knee extension). Since most of the push-off force is generated during the first third of this range where peak force occurs (i.e., at about

7.2 Strength curve for the quadriceps muscle group. In this example, peak force is achieved at roughly 118 degrees of knee extension.

Reprinted, by permission, from J.D. MacDougall and D. Sale, Department of Kinesiology, McMaster University, Hamilton, Ontario.

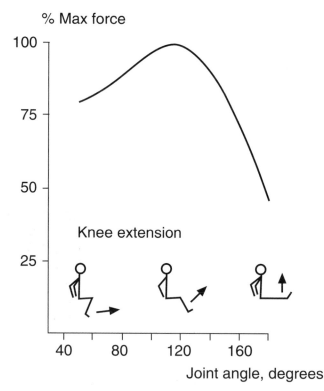

120 degrees), strength-training exercises should function to improve force levels between 110 and 130 degrees. Understanding a little about muscle strength curves, particularly of the quadriceps muscles, one can appreciate the importance of focusing strength gains at shallow knee angles.

Movement Pattern

Muscular strength can be affected by the complex movement patterns in speedskating involving multijoint actions. Consider the fact that the quadriceps muscles originate from the front of the hip-bone area and insert at the top of the patella (kneecap). These muscles, therefore, cross and affect motion of both the knee and hip joints. How much force the muscles can apply toward knee extension will depend on the rate and degree of relative flexion or extension at the hip joint.

The implication for speedskating is that resistance training for the lower body should rely almost exclusively on free-weight exercises involving the coordinated action of the hip and knee joints. Weight machines work well for building muscle mass and strength, but they do not necessarily result in physical adaptations that directly improve movement pattern strength for speedskating.

Type of Contraction

The amount of strength that a muscle can produce also depends on the type of contraction: that is, whether the muscle's length is shortening, increasing, or remaining unchanged. Here is a sketch of how the type of contraction affects force production:

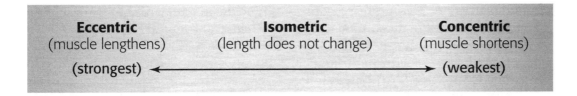

Eccentric (muscle lengthens)	Isometric (length does not change)	Concentric (muscle shortens)
(strongest) ←	→	(weakest)

Speed of Contraction

A muscle's strength potential also varies with the actual velocity, or rate, of change in the length of the muscle. With an eccentric contraction, force potential rises as the speed of muscle lengthening increases. This trend occurs up to a plateau point, whereby further increases in the velocity of lengthening fail to elicit continuously greater degrees of force generation. For concentric contractions the opposite occurs. Strength ability decreases progressively as the speed of the shortening increases. Isometric contractions lie in between these two extremes in terms of force development.

Muscle Size and Body Mass

The muscle cross-sectional area is the most important nonmechanical factor for determining absolute-strength levels. Quite simply, the larger the muscle, the more force it can develop. Since muscle mass also correlates highly to body mass, heavy athletes who are lean (not fat) typically are stronger in terms of absolute measures. This helps explain why large and heavily muscled skaters will dominate in speedskating sprint events, where high strength levels are important. For in-line racing or marathon ice skating, in contrast, it seems more important to have a high strength-to-mass ratio. Building strength through resistance training is one of the best ways to increase this index.

MUSCULAR ENDURANCE

Muscular endurance refers to the ability of a muscle or group of muscles to perform repeatedly against a submaximal load for an extended period of time. In the weight room, the term *muscular endurance* is used most often to describe a method of training where *toning* is the goal, and a high number of repetitions are done using a light load. In speedskating, however, muscular endurance usually refers to the ability to be efficient while muscles contract hundreds, or even thousands, of times throughout the course of an event. In essence, both these practical definitions are accurate. However, the story is a little more complex. In fact, muscular endurance can be expressed in two ways.

Absolute Endurance

Absolute muscular endurance refers to exercise and muscle performance observed using a predetermined standard load that is less than the maximum that could be lifted. Provided that the load is relatively high, this ability to sustain repeated contractions correlates highly to strength. Therefore, individuals with a high maximal strength usually also score well on tests of absolute endurance, while those who are less strong might score comparatively poorly. For example, skater A and skater B both perform a leg-press test to determine the maximal weight that each can lift once (one-repetition maximum test). Skater A lifts 300 pounds, while skater B can manage only 200 pounds. It is safe to say that skater A is considerably stronger than skater B. Both athletes now perform an absolute muscular *endurance* test, which in this case measures the maximum number of leg-press repetitions using an arbitrary load of 150 pounds. Skater A will outperform skater B in this test because he or she is stronger.

Relative Endurance

The second type of muscular endurance is termed relative, and it reflects the maximum number of repetitions that can be performed while using a resistance that is a percentage of maximal strength. Quite opposite to absolute endurance, relative measures *do not correlate* with maximal strength. Gains in strength actually tend to reduce the level of relative muscular endurance.

Using the previous two subjects again, skaters A and B now perform a test to measure their relative muscular endurance. This time, both are assigned a weight equal to 70 percent of their respective one-repetition maximum value. Skater A must lift 210 pounds, whereas skater B uses a load of only 140 pounds. Although skater A is the stronger of the two individuals, the benefit from being strong is lost in such a test of relative muscular endurance. In fact, skater B probably will score higher and perform more repetitions.

RELATIVE IMPORTANCE OF ABSOLUTE AND RELATIVE ENDURANCE

Whether speedskating relies more heavily on relative or absolute endurance depends essentially on whether an athlete is an in-line or ice skater. The distance one competes in also is significant in determining which kind of endurance is more significant.

Absolute Endurance, Strength, and Body Mass

Speedskating is all about applying muscular force to the skates and generating propulsion through lateral motion. Since all skaters are subjected to the same resistive forces against pushing (surface friction and air resistance), speedskating may be considered to rely most heavily on absolute muscular endurance for performance. The only factor that might argue against this view is the skater's body mass. One might contend that a heavier skater has to support more body mass, and therefore must push with more force to overcome the increased resistance. Although body weight must certainly be supported, however, pushing force is not applied in direct opposition to gravity. It might also be argued that a heavier speedskater likely has a strength-to-mass ratio that is characteristic of smaller athletes. Therefore, increased pushing resistance among heavy skaters may not significantly affect the importance of absolute strength.

All of this aside, it is understood that a high level of strength is associated with a greater ability to accelerate the body. Since strength relates highly with absolute endurance, it is safe to say that speedskating events that are highly intense and short in duration, and that require significant acceleration and top speed, will rely more on absolute levels of muscular endurance than on relative scores. The observation that most elite metric (long-track) ice skaters are tall and heavily muscled seems to support this conclusion. If we accept that short-distance speedskating performance depends more on levels of absolute muscular endurance than on relative, the importance of developing higher strength levels in the lower body is immediately apparent. Increasing strength through resistance training can indirectly improve levels of absolute endurance and facilitate personal performance.

Concluding that absolute muscular endurance is more important for short- and middle-distance skaters, however, does not necessarily mean that strength and absolute endurance levels are also most valid for in-line racers and long-distance ice skaters. To evaluate the relative importance of either type of endurance, it is important to analyze the muscular requirements of a given event. In-line and marathon ice skaters travel at slower speeds, and thus require less forceful muscular function in the pushing muscles. Also, in events of longer duration, the muscles contract countless more times than in short or middle distances.

Relative Endurance and Event Specificity

Determining whether high strength and *absolute* endurance or high *relative* endurance is more important for distance skaters is a complex issue. Developing strength is important even for speedskaters who compete in lower-intensity events of long duration. One reason for this (as has been established) is that increasing maximal strength through training reduces the relative level of tension at which blood-flow restrictions impede oxygen delivery and the removal of lactate. And a second reason is that increasing the levels of lower-body strength allow a skater to accelerate more quickly as the race's pace increases—and to heighten top speed for the sprint to the finish.

Equally important to improving strength is the ability of the muscles to resist fatigue as they contract repeatedly against submaximal loads. In this respect, muscular endurance becomes more and more important as race distances increase from sprint events up to those of moderate distance. In events of longer duration, muscular endurance holds even greater importance, although being able to push with great strength is often necessary to cope with a race's dynamics. Since relative muscular endurance does not depend on body mass, the observation that most in-line racers and marathon ice skaters are more lean-muscled than sprint skaters further supports this conclusion. In fact, the integrated importance of strength and endurance for in-line racers implies that a high strength-to-mass ratio is also vital for success.

Implications for Resistance Training

If you specialize in a particular speedskating discipline or train for a specific distance event, understanding the relative importance (and integrated value) of strength and absolute or relative muscular endurance is important. Such knowledge will help you grasp the primary purpose of resistance training and how much time should be spent developing strength—and therefore absolute endurance—versus relative muscular endurance. Weight-training methodology differs rather significantly in developing these kinds of exercises, so it is essential to differentiate among training applications.

For most all-around skaters, increasing both strength and muscular endurance should be the goal, since both types of endurance can enhance performance. When you implement such a strategy, undertaking strength and endurance training concurrently, the adaptive benefits of both will be minimized. This phenomenon is termed *antagonism*. You can reduce the detrimental effects that one form of training has on the other by using goal-specific workouts at different times of the week. This practice, termed *phasing*, is employed in the sample programs outlined later in this chapter.

PRINCIPLES OF RESISTANCE TRAINING

The same physiologic principles that govern aerobic and anaerobic training also govern developing muscular strength and endurance. The following section reviews these important principles and explains how they relate specifically to devising exercises for resistance training.

Principle of Overload

Overload involves forcing a muscle to function at a workload greater than normally encountered, with the aim to increase strength capacity. Although varying the levels of overload results in different stimuli to the muscles, the degree of overload determines the adaptation (rather than the total amount of work done). Therefore, maximal efforts do not necessarily provide the optimal stimulus for fostering gains in strength. To induce a muscular training effect, the minimum threshold required is about 35 percent of maximal strength.

Principle of Progressive Resistance

To ensure continual adaptation and increase in performance, resistance training must gradually increase both the volume and intensity of work performed. Moderate, progressive overloading actually produces faster and better results than large jumps.

Principle of Specificity

Since physiological adaptations are specific to the mode of training, resistance exercises must reflect as closely as possible the muscle dynamics of the competitive sport activity. Gains in muscular strength and endurance are achieved only in the muscles involved in the exercise.

Principle of Momentary Fatigue

To train for gains in strength, the load must be high enough to completely fatigue the working muscles by the end of the targeted number of repetitions. If more repetitions can be performed, the load may be considered too light. During the rest period, the muscles are given time to recuperate enough to again perform the same number of repetitions until fatigue once again limits the volume of any particular set.

Principle of Rest and Recovery

To allow for the repair of muscle tissue, strength workouts targeting the same muscle groups should not be performed closer together than 48 hours. This is not to say that strength training cannot be done every day; it simply means that the same muscle groups can be worked hard no sooner than every other day. Overall, the same muscles must be overloaded at least two to three times a week in order for improvement in muscular fitness to occur.

THEORY AND PRACTICE: PRIMARY GOALS

It should now be apparent that acquiring superior levels of lower-body strength is of prime importance for any skater wishing to achieve breakthrough levels in performance. In considering strength training for a speedskater, it is beneficial to isolate and prioritize the two primary goals of such training. For all skaters, according to Carl Foster (1995), the primary purposes of weight training are (1) stabilization and (2) propulsion.

Stabilization

Efficient skating requires the proper execution of a series of biomechanical events that lead to the application of force through the skate. Stability relates to both the glide and push-off phases of the skating movement. The human body functions as a series of joints and levers that are acted upon by muscles to produce force and motion. For speedskaters, stability in the pelvic area is paramount. Stabilizing the hips during the sideways extension of the pushing leg requires muscular strength applied to prevent any needless or wasted energy expenditures. The muscles stabilize the area to prevent rotation or horizontal elevation of the hips. Many young or inexperienced skaters who have not yet developed sufficient strength to keep the pelvis from tilting during push-off demonstrate this poor hip stability. By contrast, accomplished skaters are so efficient in part because their pushing forces have maximal efficiency due to the stable and motionless nature of their hips.

Propulsion

The second goal, or purpose, of weight training is to develop the specific attributes in the muscles responsible for pushing and generating propulsion. Although skating activity in itself will function to increase strength in the pushing muscles, resistance exercises can overload the muscles to a much higher degree than skate training alone.

Strength training for propulsion can involve enormous variety. Exercises for stability and propulsion should implement both static and dynamic training methods. For developing strength in this area, exercises should target *specific* strength attributes that the muscles need in speedskating, so that an athlete can push harder and ultimately go faster. Pay special attention to improving strength at the deeper knee angles—where the push begins.

Practical Application

Without hip stability, pushing efforts are largely wasted. Therefore, the first priority in implementing strength training should be to focus on the muscles that contribute directly to stabilizing the hip area. These muscles that help stabilize the hips are primarily in the abdominal wall, at both the front and sides of the body, and in the lower back. The muscles that cross the hip joint in front (hip flexors) and those of the upper-inner thigh (adductors) also play a vital role in solidifying the pelvic area.

Core strength exercises, such as squats and lunges, are the primary activities that should be used to develop hip stability. These exercises should all be done with free weights, which allow for the execution of multijoint actions. The supporting and stabilizing muscles are automatically activated during this kind of free-standing exercise, since the individual must maintain balance and equilibrium while displacing the center of gravity.

In exercises directed at improving stability, it is recommended that the amount of weight you use be limited to the maximal amount that can be *safely lifted without a weight belt*. Although a weight belt allows you to use a greater load with confidence, it takes much of the tensile stress off the key stabilizers, thus defeating the objective!

After spending several weeks to develop adequate strength in the muscles that provide hip stability, the next priority is to develop specific strength of the pushing muscles that generate propulsion. The muscles that extend the leg are the quadriceps and hamstring groups on the front and rear of the upper thighs, respectively; the gluteal muscles extend the hip, and the abductor muscles move the leg away from the body's midline. Exercises to increase propulsive strength also should rely almost exclusively on free weight forms, such as squats and lunges. Since the purpose of this training is usually to increase the level of absolute strength, considerably higher loads are used than with stability training. Consequently, using a weight belt is usually recommended to protect the smaller and weaker muscles from overstrain or injury.

Whether you perform exercises for stability or for propulsive pushing force, the amount of weight you employ should never be so great that the speed of the lift is slow. Recall that, according to the principle of specificity, resistance exercises for speedskaters should closely reflect the way the muscles function during actual skating. Using a very heavy load may beneficially stress the muscles, but the resulting adaptations still will be specific to the contraction speed to which they were attained. Strength gains achieved by using high-velocity muscle contractions transfer fairly well to low contraction speeds, but the same cannot be said for the development of low-velocity strength. That is, although there is little harm in executing lifts faster than the actual contraction speed during skating, lifts performed at speeds slower than those of skating will not effectively benefit performance.

TRAINING VARIABLES

Now that you have studied the theory supporting the importance of increasing levels of muscular strength and endurance for speedskating, it is time to examine its applicability. This next section defines some of the key terminology for resistance practice and outlines the important variables you can apply, differentiating between

Table 7.1

Training Variables for Strength and Endurance

Objective	Repetitions	# Sets per exercise	# Sets per muscle	Load (% 1RM)	Rest time (in seconds)	Frequency per week
Strength	10–12	3–4	8–12	80–86	120	2–3
Endurance	20–40	2–4	8–12	60–70	45–90	2–3
Mixed	10	2–3	8–10	75	90	2–3

training methods specific to optimal strength and muscular endurance. These points are summarized in table 7.1.

Repetitions and Load

A *repetition (rep)* consists of a concentric lifting phase, an isometric phase, and a subsequent eccentric lowering. The maximal load that can be lifted *once* for a particular exercise is termed the *one-repetition maximum* strength (1 RM). The plural term *repetitions (reps)* refers to the number of times a weight is lifted during a *continuous* bout. The number of repetitions performed within an uninterrupted effort constitutes a *set*.

The number of reps in a set and the number of sets depend on the overall physiologic effect you seek. How many reps can be performed before you experience temporary fatigue varies with the load you lift, which is expressed as a percentage of maximal strength (that is, of 1 RM) for a given muscle. Figure 7.3, a–b illustrates this relationship. Determining 1 RM strength for a certain exercise and using this figure as a general guide is an effective method to set the target number of repetitions for a given load.

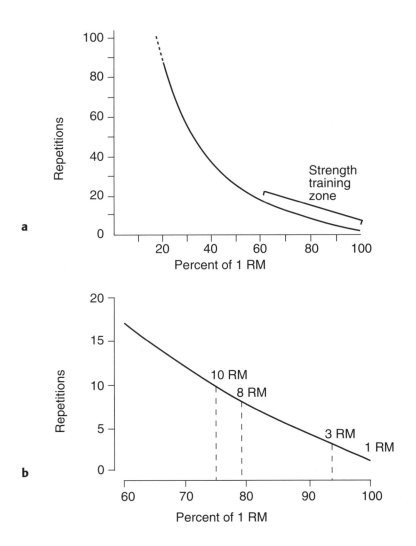

7.3 Relationship of percent of 1 RM and the number of repetitions that can be performed. *(a)* Shown for a wide range in the percent of 1 RM. Also indicated is an arbitrary strength training zone. *(b)* The strength training zone has been expanded.

Reprinted, by permission, from D. Sale and J.D. MacDougall, 1981, "Specificity in strength training: a review for the coach and athlete," *Canadian Journal of Applied Sports Sciences* 6(2):87-92.

For the development of strength, training typically employs relatively high resistance and low repetitions. Strength training for speedskating, however, should involve slightly more repetitions than normally employed. So the number of reps for a single set might range from 10 to 12, using a load equivalent to about 70 to 75 percent of 1 RM strength. Therefore, *it is not necessary to lift loads that are maximal to get improvements in maximal strength.* The overload imposed by a load that results in momentary fatigue by the end of the required number of reps is sufficient for inducing such adaptations.

If you aim to improve the level of muscular *endurance*, the required method of resistance training deviates significantly from what is optimal to build strength. Muscular endurance is most improved by using lower resistance and a higher number of repetitions. A load between 40 and 55 percent of 1 RM strength, using repetitions ranging from 20 to 40, represents a classic muscular-endurance set for speedskaters.

The purpose of muscular-endurance training is not necessarily to tax the muscles so hard that an athlete experiences momentary fatigue by the end of the targeted number of repetitions. Remember, rather, that the goal is to produce high numbers of moderate-level contractions with short rest periods, so a general rule is that a skater should feel capable of doing half a dozen more repetitions at the end of the set.

Mixed training gives mixed results. Therefore, implementing load and repetition variables that lie in between these extremes will provide gains in both strength and endurance. Performing 10 to 15 repetitions using a load of roughly 65 to 75 percent of 1 RM stimulates the muscles to improve in both capacities. This is not to say that gains will be equal. The actual development of strength versus endurance will depend somewhat on the individual. For example, such a modification can be highly desirable for beginner skaters who are first implementing resistance training.

Recovery Time and Number of Sets

The amount of time spent between sets of the same exercise depends on the specific intent of the workout. For exercises that improve muscular strength, rest time is about 90 to 120 seconds. Not only does this amount allow for almost full replenishing of creatine phosphate within the muscle cells, but it provides time for the neural muscle-control mechanisms to recover.

Two or three sets are often used for novice- to intermediate-strength training. Advanced training can involve up to five sets of a given exercise. Given the fact that several exercises may be used to target the same muscles, particularly those of the lower body, capable of handling high volume, the total number of sets can range from 10 to 12.

As discussed, muscular-endurance training involves less relative resistance and higher repetitions than does strength training. Because the goal of such endurance-type training is to increase a muscle's tolerance for repeated contractions, fewer sets may be used, with less rest in between them. This being said, a typical muscular-endurance workout would involve a recovery period of between 30 and 60 seconds. Endurance exercises using repetitions at the lower end of the adaptive spectrum (i.e., 15) would use less rest than those that involve higher numbers of reps (because fewer reps result in a lesser accumulation of lactic acid). Mixed training, involving load and repetition amounts between those of strength or endurance training, might also involve a rest period of about 60 seconds.

Frequency of Exercise

For resistance training to be effective, the muscles must be trained a minimum of two to three times a week, or three to four days in a ten-day cycle. Because 48 hours is recommended in between heavy training of the same muscle group, the most common approach is to stress all muscle groups every other day.

For advanced athletes, the routine can be broken into two separate training days, where half of the muscles are worked on day one of the program, and the other muscles groups worked on day two. This two-day format allows a higher volume and intensity to be done specific to each muscle group, but it also requires more regular visits to the gym to stress the muscles often enough.

ILLUSTRATED EXERCISE AND PRESCRIPTION GUIDELINES

Part of the beauty of using free weights is that a huge variety of exercises can be performed with them, providing the opportunity to adapt common exercises into ones that are more specific to speedskaters. Rather than trying to include every possible exercise that could benefit sport performance, this section highlights the ones that are most relevant to speedskating and those incorporated into the sample program. Readers also can apply the content from this chapter to modify other exercises, tailoring them for speedskaters.

Squats

Squats are probably the most commonly used lower-body exercise for athletes in sports that require leg and hip strength, endurance, or both (figure 7.4). Relatively simple, these exercises can be modified in several ways to best fit a speedskater.

What is most important is that the squats emphasize the deep knee bend used during skating. Full squats work the muscles through the entire range of motion, from a deep-seated position to complete extension of the knee and hip (i.e., 90 to 180 degrees in the knee joint). Half squats (figure 7.5), on the other hand, work the muscles through only half the possible range of motion (either from 90 to 135 degrees or from 135 to 180 degrees of motion). For a speedskater, working only the lower half—from a deep position to half extension—is most beneficial.

Isometric squats differ slightly in that they emphasize the static position at a given point (usually the bottom) of the working range. In an isometric squat, the chosen degree of knee flexion is held for a period between two and six seconds, followed by an explosive up-portion. Using less resistance is typical for this squat method, especially when the static position is held for longer durations.

7.4 Squats.

7.5 Half squats.

Lunges

Lunges can be directed either to the front, back, or side. They focus most of the effort on only one leg at a time. All lunges start with the feet together, followed by a step with one leg. With forward and side lunges, the leg that does the stepping then absorbs the load as it deeply flexes. With a backward, or rear, lunge, the leg that steps back is *not* the one to be worked; rather, it provides stability for the stationary leg to perform the activity. With all lunges, the exercise can either repeat on the same leg for the required number of repetitions or alternate between legs. See figures 7.6 and 7.7 for some examples of lunge exercises.

Note that when you perform these exercises, it is important that the lowest position of the lunge assimilate the knee and hip angles of the speedskating movement pattern: that is, a 90- to 100-degree bend in the knee, with the hip end sitting back.

7.6 Front lunge.

7.7 Side lunge.

Step-Ups

Step-up exercises require superior balance and coordination (figure 7.8). They use an aerobic-exercise step, a block, or a crate of appropriate height to create a knee angle of roughly 100 degrees with the leg placed atop the block. It is best to perform these exercises by alternating the leg that steps up on the block. The leg that steps up then extends powerfully to raise the body's weight over it. The knee of the free leg should be forcefully driven forward as it flexes at the hip and knee. Once both feet are back on the ground, the other leg repeats the same action. Step-ups also can involve either the entire range of knee extension (full step-ups) or strictly the bottom half (half step-ups).

7.8 Step-ups.

Hip Exercises

The best method for targeting the hip musculature is to use pulley or cable equipment or a specifically designed "multihip" machine found in many gyms. For the target muscle group to take the full effort, it is important that the hips themselves remain stable, moving the upper leg in the desired plane.

Adductor Group

The adductor muscle group consists of the muscles of the upper, inner thigh, whose function is to pull the leg *toward* the midline of the body. These muscles stabilize the body during the glide phase, and they also play a primary role in pushing the leg (the *left* leg in track skating) through and under the body during crossover steps. In adductor exercises (figure 7.9), the working leg should bend about 30 degrees, extending slightly toward the end of the range of motion.

7.9 Hip exercises, adduction.

Abductor Group

The abductor group performs the opposite function as the adductors, instead moving the leg *away* from the body's midline. In performing abduction exercises (figure 7.10), it is beneficial to perform the motion with the knee bent to about 30 degrees. Then gradually straighten the knee joint as the leg moves away from the body.

7.10 Hip exercises, abduction.

Hip Flexors and Extensors

The hip-flexor muscle group drives the recovery leg forward and under the body during speedskating recovery and set-down and stabilizes the hips during the glide. Exercises that target these muscles should also approximate the exact muscle mechanics used in skating. Therefore, the knee joint should remain flexed between 90 and 100 degrees to best simulate the movement pattern.

Although hip extension during speedskating occurs in tandem with abduction of the hip, the extensor muscle group can be selectively targeted with a cable or pulley assembly or with a multihip machine. As in the abduction exercises, for these exercises, too, it is best to begin the hip extension with a 90-degree knee bend and then gradually straighten the knee as the hip extension reaches its farthest point of movement. Figures 7.11 and 7.12 illustrate exercises for hip flexion and extension.

7.11 Hip exercises, flexion.

7.12 Hip exercises, extension.

Lower-Body Exercises Using Machines

Although free weight exercises must serve as the primary vehicle for improving strength and endurance for skaters, a well-rounded resistance program can also include the use of machines. What these machine exercises lack in versatility and specificity, they make up for in terms of heightened safety, simplicity, and a more user-friendly medium for improving muscular strength and endurance. The most common lower-body exercises using machines, and the ones most beneficial for skate-specific training, are the leg extension, leg curl, leg press, and calf raise (see figures 7.13 through 7.17). While lower-body free weight exercises involve multijoint actions and several muscle groups, their mechanical counterparts can offer the benefit of muscle (group) specific isolation.

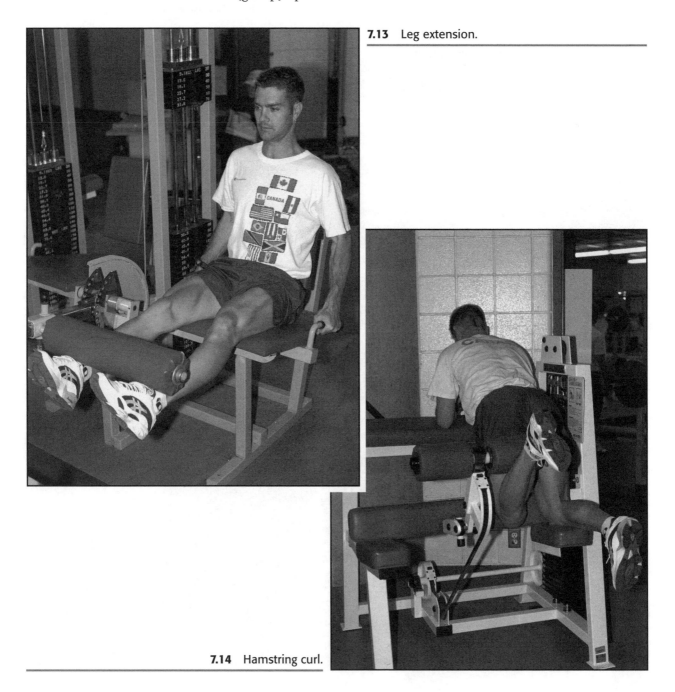

7.13 Leg extension.

7.14 Hamstring curl.

7.15 Leg press.

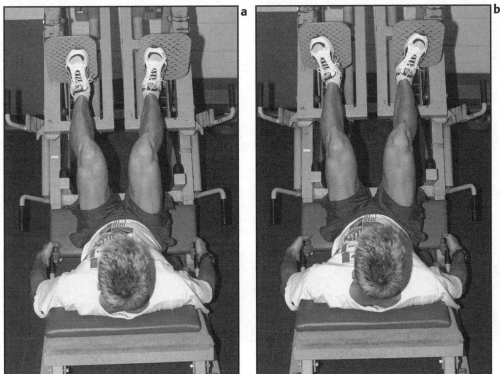

7.16 Leg press foot variations: *(a)* turning the feet slightly inward increases the stress on the medial (inner) quadriceps muscles; *(b)* turning the feet slightly outward has the opposite effect of stressing the lateral (outer) quadriceps muscles.

7.17 Calf raises.

Trunk Exercises

Trunk exercises focus on the abdominal and lower-back muscles, and should be included in all programs for speedskating. These muscles need to be strong to stabilize the hips during skating. The lower-back muscles especially need good strength and endurance for holding the trunk in a forward-flexed position for prolonged periods. The main exercises used for trunk strength are back extensions and various abdominal wall exercises. Figures 7.18 through 7.20 show several trunk exercises for the back and the abdominals.

7.18 Standing back/hamstring extension.

7.19 Prone back extension.

7.20 Abdominal curls.

Upper Body

Even for lower-body athletes such as speedskaters, building and maintaining strength in the upper body is also important. Such training makes an individual more well-rounded in strength and body proportion, enhances coordination, improves body posture during skating, and improves sprint ability (by developing more strength and power in the muscles used for swinging the arms). Training for the upper body can involve many different exercises that target a variety of muscle groups. Many coaches recommend building upper-body strength primarily in the shoulders, arms, and upper back.

SAMPLE PROGRAM FOR THE INTERMEDIATE SPEEDSKATER

The weight-training program for ice speedskaters that follows is a watered-down version of the one used by the U.S. National Speedskating Team (Hedrick 1994). Notice the use of goal-specific phasing in this program. The program is basically divided into two cycles. The lower body is trained each and every training day, as is the trunk. The upper body, however, is only incorporated into one of the workouts.

The time of year that you choose to implement this program strongly depends on whether you will use it for ice or for in-line skating. The program is designed to first develop muscular *endurance* over a six-week period and then to develop *strength* over the next six weeks. You should time the program so that the strength phase has been completed by the beginning of the competitive season. During the competitive year, you can maintain strength by simply completing the strength-cycle workout once or twice a week. Please note that sets and repetitions are expressed in these training programs as number of sets × number of repetitions per set.

Endurance Cycle: Six Weeks

Goals—Develop muscular endurance and stabilizing strength in the skating muscles. Emphasize proper lifting technique and prepare for the higher-intensity training to follow.

Intensity—Complete the required number of repetitions in good form. Select a resistance that results in near-complete, temporary fatigue by the end of the set.

Rest—Varies between 30 and 60 seconds, as specified.

Training frequency—Three times a week.

Tempo—All lifts should be done to a timing of one second up and two seconds down. The lower-body exercises should emphasize a slight delay at the bottom of the range of motion.

Table 7.2

Endurance-Training Cycle

Day 1	Day 2	Day 3
Total body	**Upper body**	**Total body**
Power cleans 3x12	Seated row 3x15	Overhead press 3x12
	Lat pull-down 3x15	
	Biceps curl 3x15	
Lower body	**Lower body**	**Lower body**
Half squat 2x30	One-leg squat 3x20	Full squat 3x40
Forward lunge 2x30	Side lunge 3x30	Rear lunge 2x40
Hip adductor 2x20	Hip abductor 3x12	Leg curl 2x15
Half step–up 2x20	Hip flexor 3x12	Isometric squat 3x20 (hold 3–5 seconds)
Trunk	**Trunk**	**Trunk**
Abdominal curl 3x15	Back extension 3x20	Abdominal curl 2x30
Oblique curl 2x15	Half sit-ups 2x15	Lateral bends 2x20
Reverse curl 2x15	Static half-sit 2x15 (hold 5 seconds)	Back extension 2x20 (hold 5 seconds)
Rest	**Rest**	**Rest**
60 seconds	30 seconds	45 seconds

Adapted, with permission, from Allen Hedrick, 1994, "Strength/power training for the national speed skating team," *Strength and Conditioning* 16(5): 33-39.

Strength Cycle: Six Weeks

Goal—Increase strength in the skating muscles by decreasing the number of repetitions and using a higher percentage of relative load. Note: because of the endurance speedskating requires, the number of repetitions here is higher than what is typically used for building strength.

Intensity—Complete the full number of targeted repetitions, resulting in momentary fatigue by the end of the last rep.

Rest—Varies between 90 and 120 seconds, as specified.

Training frequency—Three times a week; two strength days, one plyometrics day.

Tempo—Lifting rhythm should be one second up (or faster) and two seconds down, again pausing as the lower body lifts slightly at the bottom of the range (when applicable).

Table 7.3

Strength-Training Cycle

Day 1	Day 2	Day 3
Total body	**Upper body**	**Plyometric training**
Power cleans 4x12	Seated row 3x10	(see table 8.3)
	Overhead press 3x10	
Lower body	**Lower body**	
Full squat 3x12	Forward lunge 3x10	
Side lunge 4x12	Isometric squat 3x12	
Half step-up 3x10	Single-leg squat 3x10	
Leg curl 3x12	Hip abductor 3x10	
Trunk	**Trunk**	
Abdominal curl 3x20	Half sit-up 3x12	
Lateral bend 3x12	Back extension 4x12	
Back extension 2x12	Reverse curl 3x12	
Rest	**Rest**	
120 seconds	90 seconds	

Adapted, with permission, from Allen Hedrick, 1994, "Strength/power training for the national speed skating team," *Strength and Conditioning* 16(5): 33-39.

PROGRAM GUIDELINES FOR THE ADVANCED SPEEDSKATER

The sample program previously discussed is relatively simple in that it encompasses only two primary training objectives: muscular endurance and strength. For more advanced athletes willing to dedicate a longer span of time toward the development of strength and power, it is advisable to implement a more diverse approach using *periodization*. This cornerstone concept in training design is discussed in greater detail in chapter 10, Annual Training Plans. This section contains a brief outline of a more complicated strength program used by former Olympic champions Dan Jansen and Bonnie Blair of the United States (Hedrick 1994). Rather than using only two cycles, this program divides up the schedule into five goal-oriented cycles: endurance, hypertrophy, strength, power/endurance, competition.

Endurance: Five Weeks

This cycle aims to improve local muscle endurance in much the same way as the program previously discussed. Relatively light loads (40–55% of 1 RM) are used in conjunction with high repetitions (20–30) and short rest periods.

Hypertrophy: Four Weeks

The primary purpose of this phase is to achieve gains in muscle size, because of the relationship between muscle cross-sectional area and strength mentioned previously in this chapter. This phase further prepares the body for the higher intensity strength and power training to follow. High loads (80–85% of 1 RM) and low repetitions (6–10) to fatigue or failure supply the best stimulus for the muscles to grow. Rest time, however, should be kept relatively short (60–75 seconds) to emphasize the need to promote muscular endurance.

Strength: Six Weeks

The short hypertrophy cycle is followed by a strength phase where the goal is to increase specific muscular strength and prepare the body for the more explosive power cycle to follow. Training variables (load, number of repetitions, and rest time) for this phase are identical to the intermediate program previously discussed.

Power/Endurance: Seven Weeks

The major way this program differs from the simpler intermediate program is the inclusion of the power/endurance cycle. During this time, the major goal is to transform all achieved gains in strength into explosive power prior to the competitive season. Not only do specific methods for this cycle differ, but plyometric training is also infused into the training regimen (see the section titled Combining Weight Training and Plyometrics at the end of the next chapter). Since training at relatively low percentages of 1 RM strength have been shown to effectively increase power (Pedemonte 1983), lifts done at 45–60% of 1 RM for 20 seconds can be used. This approach, therefore, emphasizes speed of movement over a sustained period rather than quickly lifting heavy loads only a few times.

Competition

In this program, strength and power training continue into the competitive season, striving to maintain gains. Allen Hedrick, strength and conditioning coordinator at the U.S. Olympic training center in Colorado Springs recommends *circuit training* during this time (Hedrick 1994). Circuit training involves formatting a variety of strength/power exercises in sequence. Exercises which target the same muscles are alternated to avoid excessive fatigue. Each exercise is approached with near-maximal intensity, with little or no rest time between each one. At the end of the last activity, the entire sequence can be repeated any number of times. Circuit training is considered highly motivational for the athlete, making it a wise choice for power training during the competitive season. The highly-intense nature of each exercise is enough to maintain developments in strength and power, while the limited recovery time between exercises or sets provides supplementary endurance benefits.

While the methodology remains much the same as in the previous cycle (i.e. lower loads lifted as quickly/intensely as possible), this format continues to address the need for muscular endurance, while shortening the amount of time the athlete must spend in the weight room. Most importantly, the volume and intensity during this cycle must be varied in accord with your racing schedule. Overall, one or two workouts per week is sufficient.

SLIDEBOARD SKATING

Since the early 1970s, the slideboard has been traditionally used by ice speedskaters in the off-season as a means of developing and refining technique. Board skating also provides reasonable in-season technical and specific-strength workouts, especially when ice conditions are not good. The slideboard became even more popular with the recent growth of in-line speedskating, the inclusion of slide-aerobics in the health- and fitness-club industry, the use of lateral motion for conditioning in lower-body rehabilitation, and as cross-training for other athletes whose sport relies heavily on lateral motion.

Slideboard skating can facilitate the perfection of technique and heighten the overall process of sport-related fitness. Properly executed, it provides many benefits to speedskaters, and it has its own sequence of mechanical events that best lead to efficient technique (see pages 203–209 for slideboard skating techniques).

Slideboard skating is probably the most specific dryland training method available to speedskaters. It imitates the straightaway technique and provides a real sense of gliding. In general, slideboard workouts are meant to be technical, rather than conditioning, workouts. But there certainly are physiologic benefits to derive from a well-constructed slideboard program. Kandou et al. (1987) have shown that board skating displays many of the biomechanical and physiologic characteristics of ice and in-line speedskating. Furthermore, joint angles and the velocity of muscle contraction during slideboard skating are remarkably similar to those of true speedskating. Kandou also found that measurable physical parameters such as maximal oxygen consumption ($\dot{V}O_2$max) and blood lactate are similar to those observed during on-ice and in-line skate training.

Although sliding across a board does have certain limitations that necessitate slight modifications in technique, most of the key components of actual speedskating can be replicated accurately. Board skating allows skaters a way to develop these useful techniques:

- Practice a deep-sitting body position, emphasizing the important angles of the ankle, knee, and trunk joints.
- Work solely in a horizontal plane, promoting a straight, sideward push and a complete extension of the pushing leg.
- Perfect the lift-off, circular recovery, and set-down of the pushing leg.
- Develop a smooth, yet explosive, accelerated push.

- Promote an efficient and relaxed style of movement.
- Replicate a body position emphasizing the smooth control of weight transfer.
- Practice both single and double-arm swings.

Furthermore, board skating allows skaters to derive these physiologic benefits:

- Development and maintenance of specific strength.
- Specific adaptations in energy system efficiency (through manipulating time, intensity, and recovery variables).
- Time in the "down position" to improve specific strength and lactic-acid tolerance and removal.

And because board skating virtually replicates the time series of hip and knee angles, contraction velocities, and angular accelerations seen in ice and in-line skating, benefits from slideboard training will have maximum transfer to skating performance (Kandou et al. 1987).

SLIDEBOARD MECHANICS

Slideboard technique, like other skating strides, is easier to grasp if you divide its complete movement into sections. Each of these interrelated phases has a set of mechanical principles that must be executed correctly. Even slight misalignments or errors in execution tend to carry over to the rest of the movement pattern.

Basic Body Position

The basic body position comprises the important joint angles of the ankle, knee, and hip (trunk), and it specifies correct upper-body alignment. Here are the fundamentals for developing a good basic position:

- Keep the feet parallel, with the toes pointing straight ahead at all times.
- Flex the knees to a joint angle of about 100 to 110 degrees, where the kneecaps will be directly over the toes.
- Flex the trunk forward to an angle of roughly 60 to 80 degrees from vertical.
- Sit the hind end back slightly to focus the body mass more toward the heels.
- Square the shoulders and hips, pointing them ahead.
- Hold the head up, with the eyes focused straight ahead.
- Place both hands comfortably on the lower back.

Push Mechanics

The push should originate from a point on the foot approximately one-half to two-thirds of the way toward the heel, corresponding to a vertical line drawn down from the center of gravity. You begin the push at one end of the board, while both legs are together. The foot doing the pushing is in full contact with the bumper, and the pushing leg extends straight to the side, reaching for full extension. Keep the foot of the pushing leg flat throughout the entire extension of the hip and knee. Although plantar flexion (pointing the toes) of the pushing foot may effectively contribute to force output, this action should be avoided. Figure 7.21, a–c illustrates push mechanics.

a

7.21 Slideboard push mechanics: *(a)* as the push leg extends, the weight transfer can be clearly seen as the hips fall in toward the center of the board, *(b)* once the recovery leg sets down, *(c)* the push leg continues to extend.

b

c

Here are some additional reminders:

- The push gradually accelerates, exhibiting a definite snap of power upon complete extension.
- The heel and toe of the push leg must leave the bumper uniformly.
- At the end of the push, the foot and knee of the supporting leg are pointing directly ahead.
- Throughout the full range of pushing motion, the shoulders remain relaxed, stable, and parallel to the board—with no rotation of the trunk.
- It is acceptable for the foot to angle on the inside (invert) during the last instant of push-off, providing the foot remains pointing directly ahead.

Glide Mechanics

During the lengthy glide phase, the support leg's extensor muscles—of the hip and knee—are involved in high-level static contraction, which can result in an early onset of muscular fatigue. This accounts for the relatively short amount of work that can be performed in a single, continuous bout of board skating. Here are some guidelines for executing the glide phase:

- The foot of the support leg should be flat and pointing straight ahead, with the toes pulled slightly upward. The ability to lift the toes indicates that there is not excessive body weight on the front part of the foot.
- Maintain the support (glide) leg consistently in a deeply flexed position.
- Throughout the glide, keep the push leg in full extension, with the foot flat and aimed directly ahead.
- During the glide, the support leg is held slightly outside of the upper body in the direction of travel. This necessary positioning, caused by the feet lacking traction on the board, is the main difference between actual speedskating and board skating; it is a crucial difference to understand. Figures 7.22 and 7.23 depict two different views of the glide.

7.22 Front view of the glide.

7.23 Side view of the glide.

Recovery Mechanics

The mechanics of the recovery stroke regroup the push leg and facilitate execution of the weight transfer. It is a rather intricate process, so the recovery movement is discussed here in smaller units, defined by the function of the push leg at that specific moment in the recovery.

Impact and Lift-Off

As the support leg contacts the bumper, it gradually absorbs the shock force. The body absorbs the energy of impact, and early recovery begins, with the upper body moving directly over the support leg. Then, with the full weight balanced on the support leg, the pushing leg gently lifts off the board, remaining parallel to the surface and pointing ahead.

Recovery

As in speedskating's recovery phase, the recovery leg follows a semicircular path around the back, with upper and lower legs moving together as a unit. The recovery begins with progressive flexion of the knee, and is led by a turning-in of the recovery foot. As the foot travels around the back, the knee points downward. The ball of the foot stays close to the surface of the board throughout the recovery process. See figure 7.24.

7.24 Recovery.

Set-Down

As the foot finishes its semicircle, the knee forcefully drives through and under the body. Both legs come together, and the knees and feet should pass very close or even touch one another. The recovery foot next pushes straight forward as the knee extends slightly. The heel of the recovery foot contacts the board first, as the toes pull back. The foot continues to travel a few inches ahead of the support foot to ensure that the center of gravity falls closer to the heel.

To more closely approximate the mechanics of speedskating, it is good practice to set the foot down slightly on the outside border. Since the recovery phase is the only time the legs have to rest, make a conscious effort to ensure that the recovery process is a relaxed motion. See figure 7.25 for photos of the set-down.

7.25 Set-down.

Weight Transfer

The process of weight transfer begins during the final part of the recovery action, as the knee passes under the body and the foot drives forward. During the recovery phase, the glide leg supports the entire body's weight. During the last instant of recovery, the hip and center of gravity begin to fall inward across the board. It is important to maintain upper-body alignment and ensure that the hip initiates the "falling" motion. It is crucial that the support leg begins its lateral push to the side while the center of gravity continues to topple over to the opposite side. This process continues until the recovery leg is in place to receive the body's weight, transforming it into the support-glide leg. This "fall" and the actual timing of the weight transfer represent the true *art* of board skating. Acquiring this skill is a key part of developing a smooth, fluid, and rhythmic stride.

Arm Mechanics

Board skating is an excellent vehicle for practicing the coordination of arm mechanics with the appropriate action of the legs (the arms complement the force production of the legs). Because there is no forward motion of the body, the most effective arm swing for slideboard skating differs a bit from what you use in actual speedskating. Since the goal of board skating here is essentially technical in nature, and you want to avoid the later transfer of bad slideboard habits to speedskating, it is wise to develop and implement the same arm-swing mechanics that you would during on-ice or road training. Correct straightaway arm-swing mechanics were outlined in the earlier chapters dealing with speedskating technique. Figures 7.26 and 7.27 illustrate the single-arm and two-arm swing, respectively.

7.26 Single-arm swing.

7.27 Two-arm swing.

INSTRUCTIONS FOR BUILDING A SLIDEBOARD

Many commercially made slideboards are available on the market today. The cheaper models roll up and have detachable bumpers. Although functional, these low-end market products scratch easily and have a fairly short life span. A few manufacturers produce a "hard-body" model that merits being used for speedskate training. The cost of a good-quality board is quite significant.

For a fraction of the cost of a commercially made product, one can construct a good board that will outperform most of the mass-produced units. These guidelines can be used to build such a board. You can purchase all of the supplies from most large hardware or build-all type stores, and the entire construction process takes only about an hour.

Base

Choose a wood that is strong and durable. Particle boards and low-grade plywood will warp and further deteriorate over time; they are therefore poor choices. A good thickness for the base is a half inch or five-eighths of an inch. This makes the board heavier, but adds considerably more resilience to movement slippage while the board is in use. An ideal board width is between 35 and 40 inches with a length of eight feet (width, 89–102 centimeters; length, 2.5 meters). Extra width is nice, but it makes the board excessively large and difficult to store or move around.

Sliding Surface

The quality of surface is undoubtedly the most important part of the board, so do not cut corners on cost by purchasing anything less than the best you can find. When you shop for a good top sheet, bring a can of Pledge furniture polish, wool socks, and a rag. Spray a small area to test the level, and simply choose the surface with the least amount of friction. The two best materials for smoothness are high-grade Formica and melamine paneling. Most lumber and hardware stores have a good selection of precut four- by eight-foot sheets. Reduce the width of the sliding surface to the same dimensions as the base.

Tip: Choose a nonporous and glossy top surface. When polished it should have good luster and reflective properties. If the sheen appears duller after a quick test, this usually indicates that the material is not suitable.

Once the base and sliding surfaces are cut to the desired size, glue the top paneling sheet to the wood base with contact cement, wood glue, or a similar adhesive. Ensure that you use a thin, even layer of adhesive to prevent bubbles between the two sheets.

Bumpers

The bumpers are the ends of the board that you use to push off from. A four- by four-inch wood plank cut half an inch longer than the width of the board is simple and inexpensive. Screw the bumpers onto the ends of the board at an outward angle of about 10 degrees. This reduces the likelihood of injury by allowing the quadriceps muscles to absorb an increased proportion of the impact stress.

Bumper Padding

It is crucial to line the inside of the bumpers with an absorbent material to reduce the effect of glide impact. High-density foam, such as that used for flotation devices, works best. However, you might instead use a thick cloth or carpet lining. Figure 7.28 is a blueprint of a slideboard.

Undermat

It is important to line the base of the board with a rubberized foam material to prevent slipping during use. A carpet undermat works well, as does any thin rubber material than can be found at a local carpet or fabric store.

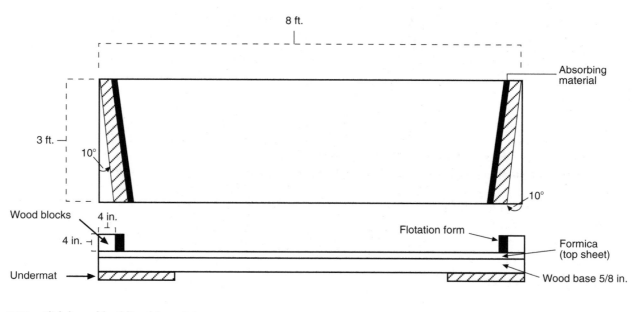

7.28 Slideboard building blueprint.

8

Power Training for Acceleration and Top Speed

Many athletes associate the term *power* so closely with both speed and strength that the true meaning of the word is lost. Power is the *rate* at which mechanical work is performed. Expressed this way, power is actually the product of the *force* of a movement multiplied by its *velocity* (Power = Force × Velocity). Power output therefore reflects the ability of a muscle or muscle group to exert force with speed as the joint moves through its range of motion.

In essence, power is what allows speedskaters to propel themselves with such velocity: it allows athletes to transmit muscular force into usable energy through the conduit of technical execution. Strength alone does not make speedskaters powerful. The ability to *utilize strength* to achieve rapid muscular contractions, moreover, can be developed only by using specific power-training methods.

Power is immensely important to speedskaters! A high level of power is associated with a greater ability to accelerate the body mass through space. Acceleration is intimately linked to power, because it reflects the rate of change in velocity with respect to time. Maximal contraction, reaction time, and the ability to move in a powerful way at the highest frequency in the least amount of time are all dominant abilities for both ice and in-line skaters. These factors enable speedskaters to achieve the highest possible level of performance capacity. It is power that essentially allows a skater to translate strength into speed and acceleration. Maximal power output levels are undoubtedly especially important for the sprinters of the world, for whom it is critical to be able to accelerate and reach top speed in as short a time as possible. However, developing superior power levels in the skating-specific musculature will benefit even middle- and long-distance skaters of both seasonal disciplines.

PLYOMETRIC TRAINING

Plyometrics refers to a specific type of power training that involves using the body's weight along with jumping exercises to load the muscles. In practical terms, a plyometric exercise involves a strong and rapid stretch and lengthening of the muscle (eccentric contraction), followed immediately by an explosive muscle contraction and subsequent "jump." The sequential staging of contractile events leads to a stronger and more powerful concentric contraction when the muscle shortens.

The actual term *plyometrics* literally means "measurable increases." Although athletes may have unknowingly used a crude form of plyometric training as early as the 1800s, it was the growing superiority of eastern-bloc track-and-field athletes in the early 1970s (who used a plyometric training regime) that led to the growing interest in and investigation of this form of training. Since plyometric exercises serve to link strength with speed of movement to produce power, these drills were originally designed to enhance the performance of athletes whose sport required such explosive strength and power. More recently, however, a consensus is growing that supplementary plyometric training serves to complement the overall training and performance of athletes within a broad variety of sport endeavors.

This chapter provides essential information on plyometric theory and its relevance to power training for speedskaters. Descriptive and illustrated exercises are included to serve the training needs and muscular requirements of the sport, followed by essential information for designing and implementing a personalized schedule of plyometric training to increase sport-specific performance.

HOW PLYOMETRICS WORKS

Plyometric exercises enable a muscle to reach maximal force development in as short a time as possible. One reason this training format is so effective is that by using it, muscular tension exceeds levels that could be induced through voluntary effort alone. Because of the high rate of force development and absolute levels of muscular tension within the muscles, plyometric exercise defines the true nature and application of physical power.

Neural Reflexes of the Muscles

When a muscle stretches, two important reflexes occur in reaction. These are called the *stretch reflex*, and the *inverse stretch reflex*. Knowledge of these processes is extremely valuable for understanding the methodology behind plyometric training.

Stretch Reflex (Myotatic Reflex)

When a muscle is elongated, small receptors called *muscle spindles* cause the muscle to contract. These structures, located in the belly of the muscle, are very sensitive to changes in muscle length. More specifically, they relay information about the actual *rate of change* in the muscle's length.

Individual muscle fibers either contract or do nothing at all. There is no such thing as a partial muscle contraction. In other words, a certain threshold of stimulation is necessary to get the fibers to shorten. Muscle spindles, on the other hand, can produce varying *degrees of resistance* to elongation. The stronger and faster the muscle is stretched, the stronger the resistive force initiated by the spindles. A familiar example of the stretch reflex is the patellar tendon (knee) reflex that doctors use to determine the integrity of the neural system. A gentle tap of the physician's mallet stretches the tendon. The muscle spindles sense this small but rapid change in length, and they respond by initiating a small muscular contraction against the resistance. The result is a subtle reflexive extension at the knee. In plyometric terminology, such a phenomenon is coined the *reflex potentiation*, because the stretch-activated muscle spindles potentiate the force production of the contraction.

Inverse Stretch Reflex

The inverse stretch reflex relies on the activity of the other key muscle receptor, the Golgi tendon organ. Much as the muscle spindles are sensitive to changes in length, the Golgi tendon organs detect both the *magnitude and rate of change of tension* resulting from muscular stretch. Opposite to the muscle spindles' response, impulses from the Golgi organs cause the muscle to relax—and inhibit muscular contraction.

The primary function of both these reflexes is to protect muscles against unexpected, violent stretching and subsequent damage. However, these two reflexes directly oppose one another in how they function. The muscle spindles' stretch reflex is typically the dominant reaction unless the Golgi tendon organs have a more intense input. If, for example, a muscle is held in a stretched position for an extended period (such as in stretching), the muscle spindles eventually "lose interest," and the Golgi tendon organs allow the *inverse* stretch reflex to predominate. A second situation in which you could expect the Golgi organ response to preside would be if a person were to jump from a high platform, where the degree of stretch due to impact would be great. Because the contraction of the muscle initiated by the spindles would likely result in muscle tearing or other serious damage, the body allows the Golgi organ response to relax the muscles.

Stretch-Shortening Cycle (Rebound Effect)

The strength of a concentric contraction can be enhanced if it is immediately *preceded by an eccentric contraction of the same muscle* or muscle group. The enhanced tension helps involve more muscle fibers, resulting in a more powerful movement and increased mechanical efficiency. This concept is the basis of the practice of plyometric training. There are four mechanisms that account for the occurrence of the rebound effect, and they deserve attention.

Elastic energy is stored in the prestretched muscle. The elastic nature of muscles allows potential energy to be stored during the eccentric movement and then released during the concentric phase. This energy is stored both in the cross-bridges that "link" the muscle protein filaments and in the elastic connective tissue within the muscle. A simple analogy is a rubber band, which releases stored kinetic energy when you let it go from a stretched position. When this muscular, tensile energy is combined with the energy of active shortening, the result is an enhanced force level and more rapid, explosive contraction.

A preparatory eccentric lengthening saves energy. The series elastic component (SEC) is the noncontractile component of the muscle-tendon unit. During a single concentric contraction, part of the muscle's shortening action is wasted when it takes up the slack in the series elastic component. Employing an eccentric lengthening prior to concentric contraction saves time and energy by ensuring the SEC is "tight" upon initialization of the concentric work phase.

The high initial-force level enhances the stretch shortening in the muscle just prior to the concentric contraction, and it is the most important factor in maximizing the stretch-shortening process. With an isolated concentric contraction, time is required to elevate muscular force to a level sufficient to initiate movement. When an eccentric stretch precedes such an action, however, the force level is already high as the muscle begins to shorten.

Reflex potentiation is related to the stretch reflex. It is estimated that the stretch-shortening cycle is 80 percent attributable to factors related to muscle mechanics, while the remaining 20 percent is made up by the action of the neural stretch reflexes previously discussed. Figure 8.1, a–c compares several protocols of a simple jumping test to demonstrate how varying the degrees of eccentric stretch can influence the potentiation of the rebound effect.

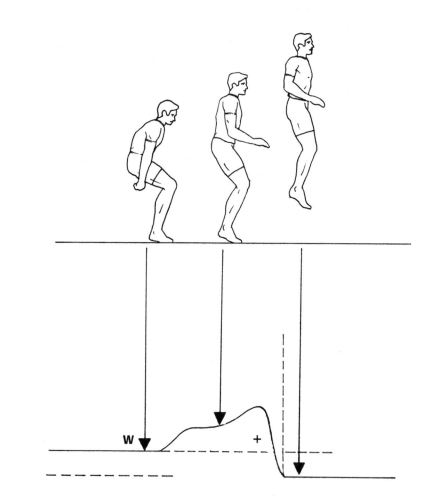

8.1 Illustration of how jump height is affected using three different protocols: (a) squat jump (SJ), (b) countermovement jump (CMJ), and (c) drop jump (DJ). Schematic representations of force platform force-time recordings are included. Positive and negative signs refer to concentric and eccentric contraction phases, respectively. SJ—the static seated position prior to the jump—eliminates the rebound effect (stretch shortening enhancement). CMJ—the rapid lowering of the body (eccentric contraction)—results in significant rebound effect. DJ—the high initial force level created by the absorption of drop force—results in the greatest rebound effect and vertical jump height. W = person's weight. UW = unweighting phase in CMJ.

Reprinted, by permission, from D.G. Sale, 1991, Testing strength and power. In *Physiological testing of the high-performance athlete*, 2nd ed., edited by J.D. MacDougall, H.A. Wenger, and H.J. Green (Champaign, IL: Human Kinetics), 63.

b

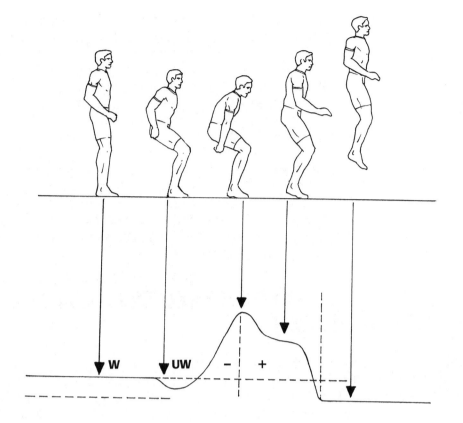

W   UW   − +

c

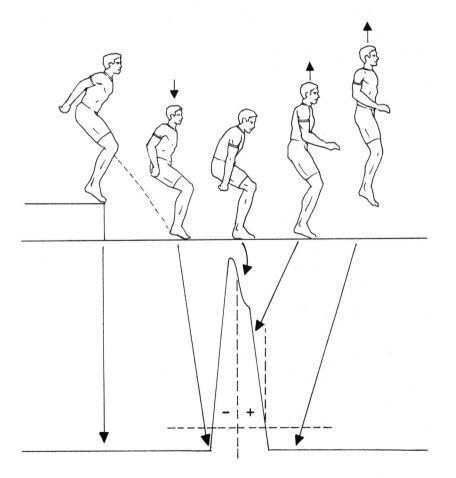

− +

The key to the rebound effect is that there must be minimal delay between the eccentric and concentric contraction phases. If the stretched position is held too long, the potentiation is lost. Thus, in 8.1a, the squat jump (SJ) involves extending from a held squat position. This does not take advantage of the stretch-shortening cycle (SSC), and the resulting vertical displacement is small. By contrast, the CMJ in 8.1b involves a rapid lowering of the center of gravity, followed by an immediate extension of the lower body. This countermovement exploits the mechanical factors discussed previously, stimulates the stretch reflex, and enhances the SSC and measured vertical jump. In 8.1c the drop jump (DJ), the result is an even greater potentiation because the intensity of the stretch reflex is stronger. The stronger reflex contraction, combined with a higher initial force level and storage of elastic energy, results in maximal recruitment of muscle fibers. In this case, an even greater vertical displacement is noted.

The exact drop height at which decreased levels of potentiation begin to occur is a topic of many debates. In plyometric exercise it is best not to approach this threshold too closely, since greater drop heights increase the chance of muscular injury.

RELEVANCE OF PLYOMETRIC TRAINING FOR THE SPEEDSKATER

The primary purpose of plyometric training is to develop muscular power by increasing the capacity to execute strong movements quickly. During skating activity, the extensor muscles of the lower leg contract powerfully in an accelerated fashion, whereby speed is generated through forward propulsion. The more rapidly a skater can develop peak force and accelerate the leg through its full range of motion, the higher will be the power output. A quicker acceleration and a higher top speed result from this higher output of power. Certainly, such attributes have more relevance for the sprinters of the world, but even long-distance and marathon skaters should be able to respond quickly to changes in pace, to accelerate, and thus to finish strongly. Therefore, any skater can benefit from the physical capacities nurtured through plyometric exercise.

In spite of the important role that power has for speedskaters, some people argue that the low body position and long, sustained glide phase mean that exercises exploiting the rebound effect have little to offer. However, remember that plyometric exercises are a means for developing power that can be effectively utilized during the push-off. Almost all exercises can be executed with specific attention to the knee joint's angle in the glide phase, and they will help skaters develop a heightened ability to increase power output from such a shallow position. Of the large number of plyometric exercises that have been developed over the years, the most beneficial are those that can be modified to allow for similar push mechanics and that emphasize a deeply seated position prior to the concentric work phase.

TRAINING SPECIFICITY

To tailor these plyometric exercises to your maximum benefit as a speedskater, it is important you perform them in a way that mimics as closely as possible the pattern of muscular activity of skating itself. Since force levels are an integral component in determining measured power and force is essentially dependent on strength, it follows that power-generating capacity can be susceptible to the same factors that influence strength.

Movement Pattern and Muscle Groups Involved

A skater generates propulsion through lateral extension to the side. The mechanical events that occur here include both extension at the knee and hip and the lateral abduction of the leg. The best plyometric exercises for the skater, therefore, involve these two movements—alone or in combination. This ensures that the prime-mover muscles of skating are specifically stressed during the plyometric drills.

Contraction Velocity and Joint Angle

Contraction velocities, because of their explosive nature, are maximal or near maximal during plyometric exercises; during skating activity, the key muscles do not always contract in this fashion. However, one must remember that the goal of plyometric exercise is to enhance the ability of the muscles to operate in the manner used for powerful accelerations and sprints. And research suggests that training done at higher velocities transfers well to slower movement, whereas adaptations made at low-contraction speeds offer little benefit for faster movements.

Regarding joint specificity, the most important factors are the angle of the knee joint at the beginning of the concentric phase, the range of motion, and the direction of force application through which the muscles act. Since improvements in muscular strength and, therefore, the ability to generate power are specific to the joint angles at which training is focused, all plyometric drills must be done very deeply to approximate the pre-extension knee angle (100 to 110 degrees) just prior to push-off in skating.

Energy System Usage

Plyometric exercises are best described as explosive and powerful, so it follows that the training relies almost exclusively on the anaerobic energy pathway. Drills of short duration (less than 10 seconds) rely almost exclusively on the low-capacity alactic pathway, whereas somewhat longer drills, lasting from 10 to 30 seconds, involve significant anaerobic lactic contribution. Plyometric training therefore is not intended to develop aerobic power or capacity, but rather the delivery systems that operate without the presence of oxygen. Provided that the plyometric movement pattern is highly specific to skating, developments in these energy systems will produce valid performance benefits for competition.

Principles of Overload and Progression

Plyometric exercises range in intensity from those that impose a modest strain on the stretch-shortening mechanisms to those that push the potential limits of this reflex to enhance contractile forces. It is crucial to increase the degree of overload in the workouts gradually as adaptations in fitness occur. This progression involves two key components: the volume (the total work performed in a single workout session or cycle) and the intensity of effort involved in performing each drill. The relative level of both should increase over time to ensure continued change and adaptation—and to provide varied stimuli to the muscles. First increase the volume of work performed before implementing progressions in intensity. Progressing too quickly or starting off with drills that are beyond the capacity of the athlete can result in long-term setbacks or serious injury.

It is imperative for any individual to start with exercises classified as low impact, and only gradually move on to those that involve stronger reflex contractions and greater levels of muscular force. Many experts feel that several weeks of resistance (weight) training should be performed before beginning plyometric training. This helps elevate the level of absolute muscular strength in the specific musculature and reduces the likelihood of damage and overuse injuries.

BASICS OF PLYOMETRIC TRAINING

Plyometrics employs the use of body weight for loading the muscles, rather than the use of weighted objects. Thus, drills are usually coded according to the intensity of the stretch-shortening enhancement.

Intensity Classification

Different authors use various terminology for classifying plyometric exercises. One method of ascribing intensity levels is to consider the *drop height* for box-jump exercises and *horizontal displacement* for jumps, bounds, or hops. For an exercise to be considered of high intensity, it must result in the greatest possible intramuscular tension, maximal recruitment of muscle fibers, and, therefore, the highest degree of rebound effect possible. The intensity classification listed in table 8.1 is a modified version of one that Tudor Bompa described in 1993.

High-Reactive Jumps

Reactive jumps involve stepping from an elevated position, landing on the balls of the feet, bending the knees to absorb force, and immediately rebounding off the ground into a maximal leap. This format requires energy to be transferred as quickly as possible from the eccentric to concentric phase and it elicits the maximal force levels in the muscles. High-reactive jump drills can be either single- or double-leg jumps. They can involve the use of multiple boxes, hurdles, or similar obstacles.

An optimal *drop height* exists for performing such exercises, one that recruits all muscle fibers and builds the highest levels of muscular force. However, the danger is that the optimal height for one individual likely is not the best for another.

Table 8.1

Five Levels of Intensity for Plyometric Exercises

Intensity	Type of exercise	Drop-height intensity of exercise
1	High-reactive jumps	Maximal
2	Bounding and hopping exercises	Submaximal
3	Low-reactive jumps	Moderate
4	Skating-specific jumps (on the spot)	Moderate/low
5	Low-impact jumps (on the spot)	Low

Adapted, by permission, from T. Bompa, 1993, *Power training for sport.* (Oakville, Ontario: Mosaic Press), 44.

Verkoshansky (1969) claims that a drop height of 80 centimeters (31.5 inches) is optimal for achieving minimal transfer time from eccentric to concentric movement, while Zanon (1977) recommends a drop height between 40 and 60 centimeters, (16 and 24 inches) which, he believes, represents the optimal stimulus to the muscle stretch receptors. The best and safest approach is to determine the optimal box height individually.

Optimal drop height can be determined using these guidelines described by Chu (1992):

- Measure the maximum standing jump and reach height by using a counter-movement jump (bobbing down before jumping) and leap as high as possible. Record the highest point where the fingers touch.
- Perform a drop jump from a height of 45 centimeters (18 inches). If the previous measure is exceeded, increase the height of the platform by 15 centimeters (6 inches) and repeat the test again. Continue to raise the platform height until you are unable to reach the standing jump-and-reach point. This is the optimal height to use for drop jumps. If you cannot reach the standing-jump measure, either lower the box height until this point can be reached or abandon this type of exercise until you have sufficient strength to reach it.

Bounding and Hopping Exercises

Bounding exercises mimic the normal running stride by exaggerating the flexion and extension of the movement but maximizing "hang time." *Hopping* exercises involve repeated hops on either one or both legs. Both types of drill develop strength and power by improving the length and frequency of the jumps and by involving multiple repetitions performed over a set distance. The distance you use must allow for the targeted number of repeats to be performed with good form. For skating specificity, the takeoff position in both types of exercises must be that the leg assumes an initial angle of 100 to 110 degrees.

Low-Reactive Jumps

A less intense version of the high-reactive jumps, low-reactive ones employ a decreased height of the box or obstacle in order to minimize the level of tension in the muscles on landing. Because of the lower intensity, these exercises typically involve more repetitions and less recovery time between sets than the high-reactive jumps.

Skating-Specific Jumps

Plyometric exercises using extension of the knee and hip as well as abduction of the leg are more specific to the movement pattern of speedskating because they involve multijoint actions and movements in the horizontal and lateral planes. These exercises are done in one area—without the use of boxes. Although these exercises are usually done with maximal effort, you can selectively manipulate these variables to fit the effect you seek: the number of repetitions, recovery time between sets, and intensity schemes.

Low-Impact Jumps

These low-intensity drills involve no drop jump prior to their execution. They are done repetitively on the spot. Much like skating-specific jumps, low-impact drills usually involve many repeats to emphasize the capacity of the anaerobic lactic system, rather than strictly to affect the development of peak force and power.

Select the intensity of the exercise, and therefore the jump height, depending on the individual qualities of the athlete. Progression through these levels is long-term and it may take years to reach the highest level of intensity. A lack of patience and discipline—incorporating high impact activities into the training program before an individual is ready—can be extremely detrimental to an athlete's performance level and can risk injury.

Volume Variables: Number of Repetitions and Sets

The number of repetitions you perform will depend essentially on the precise character of the exercises you use. For reactive, multiple box jumps of high intensity, which require high muscular force levels, limit the repetitions to between five and ten. Moderate- and low-intensity exercises, such as skating leaps and low-impact jumps, can range from 10 to 30 repetitions in one set. With such exercises, it is often more practical to equate the number of repetitions to a specific distance or time. For example, if it takes 30 meters (98 feet) to perform 15 bounding repetitions, you could do future sets of 30 meters. With skate leaps, on the other hand, it may be more appropriate to perform so many good-quality repetitions in a predetermined amount of time. This would eliminate the necessity to count individual repetitions, and it allows you to concentrate on performing the exercise with proper technique and maximal efficiency.

Recovery Interval Between Sets

The length of the recuperative recovery interval is a function of the type of drill and the intensity level of the exercise. The recovery interval between sets is important for determining the overall effectiveness of training. In general, the more intense the exercise, the longer the recovery time should be. Not only does the anaerobic alactic energy system need to charge, but also the neural mechanisms responsible for the rebound effect require time to recover. Two minutes is the minimum time to allot for a recovery interval; take up to ten minutes for the highest-intensity drills. Table 8.2 shows the recommended training variables for different plyometric exercises.

Table 8.2

Plyometric Training Variables for Each Intensity Type

Exercise type	# Reps	# Sets	Rest period between sets (in minutes)
High-reactive jumps	5–10	6–8	6–8
Bounding exercises	10–15	6–10	3–5
Low-reactive jumps	10–20	10–12	3–5
Skating jumps	10–20	10–12	3–4
Low-impact jumps	15–30	10–12	2–3

Adapted, by permission, from T. Bompa, 1993, *Power training for sport.* (Oakville, Ontario: Mosaic Press), 44.

BEFORE YOU START

Plyometric exercise is very demanding physically, particularly if you use movements of higher intensity. Before beginning a plyometric program, you should consider several points. These are recommendations that lessen the possibility of injury and maximize the effectiveness of the exercise.

Warming Up

A good warm-up is particularly important with plyometric exercise, and it can reduce the risk of injury by preparing the body for strenuous activity. The overall function of a warm-up is to enhance performance by preparing both the mind and body for the training tasks ahead. A well-constructed warm-up will increase body temperature, stimulate the respiratory and nervous systems, improve coordination, and reduce the risk of injury to the muscles, ligaments, and tendons. A good warm-up has two primary components.

A General Warm-Up

The primary purpose of the general warm-up is to prepare the body's central physiologic systems. Body temperature, muscle blood flow, respiratory function, and metabolic processes are all gradually accelerated during the general warm-up procedure. All these systems help increase the oxygen available to the working tissues. The general warm-up should begin with an initial bout of low intensity cardiovascular activity lasting 8 to 10 minutes. This phase should be followed by general exercises for upper- and lower-body flexibility and range of motion.

A Specific Warm-Up

The specific warm-up focuses on the particular muscles that will be used. For plyometric training, this phase of the warm-up functions to lightly stimulate the muscle stretch receptors and to establish the neuromuscular pathways required for the upcoming workout. To accomplish these goals, it is important to stretch the specific lower-body musculature. Next, you should perform specific low-intensity exercises. This means actually performing some of the plyometric drills that will be used in the main training session. Start with exercises at a very low intensity, and gradually progress toward those that are similar to the most intense ones in the workout. An example of an appropriate warm-up is included in the sample program at the end of this chapter.

Footwear

Because plyometric exercise involves relatively high impact, the bones, joints, and connective tissues experience levels of stress that can produce serious injury. A pair of shoes with good shock-absorbing capacity is important to lessen the risk of chronic or acute stress-induced injuries. Athletic running shoes are a poor choice because they raise the foot up off the ground, making it easy to twist an ankle. Court shoes provide good resistance to lateral instability, but they lack adequate shock absorption. The best type of footwear is "aerobic" or "cross-trainer." These shoes are more stable than running shoes, provide good cushioning against impact, and usually have a good tread to reduce the chance of slipping.

Surface Requirements

Plyometric training is extremely versatile. It requires little or no equipment, and can be performed either indoors or outdoors. For maximal effectiveness, the best type of surface is hard and one that does not absorb energy during the rebound movement. A hard surface, however, is not the friendliest to the bones and joints. For some individuals, particularly those who are first progressing to high-intensity exercises, it is a good idea to use a thin mat or piece of carpeting over a hard floor. Outdoors, a flat and soft grassy area is best to start with. Once the body has had time to adapt, you can use a hard surface. The optimal surface on which to perform plyometric exercises is a wooden platform that has a foam core. Such "plyo-boards" can be purchased or built fairly easily, using Styrofoam sandwiched between sheets of wood.

Who Should Avoid Plyometrics

Individuals with a history of muscular or skeletal injury that may be aggravated by shock forces should probably abstain from using plyometric drills. Children under the age of 13 should abstain from most plyometric exercises until their bone growth has tapered off. Stress fractures, shin splints, tendinitis, lower- or upper-back instability, and muscle strain are all signals to question the ability to perform plyometric drills without incident. If you have any doubt whatsoever, be cautious. Spend some time testing with low-intensity drills, be patient, and progress to higher levels only so long as there are no signs or symptoms of overuse or injury.

TECHNICAL ESSENTIALS

Proper technique is essential to reduce the risk of injury and to extract the most benefit out of the drills. Here are basic, yet important, "rules of thumb" to observe when you perform plyometric exercises.

Alignment

The *head* should always be kept up, with the eyes looking ahead. This posture helps maintain balance, facilitates coordination, and ensures an adequate field of vision to avoid potential obstructions. It is important to keep the *spine* and upper body as upright and relaxed as possible. Granted, the very nature of exercises such as skate-specific leaps does not permit this. Proper back posture is particularly important, however, for the high-intensity leaps and drop jumps; one function of the spinal column is to absorb the force of impact and distribute it over a greater area.

The *arms* have two primary functions: to help generate propulsive force and to enhance coordination by counterbalancing weight shifts. When the center of gravity is moving in the vertical plane, it is usually best to swing both arms symmetrically. When lateral motion is also involved, it is more appropriate to swing both arms alternately to compensate for leg activity, the same way you do when skating.

Landing Gear

In plyometric exercise, landing is a critical element. Incorrect landing mechanics may delay the transition to positive work, reduce the strength of the stretch reflex, and diminish an exercise's overall effectiveness. For high-intensity jumps, the balls of the feet should land first so that the calf muscles can be involved in force absorption. The feet should then roll to a flat-footed position to end up with slight emphasis on the heel area. This more gradual absorption pattern will reduce the risk of muscular injury by helping to distribute the impact forces over a greater surface area.

Takeoff

At the beginning of the extension, the athlete should initiate the push with the entire foot, and roll toward the ball of the foot only as leg extension proceeds. The toes should be the last anatomical part to leave the ground. This does not necessarily reflect the precise mechanics of classic speedskating, but it is necessary to help build acceleration and maximize the effectiveness of force application during liftoff. Conscious effort usually is required to ensure that this phase is executed as fast and explosively as possible.

PLYOMETRIC EXERCISES

There are virtually hundreds of plyometric exercises that can be performed alone, in series, or as a circuit. To select from this vast potential repertoire, it is important to include a significant number of exercises that are specific to your sport. Not all drills must meet this criterion, but the program should incorporate as many specific drills as possible.

Sport-specific exercises for speedskating involve extension, lateral abduction of the leg, or both, and they allow strength and power to be developed at shallow knee angles. Because the exercises that satisfy these requirements would still require many pages to describe, what follows are some of the core plyometric exercises most beneficial to speedskaters. These drills closely assimilate the requirements of speedskating. They are versatile enough to allow intensity modifications, and they require little equipment.

Single-Leg Jumps

Single-leg drills often incorporate an element of coordination into the drill to their advantage.

- Lateral leg switches (figure 8.2) involve a repetitive change in the base of support following an explosive vertical jump. This leg switch to the side requires an athlete to explode powerfully from a deep-seated single-leg squat. During flight, the free leg moves under the body, while the pushing leg moves to the side.

- Forward leg switches (figure 8.3) are much like the sideways ones, except that the legs alternate in a frontal direction. Instead of going to the side, the free leg moves behind the body and rests on the ball of the foot.

- Baby jumps are a drill to emphasize the deep body position of the skater, and they involve only a slight extension of the knee and hips. These can be performed in either single- or double-leg versions.

8.2 Leg switch side.

8.3 Leg switch forward.

Skate-Specific Jumps

With skate-specific jumps, the skater attempts to replicate the skating motion as closely as possible by involving knee and hip extension as well as abduction of the legs. Skate-specific jumps include:

- 45-degree skate leaps (figure 8.4) involve attempting to project the body sideways (hip abduction) and upwards (hip/knee extension) roughly 45 degrees from vertical. As the pushing leg extends to the side, the other leg should flex at the hip as the knee is forcefully driven away from the direction of push at an angle of 45 degrees from vertical.

8.4 45-degree skate leap.

8.5 45-degree skate leap—side and forward.

- 45-degree skate leaps to the side and forward (figure 8.5) are the same as the standard 45-degree skate leap with one major difference: the skater should travel forward roughly one to two feet each leap. For this drill, it is often more practical to ascribe a set distance for each set rather than a prescribed number of repetitions.

- Horizontal skate leaps (figure 8.6) emphasize aiming for greater horizontal distance each leap rather than vertical distance, placing the majority of stress on the muscles of hip abduction required for achieving a strong push to the side. As in the 45-degree skate leap, this exercise can be modified to involve forward travel for each subsequent leap.

8.6 Horizontal skate leap.

General Technical Variations

These drills can be done with either high or low intensity. The distinction reflects the vertical displacement and, therefore, the effort required for each jump. Another variation is between full or partial extension. Because speedskating requires explosive strength in the lower half of the leg extension, you can focus power development in this area to execute the drill with only a half knee-and-hip extension.

Bounding and Hopping

These drills can be performed as either single- or double-leg exercises. Single-leg drills often incorporate an element of coordination, and are therefore preferable. However, to aim at developing higher levels of strength and power, a double-leg version is usually preferable. Bounding and hopping drills include:

- Stair bounding (figure 8.7) emphasizes powerful extension of the hip and knee. This exercise, similar to running up a set of stairs, involves an attempt to achieve maximal vertical height when launching the body upward off each step. The hip of the other leg should flex to 90 degrees as the knee is driven forcefully upward.

8.7 Stair bounding.

- Alternate-leg bounding is similar to stair bounding but is done on a flat surface. The goal is to achieve maximal vertical height and "hang time" in the air. As in all plyometric exercises, the transition from landing to takeoff should be minimal.

- Forward squat jumps emphasize vertical height as well as leaping as far forward as possible each time. This exercise is similar to a "standing long jump" but repeated for a given distance or number of repetitions. Both arms should be used to generate power and facilitate balance.

- Crossover bounding, aimed at improving power in turn-specific musculature, is a unique plyometric exercise because it involves sideways travel. Crossover bounding begins with a skate leap to one side (as described above). Upon landing, the support leg pushes through and under the body to once again propel the body upwards and to the side (in the same direction). During this time, the initial push leg must cross over in front in preparation for landing and a continuation of the movement. Crossover bounding can be done either horizontally or in a 45-degree fashion, and can be done either on flat ground or up a set of stairs.

Low-Impact Jumps

Low-impact jumps are typically done on the spot without the use of boxes or benches, and can be performed using either single or double-leg exercises. Drills of this type impose a low to moderate level of tension or stretch-shortening reflex on the leg muscles. Therefore, these exercises require more numerous repetitions than high-reactive jumps.

- Knee-tuck jumps (figure 8.8) involve an explosive upward motion from the basic skating position. Once in the air, the knees tuck up toward the chest.

- Deep skipping is a basic drill that lowers the knee bend to that of the skating position.

- Lateral bench jumps (figure 8.9) require the use of a low stationary object such as a bench or a hockey stick spanning two traffic cones. Because these drills involve upward and lateral motion, the coordinated joint actions (knee/hip extension, hip abduction) are more specific to the speedskating movement pattern than many other low-impact jumps.

High-Reactive Jumps

High-reactive jumps are so named for two reasons: they involve either dropping from an elevated starting point (such as a box, bench, or staircase) or clearing a high obstacle (such as a hurdle); and because they impose a high level of muscular tension and stretch-activated reflex. Because of the high muscular force levels attained upon impact, these drills are most safely performed using two-leg exercises.

- Reactive box/bench jumps (figure 8.10) involve dropping from a raised platform and rebounding upward into vertical extension with minimal transfer time between landing and take-off. Both arms should be used to assist the speed of this transfer, as well as to facilitate balance. Optimal drop height for such reactive jumps was discussed on p. 219.

- Reactive hurdle jumps also impose a high level of muscular tension and stimulation to the stretch reflex, but do not involve dropping from an elevated

8.8 Knee-tuck jump.

position. Rather, these exercises require the athlete to leap over a high obstacle (such as a sprinter's hurdle) for a given number of repetitions. Again, the emphasis is on maximal vertical height and minimal transfer time. Both arms should be used, and these exercises can be done either leaping forward or to the side.

SAMPLE PLYOMETRIC PROGRAM

Warm-Up:
- Light running or biking 10 minutes (50-percent effort)
- General body stretching of the upper and lower body
- Specific muscle stretching, with particular attention to the muscles of the upper and lower leg and hip areas

Workout:
- Low-intensity plyometric exercises
    2 minutes of deep skipping
    10 knee-tuck jumps x 3 sets; 2 minutes' rest between sets
    Leg switches to the side 15 x 2 sets; 2 minutes' rest

8.9 Lateral bench jump.

8.10 Reactive box/bench jump.

- Medium-intensity plyometric exercises

  45-degree skate leap for 20 seconds x 3 sets; 3 minutes' rest
- High-intensity plyometric exercises

  Single-leg bounding x 3 sets for 20 meters; 3 minutes' rest between sets

Table 8.3

Sample Plyometric Training Program for Speedskating

Exercise	# Sets	# Reps or time	Rest between reps
Knee-tuck jumps	3	15 reps	2 min
Forward leg switches	3	20 reps	90 s
45-degree skate leaps (moderate intensity)	4	30 s	3 min
Easy skipping	NA	3 min	3 min
Reactive jumps over max. height that can be cleared	2	4–6 reps	5 min
Alternate-leg stair bounds	5	10 reps	4 min
Skate leaps with travel	3	20m	3 min
Squat jumps	1	Max. in 15 s	

COMBINING WEIGHT TRAINING AND PLYOMETRICS

There is a strong belief among speedskating coaches that using plyometric drills immediately following a strength exercise such as squats is an effective method of stressing the muscles. This method, referred to as *complex training*, forces the lower body muscles to perform powerful and explosive movements after they have been heavily fatigued and lactic acid levels are high—exactly the type of situation which occurs at the end of a race.

Combining these two supplementary forms of training in this manner should only be done with intermediate and advanced athletes. This method of training has proven to be an effective way to train for increased power. When planning to incorporate plyometrics into the training schedule, follow these guidelines:

- Pursue gains in muscular strength through resistance training for a minimum of three to four weeks before beginning a plyometric training program.
- When you begin to incorporate plyometrics into your training schedule, be sure to conduct the strength and plyometric workouts on separate days. Conduct strength training two to three times per week, and plyometric training once or twice per week. This format should continue for about four weeks.
- After time has been spent training plyometrics and strength on separate days, the two types of training can then converge to take place on the same day as

part of the same workout. The plyometric exercises, however, should be performed following the last set of resistance exercises. This type of mixed workout should be used two to three times per week for a minimum of four weeks.

- Sufficient physical preparation has now taken place to implement complex training. Following a resistance activity, move immediately into a set of plyometric exercise with little or no rest. As the competitive season begins, incorporate plyometric exercises into the circuit training format of strength–endurance training mentioned in the previous chapter. This type of workout can be performed once or twice per week, depending on the demands of the competitive schedule.

Stretching and Flexibility

Although flexibility has long been recognized as an integral component in the overall health and fitness of an individual, confusing terminology and conflicting theories about it remain common. Nor do many athletes have a conceptual framework for it. Still, most coaches, athletes, and sport scientists generally agree that flexibility is important to overall athletic performance. Proponents believe that developing and maintaining flexibility can give athletes an edge over competitors who neglect this important component.

Since a muscle's response to stretch is at the root of most contemporary techniques to increase flexibility, this chapter provides a framework for understanding this physiological issue. It also examines how increased flexibility can benefit speedskaters. This chapter also outlines what lower-body musculature is important for speedskating and provides an illustrated guide to exercises for specific muscle groups.

DEFINING FLEXIBILITY AND RANGE OF MOTION

Flexibility is not the same thing as range of motion. Flexibility reflects the actual ability of a muscle to lengthen and it determines the range of motion at a single joint or a series of joints. Range of motion refers to the degree of joint motion that can occur, given the amount of flexibility exhibited by the muscles affecting the joint. Range of motion therefore relies on flexibility to provide motion of a joint.

Static-active flexibility refers to the range of joint motion achieved when actively holding a stretch in a fixed position for an extended period, using only muscular strength to keep the limb at its farthest point of motion. This type of flexibility is most often evaluated by measuring the angular displacement that occurs at a joint. For example, a common static flexibility test for the hamstrings muscle group is a lying single-leg raise. The measure is taken simply at the terminal angle at the hip joint (e.g., 78 degrees) when the straight leg is flexed and brought up as close to the body as possible.

Static-passive flexibility is closely related to the active version, but measures flexibility held in an extended position and passively maintained with the assistance of body weight, an apparatus (such as a chair), or another person. Therefore, this measure of flexibility, although valuable, does not rely strictly on a muscle's ability to hold the limb in maximal extension.

Dynamic flexibility, in contrast, involves stretching the muscles using momentum at the end of the range of motion. This type of flexibility is associated with the resistance, or opposition, to joint movement; it reflects the ability of the limb's muscles to perform dynamic movements as they work through the joint's range of motion.

STATIC AND DYNAMIC CONTRACTIONS

Muscles come in various shapes and sizes; they supply the gift of motion by developing force and contracting across one or more joints. A contraction can shorten or lengthen a muscle's length—or not change the length at all. Static, or isometric, contractions do not involve any change in the muscle's length. They therefore do not result in joint motion. Dynamic contractions, which do result in the movement of one or more joints, involve two types of actions. When the muscle lengthens, the contraction is called eccentric. When it shortens, on the other hand, the contraction is called concentric.

IMPORTANCE OF FLEXIBILITY FOR THE SPEEDSKATER

In gymnastics, where execution relies on an extreme range of motion and places great stress on the muscles, ligaments, and tendons, flexibility is without question highly important. Perhaps surprisingly, speedskaters can equally benefit from flexibility, and often they rely heavily on this component of fitness without ever realizing it. Improved flexibility can directly affect performance for a speedskater in four key areas: injury reduction and repair, increased range of motion, reduced muscle tension, and improved back health.

Injury Reduction and Repair

Stretching to improve flexibility can be an effective method for reducing the risk of injury to the muscles, ligaments, and tendons. It also can promote the repair of muscle tissue following a hard workout. Consider that almost all the minor speedskating injuries involve the muscles. As part of the warm-up process, stretching can prepare the muscles for strenuous activity by increasing the body's temperature and blood flow to local muscles. This helps prevent injury by temporarily increasing the elasticity of the muscles, decreasing the chance of injury as a result of excessive tension or a sudden stretch.

Postexercise stretching also can assist in reducing the occurrence or severity of delayed-onset muscle soreness (DOMS). The stretching increases local blood flow, which brings in much-needed oxygen and nutrients and helps remove metabolic waste products from the muscles. Further, increased blood flow increases the rate of protein synthesis, speeding up the overall rebuilding and recovery of the muscle tissue.

The practice of postexercise stretching is also believed to reduce the occurrence of functional muscle shortening, which can result from a repeated exposure to high-level tension (such as that experienced following strength training). A muscle that is not stretched after exercising maintains a high level of tension, and thus undergoes a gradual process of adaptive shortening.

Permanent Increases in Range of Motion at the Joint

Although speedskating does not require an excessively high range of motion for the lower body joints, having tight muscles on one side of a joint may produce resistance to movement. A skater who doesn't stretch is far more likely to pull a muscle during strenuous exercise. It is a common sight in almost all speedskating disciplines to see a competitor wobble after losing balance or mixing skates with another competitor. Having poor flexibility and range of motion can cause a skater to injure a muscle or even to fall.

Fortunately, the regular execution of a well-designed flexibility program over time can have long-lasting effects on muscle length by stimulating the fibers to undergo a permanent increase in length. This "plastic deformation" elevates the range of motion about the joint, and can directly complement the muscle's force production. Such permanent increases in muscle length must be maintained through ongoing flexibility training. The old adage "If you don't use it, you'll lose it" rings true with respect to flexibility.

Increased Bodily Awareness and Reduced Muscle Tension

Regular stretching can help all speedskaters get to know their bodies. Various sensors located within the muscles give feedback during flexibility exercises on the muscles' status. These receptors—muscle spindles and Golgi tendon organs—were discussed in the preceding chapter. Because they provide information about changes in muscle length, tension, and joint position, their value to stretching exercises should be obvious. Through conditioning, skaters with a well-developed muscular system are more likely able to detect subtle signs of overuse and muscular injury. In this way, stretching exercises help to bring us in closer awareness of our bodies, and we become more cognizant of functional physical limits. These facts aside, stretching serves to reduce the level of tension in the muscles. Proper stretching exercises should not be painful but should feel pleasant, also providing a measure of psychological relief.

Improved Back Health

Many seasoned speedskaters could tell you that they have experienced at least some significant back discomfort over the years. Increasing flexibility through stretching has the potential to dramatically reduce lower-back pain and improve posture. Because speedskaters spend much time in an awkward, stressful, hunched-over position, this benefit has particular relevance. The muscles that facilitate and limit the amount of motion in the hips, trunk, and spinal areas should be the specific focus for skaters. It is no coincidence that skaters who adhere to a regular flexibility program have a considerably lower incidence of back-related maladies.

LIMITING FACTORS OF FLEXIBILITY AND RANGE OF MOTION

To have a well-rounded knowledge of flexibility and its control mechanisms, you should also know something about its limitations. For simplicity of discussion, the factors that can limit the flexibility of muscles and the range of motion at a joint are divided here into four categories of influence: individual, structural, physiological, and external.

Individual Determinants

Several variables inherent in the individual are believed to affect muscular flexibility, in spite of the fact that many of these claims have not yet been supported by research.

- Age—young children are extremely flexible, but from elementary school age, flexibility starts to decline and reaches a low point when a child is about 10 to 12 years of age. From this point onward, flexibility seems to improve going into young adulthood, but never again reaches the levels observed in early childhood.
- Gender—women, in general, are more flexible than men of similar age and activity level.
- Body proportions—because of anthropometric factors, some flexibility tests that measure the degree of movement, such as the "sit-and-reach," may favor or provide better results to those with particular body proportions (e.g., long arms).
- Injury or muscular disorders—scar tissue, for example, does not share the elastic properties of muscle fibers, and therefore can limit the flexibility and range of motion at a joint.

Structural Limitations

The soft tissue surrounding a joint can restrict motion. Tendons (links joining muscle to bone), ligaments (links between bones), fascia (the fibrous sheath that covers muscle tissue), skin, and the muscles themselves can all limit the range of motion of any joint. Some joints are meant to allow more motion than others because of their architectural design (e.g., hip, shoulder).

Physiological Determinants

As a muscle stretches, the noncontractile components provide a significant level of passive resistance. This tension provides significant opposition to muscle elongation.

Think of a rubber band: the more the band is stretched, the more resistance is developed. If a muscle is unable to "turn itself off" and fully relax during elongation, the muscle's stretch receptors can generate further tension to resist stretching. This form of tension is termed *active resistance.*

The neural reflexes associated with muscular stretch were described in the previous chapter on plyometric exercise. Understanding these processes is imperative, because these reflexes serve as the foundation of almost all stretching techniques. Here is a brief review of these important reflexes, including the stretch and inverse stretch reflexes, and the neural mechanism of reciprocal inhibition.

Stretch Reflex

The muscle spindles, located in the belly of a muscle, are extremely sensitive to changes in the muscle's length and the rate at which that change in length occurs. When a muscle is stretched, the spindles initiate impulses that cause the muscle to contract and provide resistance to stretch. The more rapid the stretch, the stronger the resistive muscle contraction. When a muscle is *held* in a stretched position for an extended period, the muscle spindles begin to lower their feedback impulses, and allow the muscle to relax.

This physiology has two important implications for flexibility training. First, stretching should be done slowly so as to minimize the activity of the muscle spindles and the reflex contraction of the muscle being stretched. Second, stretches should be held in maximal flexion to allow the stretch reflex to attenuate, so that the muscle is fully relaxed (this takes about 20 to 30 seconds).

Inverse Stretch Reflex

The Golgi organs are muscle receptors located in the tendons that detect the level and rate of change in tension during a muscle's stretching. Once tension reaches threshold level, the Golgi tendon organs initiate this reflex to cause the muscles to relax. Keep in mind that when a quickly stretched muscle initiates both neural responses, the muscle spindle-stretch reflex usually presides.

Reciprocal Inhibition

Reciprocal inhibition is a neural response; when a muscle contracts, it causes the muscle(s) on the other side of the joint to relax. That is, the stretch-reflex activity of the muscle is inhibited. This has enormous implications for stretching. Since a relaxed muscle provides no active resistance to stretch, it is highly desirable to create a situation in which you can utilize reciprocal inhibition. If for example, the hamstrings muscle group is to be stretched, active contraction of the quadriceps will inhibit the reflexes of the hamstrings and result in a more relaxed and effective stretch.

External Influences

Factors extrinsic to the body can also influence flexibility. Here are four examples of external influences.

- Muscle temperature—warmer outside temperatures are more conducive to increased levels of flexibility.
- Time of day—flexibility is usually heightened in midafternoon, likely because this is the time of the body's peak temperature.
- Clothing—it may sound silly, but tight clothing can seriously compromise the range of motion about a joint.

- Recovery stage—for athletes with recent injuries, the stage of the recovery process can affect flexibility.

MUSCLES USED FOR SKATING

In order to understand the action and relevance of the lower-body and trunk muscles used in speedskating, it helps to look at each joint involved. Keep in mind that the muscles listed for each joint are not necessarily the only ones involved in the particular joint's action. However, for skating-specific flexibility exercise they are the most valuable ones to be aware of. See the relevant skating musculature in figure 9.1.

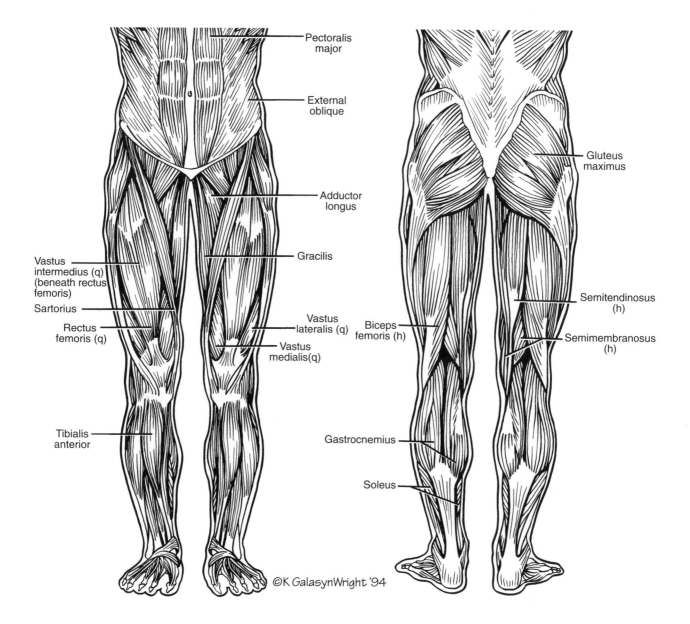

©K GalasynWright '94

9.1 Muscles of the lower body. Small q denotes muscles from the quadriceps muscle group; h denotes muscles from the hamstring muscle group.

Ankle Joint

The ankle is unique in that it is surrounded by very few muscles, but has the tendons of many muscles crossing it. For speedskaters, the muscles crossing the ankle are exceedingly important for maintaining stability—and are therefore important to keep flexible. The ankle joints can perform these four basic movements:

- Plantar flexion—pointing the toes
- Dorsiflexion—pulling the toes upward
- Inversion—collapsing the foot inward to apply more pressure on the arch
- Eversion—collapsing the foot outward

Of primary interest to skaters are the muscles of plantar flexion and dorsiflexion, namely, the calf muscles (soleus and gastrocnemius) and those of the anterior shin compartment (e.g., the tibialis anterior). These muscles contract isometrically during the glide and push-off phases and dynamically with klapskate technique. Although their dynamic function is limited because plantar flexion is an undesirable motion at the end of the classic technique push-off phase, their flexibility remains important.

Knee Joint

The knee joint is rather complex, but only performs the actions of extension (e.g., kicking a soccer ball) and flexion (e.g., pulling the heel toward the buttocks). The muscles of the knee joint are, without doubt, among the most important to speedskating. The key muscles involved in knee extension (skating push-off) are the four that constitute the quadriceps muscle group. The three muscles that form the hamstrings muscle group are responsible for knee flexion.

Hip Joint

Due to its complex structure and function, the hip joint allows a very diverse range of movements. It is affected by many muscles, which cross it from various angles. Although the hip joint provides six important motions, in skating three are most important: abduction, extension, and external rotation. Some of these muscles act on additional joints, namely the knee. These are the six movements at the hip joint:

- Flexion—the hip's flexor muscles function to move the thigh toward the chest.
- Extension—muscles that provide hip extension directly oppose those of flexion by moving the thigh backward.
- Adduction—the adductor muscle group comprises those referred to as "groin" muscles that act to move the legs toward the midline of the body.
- Abduction—the muscles of abduction move the leg away from the midline.
- Internal rotation—muscles of internal hip rotation turn the leg so that the kneecap points inward.
- External rotation—muscles of external rotation turn the leg and kneecap outward.

Trunk

The support muscles that help to stabilize the trunk area are of primary interest to the skater. These are the abdominals and the extensors of the back. Although these muscles essentially perform opposite actions, in speedskating they cocontract to maintain stability in the hip and lower back. These are the movements in the trunk:

- Flexion—the rectus abdominus muscles curl the midsection forward.
- Extension—the erector spinae muscles of the back support the spine when it flexes forward (i.e., extend the spine).
- Rotation—the internal and external oblique abdominal muscles control trunk rotation.

FLEXIBILITY TECHNIQUES

Now that sport-science research has yielded so much information about muscle physiology, neural reflexes, and the way muscles respond to being stretched, it has begun to significantly help coaches and athletes find new and improved methods for developing flexibility. Techniques that were the preferred methods years ago are now considered taboo because of their potential to cause more harm than benefit, for example, ballistic (bouncing) techniques. Instead, static-flexibility exercises and proprioceptive neuromuscular facilitation stretching are two of the more commonly accepted techniques to train for flexibility.

Static-Flexibility Training

Static-flexibility exercises involve slowly stretching the muscles to the farthest point in the range of motion and then applying light manual pressure to produce further stretch. Once in an extended position, the stretch should be held for a count of about 20 seconds. This allows the muscle stretch reflex to subside, and provides an opportunity to further stretch the relaxed muscle. Therefore, once the muscle has "let go" of its active neural tension, slightly more tension should be applied for an additional 10 to 15 seconds. It is imperative, therefore, to hold static stretches for a minimum 30 seconds in total before restretching the muscle. It is also vital to elongate the target muscle(s) slowly. Once a repetition has been performed, the limb should be returned to the initial position and allowed to relax for 20 to 30 seconds before performing another repetition. Each muscle should be stretched at least twice.

Many athletes complain that static-stretching methods are painful. If excessive manual or weight-bearing pressure is applied, pain can certainly result. However, this manifestation of pain is a direct result of overstretching: the muscle spindles become so excited that they initiate a painful reflex contraction. If a muscle is stretched *slowly* to a point of minor discomfort only, stretching can be an enjoyable and relaxing activity.

PNF Training

Proprioceptive neuromuscular facilitation (PNF) stretching is one of the fastest and most effective ways to increase flexibility. This method combines static stretching and isometric muscular contractions to achieve gains in flexibility. There are several different types of PNF stretching, but all involve techniques that partly neutralize the neural responses which cause a muscle to resist stretch. PNF stretching usually entails having a partner assist in the stretching. The partner can provide resistance for an isometric contraction (i.e., one without change in the muscle's length) and apply direct pressure to increase the effectiveness of the static stretch to follow.

The methods for PNF stretching can be very confusing, and the patterns of stretching even more so. These are two of the simpler, more easily understood techniques. They are easy to implement on joint muscles, such as those of the lower body.

Contract-Relax Technique

To stretch the targeted muscle, an initial static stretch is used to elongate the muscle to the point of mild discomfort. Keeping the joint in this stretched position, the muscle being stretched (the *agonist*) is contracted isometrically for about 10 seconds. Following this contraction, the muscle is briefly relaxed for 2 to 3 seconds, but then immediately is subjected to another passive stretch that elongates it to a higher degree than in the initial static position. This position is held for 10 to 15 seconds and followed by a relaxation period of 20 seconds before performing the next repetition.

For example, to stretch the hamstrings group in this manner, begin by lying on your back and use your hands or a towel to pull the straightened leg toward the chest. Once in this position, isometrically contract the hamstrings with near-maximal effort for 10 seconds. To do this, try to extend the leg at the hip against the resistance provided by the towel. Relax the leg for about 2 seconds, and then stretch the muscles with a more stressful static stretch, holding it for about 15 seconds. Rest for 20 seconds, and then repeat the process two or three times on the same leg.

Contract-Relax-Contract Technique

This technique is somewhat similar to the contract-relax method. To perform the contract-relax-contract technique, assume an initial passive stretch of moderate intensity. Then contract these same muscles isometrically for 10 seconds. A towel, wall bar, hands, or another person can be used to resist the isometric movement. Allow the muscle to relax next, while the muscle (or muscles) on the other side of the joint (the *antagonist*) immediately performs an isometric contraction lasting 10 seconds. The muscles are then allowed to rest for 20 seconds before performing another repetition to again stretch the agonist.

Using the hamstrings muscles again as an example, this method would be performed as follows. Begin with an initial static stretch of the hamstrings as described in the preceding example. Once in this position, contract the hamstrings isometrically for 10 seconds, using a towel to overcome the resistance to movement. Now relax the hamstrings, but keep them in slight stretch as you contract the quadriceps isometrically for 10 seconds. Release the tension from both muscle groups for 20 seconds. Then repeat the process several times for each leg.

FLEXIBILITY EXERCISES FOR THE SPEEDSKATER

Literally hundreds of flexibility exercises can target specific muscles of the body. For speedskaters, training should concentrate on the muscles of the lower body and trunk. Even for these areas alone, there are dozens of effective exercises to choose from. You will find here a selection of exercises (figures 9.2–9.9) that probably are the most beneficial to speedskaters from among the ones for flexibility and range of motion. All the stretches shown here use the static-stretching method, in which a muscle is gently stretched for 30 seconds, then repeated two or three times. You can also easily administer the advanced technique of PNF stretching for all of the target muscle groups, using the general methodology presented earlier. Table 9.1 describes a typical stretch session that focuses on specific musculature for a speedskater.

Table 9.1

Sample Stretching Session for the Speedskater

Stretch	Muscle groups targeted
Calf stretch	Calf muscles
Single-leg stretch	Hamstrings
Front-thigh stretch	Quadriceps
Spread-leg stretch (3 positions)	Adductors, hamstrings
Gluteal stretch (2 positions)	Gluteal muscles, hip rotators
ITB stretch	Abductors, iliotibial band
Lunge-position stretch (2 positions)	Hip flexors, quadriceps
Single knee to chest	Hip flexors, hip extensors

9.2 Calf stretch.

9.3 Hamstring stretch.

9.4 Quadriceps stretch.

9.5 Adductor/
hamstring stretch
–three positions.

9.6 Gluteal stretches.

9.7 Iliotibial band stretch.

9.8 Lunge position stretches.

9.9   Hip flexor/hamstring stretch.

Annual Training Plans

Taking an annual perspective can help maximize the effectiveness of physical training. It involves dividing the training year into various goal-oriented cycles. Athletes who simply approach training by performing whatever type of workout they feel like doing on a given day lose sight of the "big picture" and increase the risk of overtraining and developing chronic fatigue. More importantly, these individuals do not look beyond short-term objectives. Planning the entire training season sounds like an enormous task, but it can actually be quite simple given a little thought. Following an annual design that sequentially develops important physical attributes will optimize the process of performance adaptation and athletic potential.

The purpose of this chapter is to introduce the concept of *periodization* and the issue of cyclic-training structures. This information can help you understand and get maximum benefit from the next two chapters, which describe sample training plans for in-line and ice speedskating competition.

PERIODIZATION OF TRAINING

The practice of dividing up the annual plan into shorter, more manageable phases (cycles) of training is called periodization, a concept developed by Tudor Bompa. Adhering to this practice enhances your organizing the appropriate types of training, allows you to focus on measurable, short-term objectives, and ensures a balanced training regimen in which peak performance occurs at the desired time of year. Put very simply, periodization means doing the right thing at the right time in order to realize peak performance at the appropriate point in the competitive season.

In a study of swimmers, Matveev (1965) found that only 15 to 25 percent of the sample recorded top performances in the major competition they were training for. At the time, coaches had poor knowledge of phasic training and the seasonal development of athletes. To be successful in today's ever-growing forum of competitive sport, however, athletes are increasingly finding it necessary to develop a seasonal plan that takes into account major events.

The precise structure of this planning can be very complex, and depends essentially on the sport, the athlete's ability, and the timing of major events. As an example, some ice speedskaters who race in the Olympics plan the entire four years leading up to the next games. Such extreme long-range planning is often necessary when racing at such a high level of competition. Novice racers, too, can benefit greatly from the cyclic division of training time and the sequential development of the physical attributes important for speedskating success.

This periodization breaks down the entire training year into three main training phases, sometimes called *mesocycles*. Each mesocycle is further broken into two or more specific subphases. The planning of these phases is based on the principles of acquiring, maintaining, peaking, and temporarily losing athletic "form." Although different authors have used a variety of terms to describe these phases, they uniformly agree on the general goals of each.

For speedskating, the primary factors that determine the time frame of each mesocycle are the specific discipline (i.e., ice or in-line), the relative timing and length of the competitive season, and the dates, if any, of major events. Chapters 11 and 12 explore the specific relevance that these phases have to in-line and ice skating, respectively.

For speedskating, as in most endurance sports, the training year comprises three main mesocycle phases:

- The preparatory off-season, including early preseason and late preseason.
- The competitive season, including precompetition, peaks, and late competition.
- The off-season, including maintenance and transition.

The duration of each of these training phases can vary considerably, depending on the sport (ice or in-line speedskating) and the length of the competitive season. It is recommended that the preparatory mesocycle phase provide a minimum of two to three months to increase the levels of training volume and intensity before the racing season. Insufficient preparation at this stage will have detrimental effects on performance and will seriously limit the time to develop the intensity of training necessary for peaking to occur.

MICROCYCLES

You can think of a single workout as the basic unit for stimulating adaptation. Successive exposure to such doses, when followed by adequate rest, results in supercompensation, whereby an increased ability to perform work occurs. A *microcycle* can be defined as a *group of workout units* organized in such a manner that optimal value can be extracted from each training session. In terms of training application, a microcycle refers to a preset amount of time, usually one week, for which an overall training goal is the main criterion for determining the composition or structure. As such, the microcycle is probably the most important and functional training tool for annual planning.

It is important to realize that, although the goal of a given microcycle stays unchanged, not all training sessions within the cycle are the same in nature. Rather, the microcycle will contain workouts of varying volume and intensity. For example, a microcycle will include one or two "main" workouts of high intensity. These sessions will primarily represent the true objective of the cycle, while the other "auxiliary" days will function to enhance the overall effectiveness of the adaptation process. Since auxiliary workouts are those of low to moderate intensity, each dedicated to a specific task, the training load within a microcycle can vary considerably.

Applying the Training Variables: Volume and Intensity

The actual phase of training (i.e., early preseason, competitive season) will primarily dictate how many main workouts to include in a microcycle, as well as when in the training week they occur. In this respect, periodization serves as the medium by which volume and intensity variables are increased throughout the year in accordance with training goals and an individual's development. The microcycle functions as the smallest unit for measuring and applying these variables on a *weekly* basis. It will become apparent how microcycle structures vary in accordance with the season's training phase.

In planning a microcycle, the sequence and kind of workout sessions have great importance. For example, we know that high-intensity training sessions should be included once or twice a week, with a minimum of 48 hours between them. Still, this statement provides only sketchy information about the relevance or composition of the other training sessions for that week. In fact, the relative order of these other sessions can greatly affect the overall process of physical adaptation for that microcycle. To maximize the effect of the main workouts, the auxiliary workouts should be scheduled to give the body time to recover from the cumulative effects of the microcycle. If training days are not sequenced to allow for nearly full recovery, the adverse effects of subsequent workouts will require prolonged rest periods for the process of supercompensation to occur. Figures 10.1 and 10. 2 provide illustrations of how intensity variables can be staged in a given one-week microcycle. In figure 10.1 the microcycle contains one main workout that results in a single peak. Most of the auxiliary workouts are of moderate intensity, and one rest day is included. This microcycle would be typical of an early preseason training week.

Figure 10.2 depicts a microcycle involving two main workouts and, therefore, two peaks. Notice that after the first main workout, the auxiliary workouts slowly increase in intensity, leading up to the next session of hard training. This enhances the effectiveness of the main workout and facilitates the process of recovery. This training week would be more typical of a late preseason microcycle.

Structuring a Microcycle

The annual training program contains many microcycles, most of which aim to develop physical attributes that are specific to the sport and appropriate for the time of year. Even though the scope and purpose of the training season should already be

10.1 Typical early preseason microcycle with one peak.

Adapted, by permission, from T.O. Bompa, 1983, *Theory and methodology of training*, 3rd ed. (Dubuque, Iowa: Kendall/Hunt), 140.

10.2 Typical late preseason microcycle with two peaks.

Adapted, by permission, from T.O. Bompa, 1983, *Theory and methodology of training*, 3rd ed. (Dubuque, Iowa: Kendall/Hunt), 140.

clear to you, it is recommended that you not prepare a detailed training program for more than two microcycles into the future. This is because an individual's adaptation and performance improvement are dynamic, often necessitating adjustments in short-term training application, and they must always be taken into serious consideration in planning subsequent microcycles.

In structuring a microcycle, apply the volume and intensity variables in accordance with the phase of training and the goal of the microcycle. The content of each workout within the microcycle should depend on the previous workouts, those that will follow, and the amount of rest being taken during the cycle. Bompa (1983) proposed these general guidelines for designing a microcycle:

- Begin by identifying the objective of the cycle and its place in the annual design (e.g., introducing interval training in the early preseason).
- Determine the volume of the microcycle (e.g., six training sessions, one rest day).
- Set the relative intensity level of effort for the microcycle (i.e., how many peaks and alternations with less intense training sessions).
- Decide on the methods to be employed in each session (e.g., skating, cycling, slideboard).
- Start the microcycle with a low- or medium-intensity day, and progressively increase from there.
- Separate high-intensity training sessions by at least 48 hours.
- If training is to be done the day after a main workout, ensure that the intensity will remain low.
- Be prepared to slightly alter workouts in the cycle if fatigue limits the ability to meet the requirements of the training session.

MACROCYCLES

The macrocycle is a medium-length planning unit that is composed of several microcycle weeks, usually between four and six. The degree of volume and intensity applied within a macrocycle depends, like the microcycle, on several factors, including the time of year, the objective of the training phase, the ability of the athlete, and the individual's response to the current training load. However, training loads for a macrocycle must also follow the principle of progressive increases in load, both prior to and during the competitive season—quite often, the load pattern of a macrocycle will gradually increase, but then decrease. Bompa (1983) recommends that each subsequent step be roughly 5 to 10 percent higher than the one previous. Figure 10.3 illustrates this concept, showing consecutive microcycle weeks when the average load (volume and intensity) progressively rises and then falls.

This step approach involves three developmental microcycles followed by a fourth "tuning" cycle. This type of macrocycle structure is appropriate to use during the competitive phase, regardless of whether or not a race is to follow at the end of the macrocycle.

Figure 10.4 demonstrates how macrocycle structure can vary according to the seasonal phase. In this case, the macrocycle assumes a developmental approach, intensity levels steadily rising through each successive microcycle.

10.3 Load profile for a tuning macrocycle. Average load (volume and intensity) increases roughly 5 to 10 percent for each of three successive microcycles, then declines for the last microcycle. This approach is used during the competitive season.

Reprinted, by permission, from T.O. Bompa, 1983, *Theory and methodology of training*, 3rd ed. (Dubuque, Iowa: Kendall/Hunt), 147.

10.4 Load profile for a developmental macrocycle. Intensity and/or volume steadily increase for each successive microcycle.

Reprinted, by permission, from T.O. Bompa, 1983, *Theory and methodology of training,* 3rd ed. (Dubuque, Iowa: Kendall/Hunt), 147.

YEARLY TRAINING DESIGN

The annual training plan is the most important tool for guiding athletic training throughout the entire year. As mentioned previously, each training phase of the annual plan is considered a mesocycle. The decreasing hierarchy follows from here to the subphases, macrocycles and microcycles. Figure 10.5 presents a general scheme, depicting the division between these cyclic phases. This representation will serve as the model for the dynamics of seasonal training in the next two chapters.

When you compile an individualized annual plan, the first step is to outline the overall goals of the season and to identify the presence of major events, if there will be any. In some instances, novice and intermediate speedskaters have no true major events in the year ahead, and the goal is simply to do as well as possible for each and every event during the racing season. If this is the case and the racing season exceeds two to three months (as it does for both ice and in-line racing), it is still advisable to schedule at least two arbitrary peaks into the plan. This is important, since it is impossible to maintain maximal performance ability for a sustained period of time. Sometimes the length of the competitive season may be up to five months, and in such a case three or even four moderate peaks can be scheduled, provided they are separated by at least three weeks or more.

Once the performance objectives have been determined and incorporated into the annual plan, the next step is to determine the intensity for each macrocycle governing the quality of work to be performed by the skater. The simplest way to express intensity is to use a high, medium, and low scale. A more precise method would be to include "submaximal" and "maximal" as categories above "high." This intensity scheme is applied to identify the primary physical skills and energy systems important for the event and the order in which they should be developed. In any case, it is important to ensure that the load (volume and intensity) gradually increases, leading up to the competitive season.

10.5 Generalized annual training design.

Reprinted, by permission, from T.O. Bompa, 1983, *Theory and methodology of training,* 3rd ed. (Dubuque, Iowa: Kendall/Hunt), 147.

11

An In-Line Training Plan With Sample Weeks

Since the purpose of periodization is to employ the appropriate type of training at the desired time of year to achieve peak performance, the annual plan for an in-line speedskater must revolve around the timing of the competitive season. In the more northern reaches of the hemisphere, this scheduling is affected a bit by when outdoor skating can begin. In the northern United States and Canada, it is impossible to begin regular in-line training until March, when the weather warms up and the roads are free of snow. Although timing of the competitive season will therefore vary between skaters, this discussion will assume that the racing season begins in May and that two major competitions (peaks) are planned. Each major phase of training focuses on specific goals and training adaptations (see chapter 10). These are the components of the broad sample schedule:

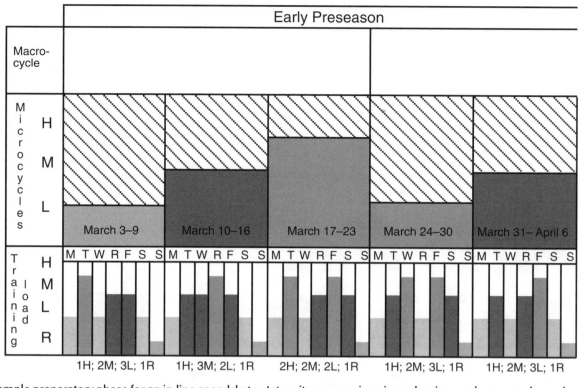

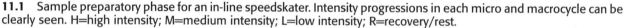

11.1 Sample preparatory phase for an in-line speedskater. Intensity progressions in each micro and macrocycle can be clearly seen. H=high intensity; M=medium intensity; L=low intensity; R=recovery/rest.

Off-Season Phase	**October to mid-February**
Maintenance subphase	October to mid-January
Transition subphase	Mid-January to mid-February
Preparatory Phase	**Mid-February to end of April**
Early preseason	Mid-February to March
Late preseason	April
Competitive Phase	**May to end of September**
Precompetition	May
Competition	June-September
Peaking and tapering	July 12 and September 3

In this chapter we discuss an annual training plan for the in-line skater with respect to the three main training phases. We highlight the training goals and objectives and describe the appropriate training methods for each cycle. Furthermore, the structure of a typical microcycle for each phase is included, as well as insight into the division of training time for developing the appropriate energy systems. We present sample training weeks for an intermediate in-line racer for each main phase, providing more specific instruction for the application of volume and intensity variables. Figure 11.1 diagrams a portion of an annual plan that might be typical for an in-line speedskater.

OFF-SEASON PHASE

The off-season phase has unique goals and objectives. Throughout this cycle, the primary directive is to maintain a reasonable level of aerobic fitness and specific

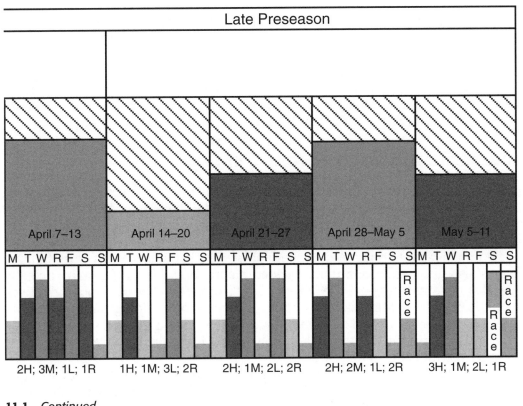

11.1 *Continued*

muscular strength. At the end of the competitive season, when skaters enter the maintenance subphase, they should take several weeks of rest. This does not necessarily imply that training should cease, but that the beginning of the cycle should reflect a major decrease in the training load that still will ensure that gains in oxygen uptake previously attained are kept (see next section, Concept of Maintenance). During this time, skaters should also reflect on the previous season, evaluating whether goals were met, what mistakes were made, how effective the training was, and what kinds of improvements might be made for the following season. In sum, the off-season phase is an important part of the annual planning process in terms of both mental and physical preparation.

The off-season is also the ideal time to work on refining skating technique. For "developmental" or novice in-liners who are able to skate during this phase, an important goal is to work on fine-tuning the critical aspects of body position, weight transfer, and push mechanics. For more advanced skaters, the off-season phase is the optimal time to try to learn the double-push technique (see chapter 1). It is good to focus on technical matters at this time of year because most skaters feel more energetic and keen to learn, and will respond better to new information when their bodies are not in a state of chronic physical overload.

Concept of Maintenance

Since it takes much less effort to maintain a training effect than it does to develop fitness, the initial cycle should be marked by a progressive diminution of both volume and intensity. This will allow the skater to begin the regenerative process in preparation for the following season.

The transition subphase marks the point where off-season training methods make a small but significant shift in purpose and application. The goal of this shorter cycle is to gradually increase the volume dedicated to specific training methods. For example, in-line skaters should continue to skate on either ice or wheels during the off-season to maintain specific conditioning. During the maintenance phase, this may take only one or two such workouts a week. Upon entering the transition phase, the proportion of time spent training in the specific activity should increase slightly. The intensity should not be significantly elevated, but the number of training sessions in the microcycle should slightly increase (to three days a week, for example).

Incorporating Variety—Cross-Training

Since the goal in the early off-season phase is to maintain the baseline of endurance fitness, a variety of aerobic activities can and should be employed. Cross-country skiing, cycling, running, and even aerobics classes can be valuable maintenance activities. Since these activities develop central physiologic factors, their effects are widely transferable to other endurance-type activities. Using several cross-training formats also gives athletes a much-needed mental break from the many miles of speedskating, and it provides the muscles with a broader range of stimulation. Even so, if it is possible, in-line skating should remain a core training mode in the off-season whenever possible. The proportion of time spent on the specific activity can be fairly low during the maintenance subphase, but it should moderately increase as you enter the transition subcycle.

Although the primary objective of the off-season mesocycle is to maintain aerobic power output, an important secondary goal is to sustain a reasonable level of specific muscular strength. Resistance training serves an important role here, but other activities—such as slideboard skating, plyometrics, and dryland exercises—can also help you meet this goal.

Weight Training and Plyometrics

The off-season is the ideal time to begin building muscular strength and endurance in the skating-specific musculature. As discussed in chapter 7 (Building Strength and Muscular Endurance), you can manipulate resistance exercises in various ways to imitate the speedskating patterns of muscular involvement. At the beginning of the maintenance phase, the first emphasis should be on developing muscular endurance and strength in the muscles that are vital *for hip stability*. Early on, such training should take place twice a week. After six weeks of muscular endurance training, the cycle should emphasize the development of *maximal strength*, using fewer repetitions and heavier weights. Midway through the strength cycle, plyometric exercises can be added, both on separate training days and as part of the strength workout. This procedure was discussed in chapter 8.

After completing the strength-training cycle, athletes enter the transition subphase where more time is spent on the specific activity (i.e., in-line or ice skating). At this time, resistance-training methods should shift again: the goal is now to translate gains in maximal strength into power. Plyometrics, therefore, takes on a key role at this time, and the number of plyometrics workouts in each microcycle can be increased by one. Weight training should continue twice a week, leading to early preseason, but the emphasis changes, so that all lifts are done in a more explosive manner.

Division of Training Time

In the off-season, training time can be divided into the distinct categories of (1) specific endurance skating, (2) moderate-intensity cross-training workouts, (3) recovery and endurance cross-training, and (4) specific strength training. Figure 11.2 shows the approximate division of training time in the maintenance subphase. To apply this recommendation, first identify the number of training days in the microcycle and how many of those days (if any) will involve more than one training session.

• *Specific endurance skating* can be on ice or in-line skating, but in-line is preferable. These training sessions should be steady-state workouts of prolonged duration (a minimum of 30 minutes). The intensity should elicit heart rate values below the level of the anaerobic threshold (HR zone 2). At this level lactic acid does not accumulate. Furthermore, the exercise duration is limited only by fuel supply. For an in-liner who trains six days a week, this workout would likely occur twice within one microcycle.

• *Medium-intensity cross-training workouts* can include skiing, cycling, running, or any other aerobic activity. Work times should be more than 20 minutes, but the intensity level here is moderate, designed to elevate heart rate to a level hovering around and slightly above the anaerobic threshold (HR zone 3). With only one rest day, this training session would occur once weekly.

• *Endurance cross-training workouts and recovery* involve the greatest amount of training time for the off-season phase. Again, any aerobic activity can be used. These training sessions should be greater than 30 minutes in duration, and reach heart rate zone 2 in intensity. Most athletes would take one rest day and employ three endurance cross-training sessions in a typical microcycle.

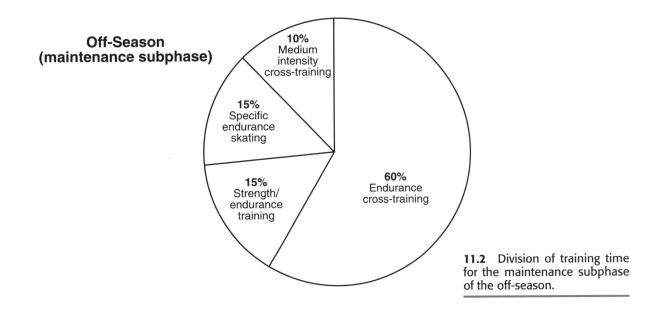

**Off-Season
(maintenance subphase)**

10%
Medium
intensity
cross-training

15%
Specific
endurance
skating

15%
Strength/
endurance
training

60%
Endurance
cross-training

11.2 Division of training time for the maintenance subphase of the off-season.

Figure 11.3 illustrates the subtle but significant changes in training time for the transition subphase of the off-season. Notice how a greater proportion of time is dedicated to skating and strength components, and less time to endurance cross-training. It is important to be aware that this division does not necessarily reflect the number of days or workouts for each type within a microcycle, but simply is a measure of overall volume.

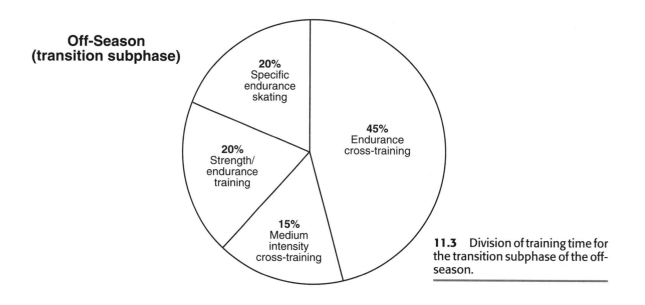

**Off-Season
(transition subphase)**

20%
Specific
endurance
skating

45%
Endurance
cross-training

20%
Strength/
endurance
training

15%
Medium
intensity
cross-training

11.3 Division of training time for the transition subphase of the off-season.

Microcycle Structure

During the off-season, the structure of a typical microcycle can be fairly regular, since the goal is primarily maintenance. Over successive weeks, microcycles should gradually increase in training volume (number per macrocycle), but the degree of the increments should be fairly small. Absolute volume increments can reflect longer training sessions and/or more workouts per microcycle. Many microcycles (upwards of six or eight) can compose a macrocycle during this time of year.

Although almost identical microcycles may be repeated, in structure you should include the moderate-intensity training session followed by a day of rest or of very low-intensity exercise. Figure 11.4 illustrates a typical low-intensity microcycle during the off-season. The early part of the week involves a steadily increasing intensity load, peaking with the moderate- to high-intensity cross-training session. The following day is a low-effort workout, followed by two days of moderate-intensity sessions. The last day of the cycle is one of complete rest.

Sample Off-Season Training Week

Monday:

a.m.—Endurance cross-training, with a cycling workout of 40 minutes; HR between zones 1 and 2.

p.m.—Specific-strength session, with muscular-endurance weight training for the lower and upper body (sets of 20 to 25 repetitions using low weight).

Tuesday:

Specific-endurance skating, with 15 minutes of easy technical work and 60 minutes of steady-tempo in-line skating; HR zone 2.

Wednesday:

Medium-intensity cross-training workout, with cross-country skiing at variable pace; HR fluctuating within zones 2 and 3.

Thursday:

Endurance cross-training workout, with Stairmaster for 20 minutes, running for 15 minutes; HR in zone 2.

Friday:

a.m.—Muscular-endurance weight training for the lower body (high repetitions, low weight).

p.m.—Specific-endurance skate session, with 2 sets of moderate skating for 20 minutes, with 5 minutes' recovery between them; HR zone 2.

Saturday:

Endurance cross-training session, with 20 minutes of cycling plus slideboard training, with 5 sets of 8 minutes each, with 3 minutes recovery; HR zone 2 to 3.

Sunday:

Complete rest with stretching.

11.4 Low-intensity microcycle during the off-season.

Adapted, by permission, from T.O. Bompa, 1983, *Theory and methodology of training*, 3rd ed. (Dubuque, Iowa: Kendall/Hunt), 140.

PREPARATORY PHASE

The preparatory mesocycle is a transitory phase involving a significant shift in training methods. This cycle has early preseason and late preseason subphases, each lasting roughly a month. In the first stages of this cycle, the goal is to introduce higher-intensity levels to prepare the body for the strenuous demands of upcoming competition. More specifically, this phase elevates the absolute levels of volume and intensity to allow the body to adapt to the technique, to higher-intensity training sessions, and to the greater use of skating-specific musculature. The late preseason is a good time to introduce more intense interval-training methods and a general increase in the absolute training load.

Interval Training

In the schedule (temporal) model given at the beginning of this chapter, the preparatory phase falls in March and April. Moving from the transition phase of the off-season to the first stage of the *preparatory mesocycle* involves several major changes. Aside from spending more time on specific endurance skating, you begin to incorporate skating intervals into the preseason training. The aerobic base you developed during off-season training now acts as a sort of reservoir to draw from for higher-intensity training.

The first type of interval session to use in the early preseason involves endurance-type "cruise" intervals, performed at or just below race pace. These are moderate-intensity repetitions, usually about three to four minutes long and having a work-to-recovery ratio of one-to-one. Intervals of this type help to develop aerobic fitness while they also moderately tax the anaerobic system. In the late preseason, your interval-training methods will focus more selectively on the anaerobic energy pathway, become more intense, and use shorter work times.

What is most important to remember in designing the sequence from early to late preseason is that the volume and intensity overload should increase either gradually or in each and every successive microcycle. In the early preseason, interval training should initially be used once a microcycle—for a period of two or three weeks. You can then increase this training to twice per microcycle as you enter the late preseason.

Specific-Strength Training

During the preparatory phase, specific-strength training continues to play an important role. The point of this method is essentially to transfer the gains in strength achieved during the off-season into more dynamic power. Therefore, you should now limit weight exercises to using loads that can be "lifted" in the explosive and powerful manner that is characteristic of the *speedskating push*. However, you can diminish the frequency of these workouts to once weekly.

Also continue plyometric training during the preparatory phase, with the emphasis on powerful movements using higher repetitions. You can use one session per microcycle or, even better, incorporate the plyometric training into the weight-training workout. These specific strength and power sessions can be quite valuable when the weather is not good for outdoor skating.

Division of Training Time

How you divide the training time in the preparatory phase reflects the major changes in training methods you will be using. Because you will be gradually increasing interval workouts from one to two times per microcycle and because the nature of the interval session changes from early to late preseason, there are two different divisions included here. Figures 11.5 and 11.6 not only show the change in relative importance of the different methods, but they also highlight the sequential nature of energy-system training.

Microcycle Structure

The sequential staging of training sessions becomes increasingly relevant as the intensity of activity rises. As a consequence, microcycle structure in the preparatory phase becomes even more important. Once you have introduced interval training, the day following the training session must be limited to either a low-intensity workout or rest, leaving *a minimum of 48 hours* between intense work bouts if you will be including more than two of them within the same microcycle.

In the most *basic microcycle,* the first day of the week is low in intensity and the last day is for rest. When you use only one high-intensity interval session in an early preseason microcycle, the load should rise gradually over the first few days to reach a peak at midweek. When the interval session occurs in the microcycle does not

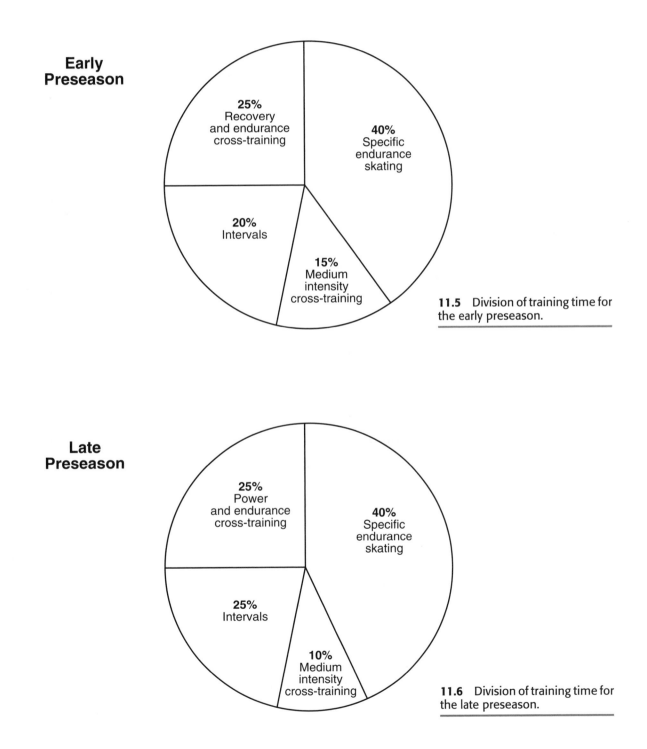

Early Preseason

25%
Recovery and endurance cross-training

40%
Specific endurance skating

20%
Intervals

15%
Medium intensity cross-training

11.5 Division of training time for the early preseason.

Late Preseason

25%
Power and endurance cross-training

40%
Specific endurance skating

25%
Intervals

10%
Medium intensity cross-training

11.6 Division of training time for the late preseason.

matter, provided that strenuous workouts are not staged back-to-back. Figure 11.7 depicts an early preseason microcycle, using one interval session. Figure 11.8 represents a late preseason microcycle with two peaks. You can see the desirable structure of a typical developmental macrocycle containing four microcycles by referring back to figure 10.4 (page 256).

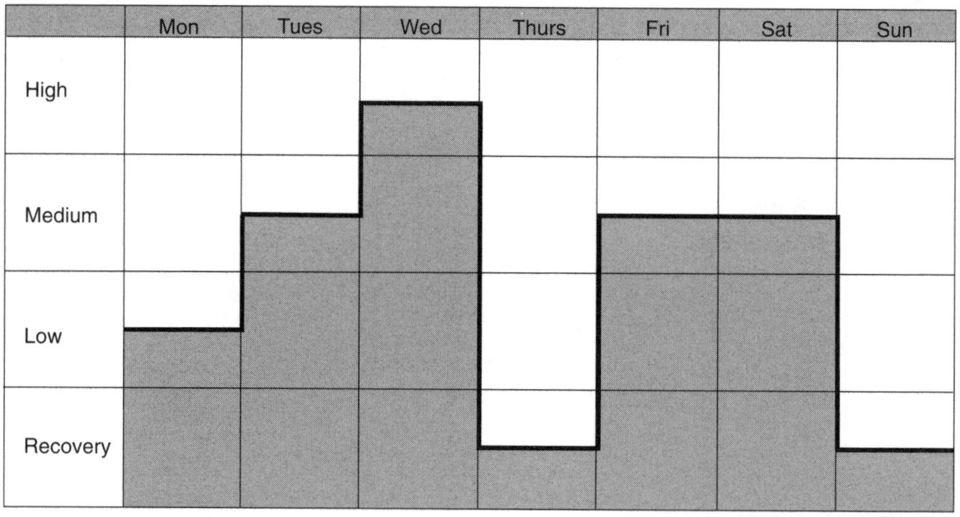

11.7 Early preseason microcycle with one peak.

Adapted, by permission, from T.O. Bompa, 1983, *Theory and methodology of training,* 3rd ed. (Dubuque, Iowa: Kendall/Hunt), 140.

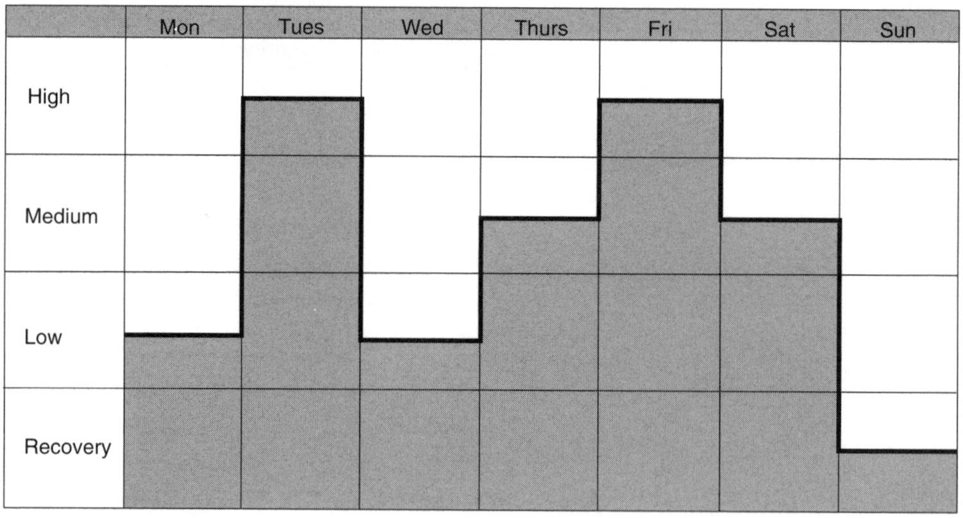

11.8 Late preseason microcycle with two peaks.

Adapted, by permission, from T.O. Bompa, 1983, *Theory and methodology of training,* 3rd ed. (Dubuque, Iowa: Kendall/Hunt), 140.

Sample Preparatory Phase Training Week

Monday:

a.m.—Strength-training workout, with plyometric exercises (10 to 12 repetitions, load equivalent to 65 percent of 1RM strength lifted as explosively as possible).

p.m.—Specific-endurance skating, with 40 minutes of low-to-moderate tempo skating; HR zone 2.

Tuesday:

Specific-endurance intervals, 8 repetitions x 3-minute skating intervals at or just below race pace; equal recovery time; HR zone 3.

Wednesday:

Recovery cross-training workout, using 30 minutes of light cycling; HR zone 1 to 2.

Thursday:

a.m.—Strength and power weight-training session, with 10 to 12 repetitions at 65 percent of 1RM strength, incorporating plyometrics in the workout.

p.m.—Specific-endurance skating, 3 x 20 minutes, with 5 minutes' recovery; HR zone 2 to 3.

Friday:

Skating-interval session, with 6 x 1 minute using 85 percent effort, 2 minutes of recovery between repetitions, and 10 minutes of set recovery; 5 x 90 seconds using 80 percent effort to achieve HR zone 4; and 15 minutes of easy cooling down and stretching.

Saturday:

Medium-intensity cross-training, using a 45-minute hilly (fartlek of variable intensity) bike ride, achieving HR zone 2 to 3.

Sunday:

Full day's rest with stretching.

COMPETITIVE SEASON

The primary goal of the competitive season is to modify training so that all of the earlier gains in conditioning translate to achieve peak performances at the desired events. For in-liners who do not train specifically for a major competition, you should still plan the competitive season as if such an event exists. Since it is impossible to maintain top physical shape for an entire season, you must format training so that performance capability fluctuates mildly over the course of the competitive season.

The competitive season signifies yet another dramatic shift in training methods. By this point in the year, skaters will have gradually increased the volume of training so that the peak was reached prior to the beginning of this mesocycle. Unless, of course, you plan to skate an ultra-marathon event in the fall. However, the degree of relative load continues to increase *during* most of this cycle. The high-intensity main workouts become the focal points for further adaptations, while the auxiliary workouts simply increase the effectiveness of hard training and facilitate speedy recovery.

It is the decline in training volume during this phase that allows you to use increasingly intense training sessions without developing cumulative fatigue. This honing process is the basis behind the practice of peaking and tapering.

Overreaching and Overtraining

Many skaters burn out midway through the competitive season by overly increasing volume and/or intensity levels. The mistaken theory that large amounts of regular hard training yield great results is a prevalent belief among athletes. When training incorporates excessive main workouts into a microcycle without sufficient rest and recovery, the process of adaptation is ultimately delayed significantly because of fatigue. This process, called *overreaching*, can actually be desirable because, following adequate recovery, the degree of adaptation and level of performance is greatest. When an athlete is exposed to further high-intensity stimuli while fatigued, however, overreaching can become transformed into a chronic pathological state called *overtraining*. Skaters, like all other athletes, must be very cautious when training hard several times a week, especially in the competitive phase.

Listen to your body, monitor your resting heart rate, and—at the first sign of significantly delayed recovery or chronically poor performance—lower the intensity of training or take several recovery days until the symptoms subside.

Interval Training

During the competitive season, interval training is the main form of activity which further improves performance capacity. The number of interval sessions in a week should depend primarily on the presence of a competition during the microcycle. When you plan for a race, two interval sessions can be performed. When you will not be racing, the microcycle can include either two or three interval workouts. Regardless of how many high-intensity sessions you include, it is important that you have sufficient recovery time between main bouts.

During the competitive season, the shift will focus toward those interval-training methods that are the most intense. They are the short work bouts (i.e., aimed at elevating lactic acid tolerance) that develop the anaerobic pathways. Training during this time can also begin to include sprint-type intervals for the development of the ATP/CP system.

Specific-Strength Training

Many skaters will cease weight training during the competitive season, because their focus is now primarily on developing lower-body power through actual skating. The

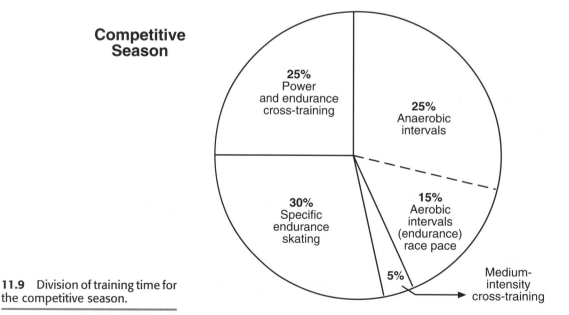

11.9 Division of training time for the competitive season.

rationale here is that the overall intensity of skating, applied through the use of interval training, is sufficient for maintaining the gains in strength and power you should have already achieved. You may wish, however, to continue having a plyometric training session once a week. You can also use slideboard skating as an occasional supplement when weather conditions do not permit skating outdoors.

Division of Training Time

The competitive season is distinguished by its increased proportion of time spent on high-intensity training methods. In addition, you will decrease time spent in moderate-intensity cross-training, using it almost exclusively to facilitate recovery. Figure 11.9 shows the approximate division of training time for a typical week during the competitive season.

Microcycle Structure

During the competitive season the microcycle format can vary, depending on whether the week includes a competition. Even when no race is held, however, it is important that the weeks within the macrocycle always conclude with a "tuning" microcycle, where the overall intensity of the final week is reduced. Refer back to figure 10.3 (page 255) for an illustration of the succession of microcycles in the competitive season.

In a week when no race is planned, the microcycle can include two or even three main workouts, as depicted in figure 11.10. When the macrocycle consists of four microcycles, such a high-intensity workweek should be the third one in the cycle.

When a race is scheduled (usually on the weekend), the microcycle may involve only one main workout, and therefore only one peak. It is best for this peak to occur early on in the week, perhaps on a Tuesday or Wednesday (three to five days before the competition). This allows the intensity of the microcycle to decline as the event approaches, so that two "unloading" training sessions can be implemented. These unloading days provide opportunities for the body to recover and experience a

11.10 Competitive season microcycle with three peaks (no race).

Adapted, by permission, from T.O. Bompa, 1983, *Theory and methodology of training*, 3rd ed. (Dubuque, Iowa: Kendall/Hunt), 140.

significant supercompensation (where performance capability rises above the prefatigued state). Figure 11.11 diagrams a one-peak microcycle before a race. The second peak represents the race itself.

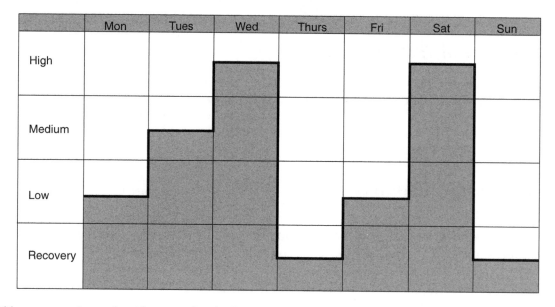

11.11 Competitive season microcycle with two peaks. The first peak is a workout, the other a race. In this example, the Saturday event is preceded by a low-intensity day and a recovery day.

Sample Training Week for the Competitive Season

This sample training week is for a microcycle that does not involve a race on the weekend. In this example, the microcycle includes three main workouts, providing three separate peaks.

Monday:
Specific-endurance skating, with 35 minutes at a low intensity; HR zone 2.

Tuesday:
a.m.—Warm up with 10 minutes of easy skating in HR zone 1; follow with an equal amount of stretching.

Interval session of 3 repetitions x 3 minutes at 80 percent effort, with equal recovery between repetitions; 5 minutes for a set recovery.

4 x 2 minutes at 85 percent effort, with equal recovery, 8 minutes for a set recovery.

5 x 1 minute at 90 percent effort, with 2 minutes of recovery between repetitions; 10 minutes of cool-down skating.

Note that to maximize recovery time, this workout should be done in the morning, with the Wednesday workout done in the afternoon.

Wednesday:
p.m.—Low-intensity cross-training, with a 30-minute bike ride, achieving HR zone 2.

Thursday:
Warm up with 6 to 8 minutes' easy skating; 5 x 100-meter accelerations, building up to 100 percent effort by the final repetition.

Lower-body stretching.

Interval session to include 4 x 30 seconds at 90 percent effort, with 2 minutes of recovery time and 6 minutes of set recovery; 6 x 30 seconds at 95 percent effort, with 3 minutes of recovery time and 10 minutes of set recovery; and 5 x 15 seconds at 100 percent effort, with 3 minutes of recovery.

Cool down with 10 minutes of skating.

Friday:

Low-intensity recovery skating, with 20 minutes of steady and easy skating in HR zone 1.

Saturday:

Warm up with 10 minutes of easy skating, slowly accelerating from about 40 percent effort to 65 percent effort by the end; lower-body stretching.

Interval session with 4 minutes of 15 seconds "on" and 15 seconds "off." There are 8 "on" periods of 100 percent effort and 8 "off" periods of very slow skating (i.e., just keep the legs moving); 5 minutes of set recovery.

Follow with 6 x 10 seconds at maximal effort from a standing start, 2 minutes of recovery; 10 minutes of set recovery. Then, 8 x 6 to 8 seconds at maximal effort from slow-skating speed, 3 minutes of recovery between repetitions; 5 minutes of set recovery.

Cool down with 10 minutes of easy skating.

Sunday:

Day of complete rest.

USING A TAPER TO REACH PEAK PERFORMANCE

The term *taper* is commonly used to describe a reduction in training before a competition. The rationale behind the taper is that after a training period of high overload, you can enhance performance by including a brief period when training is sharply reduced. Some evidence seems to suggest that heavy, chronic training can depress leg strength. If the training load is sharply reduced while intensity remains high enough to avoid detraining, on the other hand, performance can be potentiated, because the fatigue level declines (see figure 11.12). Quite simply, tapering is a method for achieving maximal supercompensation by unloading fatigue prior to competition.

A great deal of research on tapering has focused on what specific method produces the best performance. One study on middle-distance runners suggested that the best taper method is to reduce volume drastically the week before the event to allow for fatigue compensation, but to keep the intensity levels high (Shepley et al. 1992). This tapering method normally requires a seven-day period, and includes two rest days and four intense workout days preceding the major race. A warm-up and stretching should be done before each intense workout. The example of a microcycle taper that follows, which was adapted from this study, assumes that the event occurs on a Sunday. If the race were to take place on Saturday, instead, then the whole sequence must begin one day earlier.

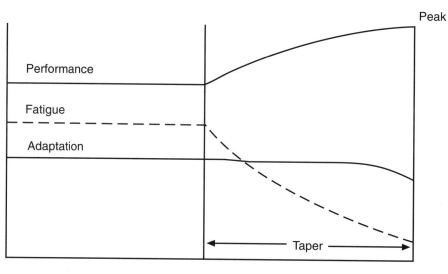

High volume and intensity   Reduced-volume intensity maintained

11.12   The tapering process facilitates performance by unloading muscular fatigue.

Reprinted, with permission, from J.D. MacDougall and D. Sale, Department of Kinesiology, McMaster University, Hamilton, Ontario.

Microcycle Taper With Five Training Days

For simplicity, the intensity is expressed as a percentage of maximal effort. The recovery period between repetitions is four to six minutes, and it should allow for full recovery. Often, some experimentation with recovery time is required—the recovery interval must be of sufficient duration that each subsequent interval can be performed with the same speed and intensity.

Monday:

Rest.

Tuesday:

5 repetitions x 60 seconds at 95 percent effort.

Wednesday:

4 x 70 seconds at 100 percent.

Thursday:

3 x 70 seconds at 90 percent.

Friday:

2 x 70 seconds at 100 percent.

Saturday:

Rest.

Sunday:

Race.

Some skaters prefer to take two full rest days before the major event, making the taper eight days in total. In that case, you would back up the procedure one day ,so that the same number of workouts is completed.

Sunday:

Rest.

Monday:

5 x 60 seconds at 95 percent effort.

Tuesday:

4 x 70 seconds at 100 percent.

Wednesday:

3 x 70 seconds at 90 percent.

Thursday:

2 x 70 seconds at 100 percent.

Friday:

Rest.

Saturday:

Rest.

Sunday:

Race.

CHAPTER 12

An Ice-Skating Training Plan With Sample Weeks

Using the principle of periodization will help an ice skater formulate an annual training plan to reach peak success at the appropriate time. The entire year's training must revolve around the competitive season. What makes the yearly design somewhat more complicated for ice skaters than for in-line skaters is that there can be greater diversity in the scheduling of events and the time of year when you begin specific on-ice training. For example, most short-track skaters who train with a club will begin to skate on the ice in September, with early competitions beginning the next month. For long-track skaters, their proximity to an indoor oval has an enormous impact on the planning of annual training. Those who have access to such a facility can skate year-round, and they often begin competing in November. But for those long-track skaters who lack the luxury of artificial ice, it is impossible to begin specific skating until late in December or even early in January. This shortens the ice season greatly, and competitions begin only a few weeks after the ice is available. For these reasons, it isn't possible to prescribe a schedule for all ice speedskaters in terms of ascribing specific dates to mesocycles. This chapter, therefore, simply provides basic guidelines so that each individual can format the training cycles according to the availability of ice and the onset of competition.

As with the in-line training plan, ice skaters should divide up the year into these main cycles:

Off-Season Phase
> Maintenance subphase
>
> Transition subphase

Preparatory Phase
> Early preseason
>
> Late preseason

Competitive Phase
> Early competition
>
> Peaking and tapering
>
> Late competition

OFF-SEASON PHASE

As in all endurance sports, the primary goal during the off-season is to maintain a reasonable level of aerobic fitness. Even for ice skaters who specialize in sprint distances, sustaining gains in oxygen uptake during such seasonal "down time" will enhance overall effectiveness. It will support the higher intensity training to come later in the training year's preparatory cycle. An important secondary goal of this phase, as it is also with in-line skaters, is to maintain specific strength in the skating muscles. This is usually accomplished through weight training, slideboard skating, dryland exercises, and (for some) in-line skating in the summer months. The off-season is also a time to reflect on the past season, begin strategic planning for the upcoming year, and focus on refining speedskating technique.

You can refer to the previous chapter to see how to divide training time and the structure of a typical microcycle in the off-season (figures 11.2 to 11.4, pages 261–263). For all practical purposes, the same guidelines and methodology that are useful for in-line training will apply as well for ice skaters. In the transition subphase of the off-season, you should dedicate a slightly greater proportion of time to more specific training methods. Since the off-season for ice skaters corresponds to the warm summer months, the best method to use for specific training is in-line skating.

Sample Off-Season Training Week

Monday:

Endurance cross-training, with a 20-minute run followed by several dryland skating imitations and stretching; HR zone 2.

Tuesday:

In-line skating, with a 45-minute, easy skate including a few mild tempo surges; HR zone 2.

Wednesday:

Specific-strength training, focusing on lower-body muscular endurance (high repetitions, low weight), followed by stretching and a few low-intensity plyometric exercises (45-degree skating leaps).

Thursday:

Rest.

Friday:

Moderate-intensity cross-training, with 50 minutes of cycling, picking up the pace for 2 to 3 minutes after every 10 minutes; HR zone 2 to 3.

Saturday:

In-line skating for 30 minutes at a moderate pace; HR zone 2.

Sunday:

a.m.—Specific-strength training for lower-body muscular endurance.

p.m.—Endurance cross-training, with an easy 20-minute bike ride; HR zone 2.

PREPARATORY PHASE

This cycle should begin roughly two to three months before the start of the competitive season. One of the biggest changes in this phase concerns the increased volume and intensity of specific training. The problem is that it is often impossible to gain access to ice this far ahead of the racing season. Those who live near or train at an indoor facility can manage this timing. But those who rely on cold weather's natural ice supplies, or even those who skate at an outdoor artificial track, may face seriously limited ice-training time before the first event.

The key to this problem is studying the training methods of ice speedskaters before the emergence of year-round facilities. That is, using a variety of dryland activities can help prepare the skater physically, so that intense training can be implemented as soon as the ice "comes in." Weight training is a valuable tool for building specific strength during this time. Most athletes of the past, however, also relied heavily on dryland training methods, such as skating imitations, plyometric training, and an increased level of moderate- to high-intensity cross-training. If you lack year-round facilities, turning to in-line skating is undoubtedly the most specific alternative training form. Many such athletes have been reluctant to use in-line skating as a primary method for preparing for competition, mainly because they have been influenced by some coaches who mistakenly believe that the differences between the two sport forms will destroy or alter ice technique. So long as an athlete is aware of the distinctions between the two skating forms, this damaging effect will not occur.

The microcycle structure, division of training time, and application of volume and intensity variables for this cycle were discussed in chapter 11 (pages 263–267). Therefore, this section will simply add general guidelines for modifying training to be appropriate to ice speedskating and provide an example of a typical training week.

Interval Training

Because the goal of this preparatory cycle is to help prepare the skater for competition, training methods should begin to more closely approximate the specific demands of competition. This having been said, you should now incorporate interval training into the microcycles.

All speedskating distances rely heavily on the anaerobic energy pathways. So you want to direct interval training at adaptations to these specific systems. It is paramount that the training mode be the same as what an athlete is training for. If ice is available, interval training should therefore take place on ice. However, if a rink is not available, you can use slideboard training or in-line skating instead.

Assuming that a good aerobic base has been built, you should begin with intervals directed at the anaerobic lactic system. You can include such higher-intensity training once a week for several weeks, and then increase it to twice a week. Remember that a minimum of 48 hours must separate each main workout whenever two or more interval sessions are staged in the same microcycle. Consider the day following hard training as either a low-intensity or recovery day.

Sample Preparatory Phase Training Week

The following sample week assumes that ice is not yet available. If you are able to ice skate, on-ice training can replace the in-line skating intervals.

Monday:

Endurance cross-training, using a 40-minute bike ride: 15 minutes at an easy pace, 10 minutes moderate, and the last 15 minutes again easy.

Tuesday:

In-line skating intervals, using 6 repitions x 5 minutes at 75 percent effort, followed by 3 minutes of rest; HR zone 3.

Wednesday:

Moderate-intensity cross-training, using a 30-minute run, elevating the pace for 2 minutes after every 5 minutes; HR zone 2 to 3.

Thursday:

Warm up with 10 minutes of easy skating; do 5 x 100-meter accelerations, building up to 100 percent by the last repetition.

Follow with in-line skating intervals of 8 x 1 minute at 1,500-meter pace, taking equal rest; HR zone 3 to 4; take 6 minutes of set rest.

Add 6 x 30 seconds at 1,000-meter pace, with 90 seconds of rest; HR zone 4.

Cool down and stretch.

Friday:

Recovery cross-training, using 25 minutes of steady cycling; HR zone 1.

Saturday:

a.m.—Plyometric training, with an emphasis on combination movements most specific to skating.

p.m.—Slideboard skating, doing 10 x 2 minutes at 70 percent, with the emphasis on proper technique and steady tempo.

Sunday:

Rest.

COMPETITIVE PHASE

The primary goal of the competitive season is to adjust training methods so that all of the adaptations achieved to this point will produce optimal performance in competition. Once again, the timing of the competitive season that skaters encounter can vary greatly, as can the availability of ice time. Moreover, ice skating involves several distances, which require specific training methods to exploit the necessary physiologic requirements, so it is impossible to provide exact guidelines for training in this phase.

For ice skaters, the number of competitions in the racing season is far fewer than for an in-line skater, who may race every weekend for many months. Most ice skaters compete in local and regional competitions, and then they may qualify for higher-level events, depending on their performances. So, many ice skaters can easily identify at least one or two dates when performance peaks are desirable. This being true, training during the competitive season should be based around these major events.

When you enter the competitive season, you should have already experienced a peak in training volume that will sustain performance level through the application of two or three intense workouts every microcycle. Interval training, therefore, becomes the primary means of fine-tuning during the competitive season. Some skaters focus on a particular or specific distance, and the composition of the interval sessions must be specific to the energy system (and speed) mainly used for the event for which you are training. Even so, almost all ice speedskating races rely most heavily on the anaerobic lactic pathway. Sprint distances also require the development of the ATP/CP energy system, which is responsible for accelerating and getting up to top speed as quickly as possible. So as you plan each microcycle in the competitive season, you should examine the demands of the event and then apply the appropriate type of interval training for the energy system you are targeting.

Microcycle Structure

If you are not planning on a race in a given microcycle, the training week can include two or three main workout days. What is important, again, is that the rest of the microcycle be structured so that the interval sessions are of maximal value. Generally speaking, this means that 48 hours should pass between main workouts—to give the body a chance to fully recover and regenerate its fuel supplies. You should also balance the intense workouts with low-intensity and rest days to avoid delaying the compensation and adaptation processes that occur after the body is fatigued.

Successive microcycles should always provide a progressive rise in the first few weeks, followed by a tuning microcycle, in which you significantly reduce the absolute intensity load. Figure 10.3 (page 255) illustrates this design.

When the microcycle involves a weekend race, the week can consist of only one intense workout, which should be performed early to midweek. Following this workout, the intensity of training bouts leading up to the race should decline, so that you implement two low-intensity workouts to "unload" cumulative fatigue. You can find an example of this preseason, single-peak microcycle in the previous chapter (see figure 11.7, page 266).

Sample Long-Track Training Week in the Competitive Season With a Weekend Race

Monday:

Endurance cross-training, with 30 minutes of low-intensity cycling; HR zone 2.

Tuesday:

Endurance skating, including 4 repetitions x 6 laps at 80 percent effort, building up speed each turn and relaxing on the straight, with 2 minutes' recovery between reps; HR zone 2 to 3. Take 5 minutes' set recovery. Continue with 2 x 20 laps at 70 percent steady effort, accelerating each straightaway; HR zone 2. Eight minutes' recovery between sets.

Wednesday:

Recovery cross-training, using 20 minutes of easy cycling; HR zone 1.

Thursday:

Interval session, with a 12-lap warm-up. For the first 4 laps, skate steadily; for the middle 4 laps, build speed in the turns; for the last 4 laps, build speed in the straightaways. Follow with 6 x 600 meters at 1,500-meter race pace and 2 minutes' recovery; HR zone 3 to 4. Take 10 minutes' set recovery. Do 8 x 300 meters at 500-meter race pace, taking 3 minutes of recovery for the first 4 reps, 4 minutes of recovery for the last 4; HR zone 4. Take 10 minutes of set recovery. Cool down with 10 laps at 50 percent effort.

Friday:

Low-intensity skating, with 10 laps of a steady warm-up, very easy. Add 4 x 3 laps at 75 percent effort, followed by 3 minutes of recovery; HR zone 2. Take 5 minutes of set recovery. Add 3 sprint starts, ending after the first corner. Effort should slowly increase for each rep (i.e., 80, 90, 100 percent). Take 2 minutes of recovery between reps.

Saturday:

Rest.

Sunday:

Race.

PART III

Racing

13

In-Line Competition

In-line speedskating is an exciting, fast-paced pack sport that is growing rapidly. Although outdoor racing dominates in participation rates, the sport takes its roots from indoor, four-wheel "quad" rollerskating. The first recorded roller speedskating competition on this continent took place in Cincinnati, Ohio in 1938. Since then, much has changed in the sport. With the advent of in-line skates, wheel athletes soon realized the superior speed and versatility that five wheels in single file could offer. Progressively fewer athletes race on quad skates indoors. Most athletes have made the permanent transition to in-lines.

DOMESTIC RACING

Domestic racing is growing by leaps and bounds. In some of the larger events, over 2,000 competitors show up on the start line. Hundreds of races are held throughout the country each year. The sport has grown to the point where commercial endorsements and cash purses can support a small, diverse number of professional skaters. Although each individual may excel in either short or long races, it is typically the same skaters who dominate, regardless of the specific distance or race format. Domestic in-line racing demonstrates enormous variety in terms of race distance, course layout and design, and the variability of course conditions such as turns, hills, and the quality of the asphalt. This next section serves to briefly describe the race characteristics of events you would typically enter.

Race Distance

Due in part to the simple logistics of coordinating a relatively short event, 10 kilometers has become the standard distance for most in-line races. In the more prestigious outdoor events where many elite skaters are present, the male winner often crosses the finish line with a time of around 15 minutes (an average speed of 40 kilometers/25 miles per hour!). The fastest times for their female counterparts are about 10–15 percent slower (16.5–17 minutes).

For most intermediate in-line racers, a time of 20–22 minutes is considered a good performance. The attainment of such speedy times, however, can depend on any number of things such as the course design, the presence of hills, and the aggressiveness of the pack. Poor asphalt can also significantly slow race times. Race times may be as much as 20% slower in events which are affected by these factors.

Even though 10 kilometers is the most common in-line race distance, others, ranging from 5 to 50 kilometers are commonplace. Forty-two kilometers is the true marathon distance, yet any event longer than about 40 kilometers is typically referred to as such. Ultra-marathons are events which are 100 kilometers or more. The annual New York 100K Championship or infamous Athens-to-Atlanta (130 kilometers) are such examples.

The Dutch System of Race Format

Holland, the pride-land for long-distance ice and in-line racing, is a nation which has developed a rather unique approach to race format. So abundant are the number of competitive racers in the Netherlands that in-line races are often staged several nights a week in addition to the weekend events. Moreover, the sheer number of entrants requires the division of ability-oriented classes—A, B, C, and Veterans. Because a separate race is scheduled for each class, the Dutch have developed a unique system which allows numerous races to be held in a relatively short time period.

When a given race distance is ascribed to an event, the time between the first and last skater is often large. Therefore, this method is a poor choice when sequential races are to be staged. Dutch officials realized this and responded by developing the time plus laps method (e.g., 30 minutes + 2 laps, 45 minutes + 3 laps). This type of race is being implemented sporadically in North America. To work effectively, this format requires that the racecourse be a criterium or short circuit where typical lap times range from 1 to 4 minutes. In the 30 minutes + 2 laps race, competitors skate for a minimum of 30 minutes. Once this time has elapsed, a bell is rung as soon as the lead skater finishes his current lap. From this point, everyone, including lapped skaters, completes only 2 more laps to the finish. The result is that the last skater will finish only a short time behind the first, allowing the next event to begin considerably sooner. It is important that officials take note of skaters who fall one or more laps down on the field, and rank them accordingly once they finish.

Race Types and Course Layout

Of all the in-line races which take place in a typical season, the majority of events can be lumped into five categories: criterium, point-to-point, out-and-back, circuit, and time-trial. These race types are based on the event format, course description, or both. A brief description of each follows.

© Bob Justice/Mach Five Sports

13.1 American skaters are dominant in the world of inline racing.

Criterium Race

This type of course, borrowed from bike racing, usually measures between 1,000 and 2,000 meters for one lap. The loop is usually a square or rectangle, such as a city block, but may also take on a less-defined shape. All corners in a true criterium should be in the same direction. Although the rotation is almost always counterclockwise, the race can proceed in either direction. These courses are usually flat, but may occasionally have an uphill and downhill section. Because of the relatively short distance for one lap, the race will involve numerous rotations around the loop (e.g., 5–10 laps for a 10K).

The criterium format usually results in very fast-paced racing. Tempo changes often, and skaters rarely have a chance to settle into a regular rhythm. The numerous corners provide an exceptional opportunity for breakaways, and allow team skaters to fully exploit their tactical strength. Because skaters complete numerous laps of the course, this layout is undoubtedly the most spectator-friendly.

Point-to-Point (Road) Race

As the name implies, this open-ended type of racecourse has start and finish areas which do not coincide. Most often these courses are relatively straight, but can involve a number of corners in both directions and varying degrees of incline or decline.

Skaters often record fast times on point-to-point courses, especially if they are relatively straight and/or there is a tailwind. This racing format provides skaters with the opportunity to launch long, sustained breakaways. These can be very psychologically damaging to other competitors because it is easy for the breakaway group to extend their lead out of sight. You might be led to believe that straight out-and-back courses facilitate a more steady race pace, but don't be fooled. The tempo is often fast and sporadic. This format is the least interesting for spectators because skaters will only pass a given point on the course once.

Out-and-Back Race

This course format is the same as the point-to-point race described above, but involves one major difference: the start and finish areas coincide. The skaters skate out to a predetermined point, then turn around and retrace their path to finish the race where they initially started. Some out-and-back races only involve one such turnaround, while others may involve several loops of the course.

Much like the point-to-point race, this format can bring some fast and exciting racing with numerous breakaway attempts. When this occurs, however, the chase pack is given the opportunity to measure their losses at each turnaround. Because skaters must slow when approaching these points, many tactical maneuvers are initiated just prior to or following the turnaround.

Circuit Race

A circuit is a continuous closed course which usually measures between 1,500 and 4,000 meters (4 kilometer) for one lap. The course can be circled in either direction and can involve both left- and right-hand turns. Although a circuit race usually involves two or more laps, it is possible that only one may be completed. Circuit races are usually held in parks, at (car) race tracks, or in industrial or suburban areas.

The circuit race typically yields marginally slower race times than other course formats, yet not always. The numerous twists, turns, and the occasional hill of most circuit courses means that the pack tends to spread out often. Although breakaway attempts can be relentless in some races, the group is usually unwilling to let others escape from the pack. Knowledge of the course that comes from having performed several laps often leads skaters to wait until the end of the race to attack. The beauty of in-line racing, however, is that no two races are exactly alike. Therefore, this and all other characteristics attributed to each course layout are only generalizations.

Time-Trial Race

This event format, commonly referred to as the race of truth, pits the solo skater against the clock. Although slight variations in event coordination exist (such as the amount of time between the start of each skater), the premise is the same—each athlete completes the course solo without the benefit of drafting. The time trial can take place over any distance, and involve any course setting. Most commonly, the time trial is held on a point-to-point or out-and-back course.

More than any race format, the time trial tests the fitness, motivation, and pain threshold of the competitors. With drafting, strategy, and team tactics removed, race results often deviate from the norm. That is, skaters who do not necessarily perform well in a pack environment often excel in the time trial. Like long-track ice skating, the clock is the sole means of measuring performance, and competitors are rarely, if ever, aware of how well they are doing while racing.

INTERNATIONAL RACING

In the U.S., the United States Amateur Confederation of Roller Skating (USAC/RS), also known as USA Rollerskating, is the governing body responsible for selecting the best in-line skaters to represent the nation in competition. Many countries have similar associations. At the international level, the governing body for the sport is called the Federation Internationale de Roller Skating, or FIRS. Every year a World Championship is held to determine the best skaters on the globe. In addition to roller speedskating having its own independant World Championships, it has been part of the Pan American Games since 1979.

Course Descriptions

Traditionally, the World Championships alternated between a "road" course one year and a "track" competition the next. At the 1994 World Championships in Gujan Mestras, France, competition took place in both venues, with three days alloted for each. This trend continues today at both the World Championships and most Pan American Games.

The Road Venue

Road courses can be either open or closed-circuit. In an open-road course, the start and finish lines do not coincide, and the gradient cannot exceed 5% (exceptions to this rule shall never exceed 25% of the whole course). This type of course is employed in the 42K marathon for men and 21K half-marathon for women. A closed-circuit course is one where competitors must complete multiple laps in accordance with the distance of the race. The distance for one lap can be anywhere between 250 and 1,000 meters, with a minimum course width of 5 meters. This type of course is used for distances between 300 meters and 10 kilometers for women and up to 20 kilometers for men. The direction of the race is always counterclockwise.

The Track Venue

The word track refers to a banked track. The track can range between 150 and 300 meters in size. Unlike cycling velodromes, banked tracks for skating are parabolic in shape. That is, the corners are banked, while the straightaways are flat. In addition, the corners are not uniformly banked. The inside of each turn is flat (figure 13.2), with the banking growing progressively greater toward the outside of the turn. This design allows skaters to take the shorter inside of the turn at slower speeds; at the same time, it provides adequate banking on the outside of the corner to prevent slippage at higher speeds. The surfaces of banked tracks are usually made of concrete, granite, wood, or tile.

Race Formats

There are four different types of races employed at both World Championships and Pan Am Games: time trials, elimination races, points races, and heat races (discussed in the next section on race structure). This section describes the first three formats and gives the distances of each race.

Time Trials

The only race that is skated solo on both road and track is the 300-meter sprint against the clock. In this time trial, the start is not initiated by a starter's pistol. Rather, the

13.2 200m banked track events often lead to fast-paced, exciting racing. The skaters in this figure are taking the shortest route through the turn using the flat inner portion of the track.

skater starts whenever he or she wants to. The time clock begins when the skater trips the electronic eye at the start, and it stops when the beam is broken at the end. The fastest male skaters in the world can do the 300-meter road sprint in under 25 seconds, while the banked-track times are slightly slower (27-second range). The top female sprinters record 300-meter road and track times around 28 and 30 seconds, respectively.

Elimination Races

This competition, also called "last man out," uses direct elimination of one competitor at each of several fixed points in the race. Once eliminated, a skater must pull out of the race and leave the course.

A skater is eliminated from this event if, on a prescribed lap, that contestant crosses the finish line in last place. The rules have been recently modified so that the back of the trailing skate is used to determine who should be eliminated when two or more skaters are very close. As the skaters pass the finish line on the lap before the elimination lap begins, an official will ring the bell. The bell schedule is predetermined so that five skaters stay in the race with four laps remaining. The five skaters who survive down to the final cut then battle out the end of the race. These skaters are placed in the order by which they cross the finish line, with the rest of the field ranked according to elimination order. Men skate a 20-kilometer elimination race, whereas the women use a 10-kilometer distance. These distances are used for competition on both road and track.

Points Races

In these races, each skater is eligible to accumulate points throughout the duration of the event. Points are awarded at preset intervals. For the men's 10,000-meter points race, 14 point laps are included. The women compete in a 5,000-meter event, in which points are attainable on 7 sprint laps. Therefore, the number of laps between sprint laps, as well as how many preliminary laps are prescribed before point laps begin, will essentially depend on the size of the course.

When the skaters complete the lap prior to the one for which points will be awarded, the lap counter will ring a bell to signify that at the next time across the finish line points will be awarded to the first three skaters. For the men's race, the first seven sprint laps reward the first three skaters across the line with point totals of 3, 2, and 1, respectively. In the women's event, the first four sprit laps also award point totals of 3,2, and 1 for the top three skaters. The interesting aspect of the points race is that the awarding of points for sprint laps changes for the last half of the race. In the men's race, the points awarded for the final seven sprint laps are 5, 3, and 2. In the women's 5,000 meter, the identical points (5, 3, 2) are awarded for the final three sprint laps. And finally, points are awarded after the final lap on the basis of finishing order. The winner receives 10 points, second place gets 9, third is awarded 8, and so on, with the tenth place finisher receiving 1 point.

To succeed in the points race, a skater must be able to implement a flexible strategy that will provide for the maximum number of points by the end of the race. Some skaters prefer to try and get points early on, relax in the middle laps, and then finish strong. Others may take it easy early on, and then try to break away late in the race to win the more valuable sprint laps and finish in the top few placings. Because of the complex nature of this race format, quite often the skaters themselves do not know who has won the race until officials tabulate the totals at the end.

Race Structure

As mentioned, the 300-meter sprint is the only solo race. For the points races, a single final is run when the number of participants is less than 20. Beyond this, two or more heats are used to qualify a predetermined number of skaters to the next round. In the elimination races, the maximum number of skaters is 30, with qualifying heats being used when the total number of entrants exceed this number.

Two other race distances have not yet been mentioned: the 500 meter and 1,500 meter. The 500 meter is a true sprint event; skaters perform at near maximum for the entire race. This event is skated in heats. Although the number of heats and semifinals will depend on the number of participants, the maximum number of skaters who can compete at once is six. Heats are determined based on 300-meter sprint times, with the top one or two skaters from each heat moving on to the next round.

The 1,500 meter is also skated in heats that are based on performance in the 300-meter time trial. In this event, both placement and time determine qualifications to the next round. That is, the winners of each heat plus a designated number of skaters with the fastest times move on to the next round of competition. The heats and final may involve up to six skaters. Although this distance can be completed in just over two minutes, some races will take up to three and a half. This event is the classic cat and mouse race, where the first half to two-thirds of the race is often a lot of playing and jockeying for position. The pace often doesn't become intense until the last 500 to 600 meters. Both men and women skate the 500- and 1,500-meter distances, using both road and track venues. Table 13.1 summarizes the race format and distances for men and women at the World Championships and Pan American Games.

Table 13.1					
Summary of Men's and Women's Distances Used for Road and Track Competition at the International Level					
Men 300m solo	500m	1,500m	10,000m	20,000m	42K
(time trial)	(heats)	(heats)	(points race)	(elimination)	(pack marathon)
Women 300m solo	500m	1,500m	5,000m	10,000m	21K
(time trial)	(heats)	(heats)	(points race)	(elimination)	(pack marathon)

OUTDOOR RACING—SOLO TACTICS

Succeeding as an in-line athlete requires more than having superhuman fitness. Aside from being able to cope with the technical demands of the sport, an athlete must devise and implement some form of strategy. In-line racing basically involves two kinds of skaters: those who race solo and those who compete as part of a team. Since most in-liners race without the benefit of teammates, more attention will be given to tactics that have proved valuable to the solo skater.

Outdoor road racing on in-line skates is an exhilarating sport. Given variables such as course design, elevation (hills), race distance, environment, composition, size of the field, and dynamics of the pack, no two races are ever the same. Various tactics and strategies that the competitors themselves implement are equally influential on the outcome of a race.

Strategy Versus Tactics

The terms strategy and tactics are often used interchangeably. However, they mean distinctly different things. Tactics refer to specific methods for executing race maneuvers to improve success and performance. Strategy, on the other hand, refers to the actual plan that is implemented for an event. Strategy is directed to a goal, therefore, whereas tactics are the specific methods for achieving this goal. A building's blueprint is somewhat analogous to strategy, it being a plan for the goal of constructing the building. The step-by-step instructions, on the other hand, would be the tactics for implementing the blueprint, the ways to get the building built.

Developing a Prerace Strategy

Every skater can benefit from developing a strategy before the event. Knowing the course and your competitors' ability, for example, is often essential for forming an effective strategy. Even more important, however, is to implement your strategy by using tactics that exploit your strengths. As you develop a prerace strategy, there are two important points to keep in mind: flexibility and how valid your goal is.

- Flexibility. The strategy you employ must be flexible enough to accommodate unexpected events. Consider an example. For skaters who are not good sprinters, it is a good idea to keep the race pace high, so that the sprinters of the pack already grow tired when it comes time to make a hard effort toward the finish. Let's say a skater's plan is to lead the race from the start, in order to stimulate a high initial pace. It is possible that another skater may be planning to do the same thing, or perhaps the field will not give chase. Therefore, a backup plan should always be available to cover unforeseen events.

• Goal validity. A strategy must be both realistic and achievable. If the strategy is to win a particular race and several pro skaters are present, the plan may not be reachable. In such a case, last-minute adjustments to the goal may be necessary. A strategy must also be measurable, so that you can provide or receive feedback on its effectiveness. The tactics must be precise enough so that a skater can not only evaluate performance during the race, but also later can reflect on the relative success of the strategy and tactics once the competition is over.

Drafting

The practice of drafting was discussed in some detail in chapter 4. Because drafting has immense importance for success, its relevance for initiating tactical maneuvers should also be mentioned. Quite simply, all skaters should draft whenever and wherever possible. Drafting reduces the level of effort required to sustain a given speed, and it reduces back strain by allowing a more upright skating position. It helps in implementing strategy in that the energy savings experienced during drafting allow a skater to rest; prepare for upcoming, self-initiated tactics; respond to maneuvers by other competitors; and recover from previous high-intensity efforts. Drafting is fundamental to implementing all facets of race tactics.

Breakaways

Much as drafting is the fundamental technical aspect of pack skating, the breakaway, also called an *attack* or *flyer*, is the most basic tactical unit employed in a pack-style in-line race. Quite simply, a breakaway can be defined as an attempt to strongly accelerate ahead of the pack, breaking the draft of skaters behind you. To optimize success, a breakaway should involve some element of surprise, so that by the time other skaters realize what is happening, the breakaway already has so much momentum that rivals cannot accelerate quickly enough to get back in a drafting position.

Although breakaways all share certain elements, the purpose of the break can vary. You should realize that the reaction of the field ultimately determines the specific nature and effect of the flyer. The three different types of breakaways (tempo, terminal, and cooperative), as well as the purpose of each, are discussed next.

Tempo Breakaways

The purpose of a tempo breakaway is to tire the field by suddenly accelerating out of the pack, which forces others to chase. The intended purpose is to surprise the pack by picking up the pace, wean down its size, and tire the chasing members. The hope is that when the break is made, the pack will chase and string out as each successive skater responds to the increase in speed and follows the effort of the skater in front.

Tempo breaks are not necessarily maximal in effort, but intense enough to make members of the pack nervous about the intended purpose of the flyer and to temporarily put significant distance between the break and the field behind. The intensity of the break should also reflect how long the skater plans to stay away from the pack. For breakaways intended to tire the field, the skater who initiates the flyer usually anticipates being caught after an undetermined period of time. Therefore, excessive energy should not be expended if the intent is to eventually get reeled back in. Most often, a tempo break where the pack begins immediate chase lasts between 5 and 15 seconds before at least one skater latches on.

In some instances the pack does not follow a tempo break, either because the field is genuinely too tired to chase or its members are confident that the break will eventually be caught without having to instigate immediate chase. If the skater who makes the break is unknown to the field, quite often the pack is willing to let a small gap open up. However, if a "player" known to the pack makes a similar move, that skater is almost always followed—particularly late in the race.

If the skater who makes the break is not followed, two options become available to him or her. The conservative choice is to ease off and slowly regroup with the pack. This may be a safer choice, since tempo breaks are rarely initiated with the intent to complete the remainder of the race alone. However, a confident or gutsy skater can choose the other option and continue on the break, trying to gain as much distance on the field as possible. The hope in such a move is that the field will either relinquish the win to the skater on the flyer or simply not be able to close the gap before the finish. Such an option involves considerable risk, because staying out in front of the pack, exposed to the air for an extended period, is very fatiguing. Once the chase group catches up, a counterbreak may be so intense that the original breakaway skater cannot remain in contact with the pack.

Terminal Breakaways

The second purpose of a breakaway can be to initiate a sudden sprint with maximum intensity, trying to open up a margin that will never be closed by the chasing skaters. Such a tactic, called a terminal break, is intended to be the "winning move." It must achieve the element of surprise to succeed optimally. A terminal break must also have maximal speed and momentum: full commitment must be applied without hesitation. Sometimes the breakaway fails if two or three skaters react quickly enough to jump on the break. A cooperative unit can then be formed to attempt to add distance between it and the remainder of the pack. A terminal type of break is usually intended to be solo, with the goal of accelerating so quickly that no other skater can latch on. Attempt this tactic only if you are confident that you can skate the rest of the race without being caught.

Sometimes, a skater will take a gamble and launch what is intended to be a terminal break early in the race. Surprisingly enough, this tactic is often successful— either because the pack delays excessively in giving chase or because the skater on the flyer is significantly superior in ability. Most terminal breaks, however, are launched in the last part of the race. Occasionally, athletes with a high ability to sustain heavy efforts for an extended period may break away despite several kilometers remaining in the race. However, most terminal breaks occur in the last 600 to 1,200 meters to the finish. To optimize chances for success, initiate this type of break when the pack is tired and you can take it by surprise. To conserve energy for the break, try to skate a conservative race before you use this tactic. This may mean letting a few other breaks go (and hoping they are caught), leading as little as possible, and doing as little chasing as possible. From a defensive perspective, it is valuable to try to identify the skaters who are doing the least amount of work, since they may be planning to make terminal break attempts of their own.

Cooperative Breakaways

Although the outcome of a break is often an unexpected result, the terminal and tempo breakaway types are both intended to be solo missions. When the break is meant to open a gap on the field and bring along one or more skaters behind (either teammates or opponents), however, the tactic is called a cooperative breakaway (figure 13.3). Because strong skaters will almost always (try to) jump on a flyer that looks serious, a cooperative break is not always planned: it may simply form as the result of a skater's attempt at a solo attack. Nevertheless, regardless of how it is formed, a cooperative break can be considered a positive result of any tactical maneuver because it achieves the mutually desirable outcome of opening a gap on the field.

What is important is that once a gap is opened, the skaters of the cooperative break form an allegiance and work together to maintain or increase distance on the pack. As you will see in the next section, the timing of a cooperative breakaway— and the position in the pack where the attack originates—can facilitate and even target select skaters to join the break.

Timing the Breakaway

The timing of a breakaway is critical for its success. It is wise to be alert to inattention or fatigue in your rivals and to take them by surprise. These are essentially the three times when it is best to launch a flyer.

© Photo by Tom Cole

13.3 Cooperative breakaway: opposing teammates may form a strategic alliance for the sake of mutual benefit.

- Periods of momentary inattention or hesitation on the part of either the pack or a specific rival are opportune times to launch an attack. Road obstacles, turns, or periods of slow pace are good examples of such opportunities.

- Breakaways are often most successful when the pack or a rival skater is in an obvious state of fatigue.

- To fully exploit the element of surprise, a break should begin at a time when it would be least expected or suspected (e.g., the start of a race or immediately after a previous breakaway).

The question of location in the pack—from where you should initiate such a tactic—is closely related to the issue of timing the breakaway. A break should never be initiated from the front, where everybody can see what is happening. As a general rule, a flyer should be initiated from the middle to rear of the pack. This allows you time to accelerate and reach top speed by the time you pass the skaters at the front of the group. There is, however, one major drawback to this rule. If a break is begun from the back of a large group, skaters toward the rear will be the first ones to notice the move, and they can often notify those ahead, especially if teams are present. Even if no teams are represented in the pack, skaters will often notify others if they think it is in their own best interest to deter a breakaway from occurring. By the time the skater reaches the front of the group, other skaters may already be in tow.

When you prepare to launch an attack, you must first determine the depth and size of the pack, the location of key rivals, and whether you intend the attack to bring tag-on skaters. For tempo and terminal breaks (whose purpose is a solo flyer), the break should begin far enough to the rear to allow you a high degree of acceleration and to decrease the chance of competitors coming along for the ride. It is important to make sure that the break occurs when your known rivals are in front!

The timing of a planned cooperative breakaway, and your position within the pack when you initiate the attack, can facilitate the enlistment of other skaters. In fact, you might target good skaters and tempt them to join a break by initiating the attack near the back—but just ahead of the desired cohorts. This way, they will be the first ones to see the break and will have the best chance of joining it.

Often times, the goal of a skater is not to win the race, but to beat one or more individuals to the finish line. In that case, one of the best times to make a breakaway is when the particular competitor is tired. For example, the best time to make a break is either immediately after your rival has just finished a break of his own, when he is leading, or when he is in a position in the pack that would make it difficult to follow you.

Regardless of where in the pack a breakaway begins, it is important to accelerate at an effective distance alongside the pack. The worst choice is to accelerate past the pack about 5 to 10 feet off to one side. This would allow skaters to pull out of the pack as soon as they realize your break is occurring—and perhaps to even do so before you pass them with your break. A close proximity to the pack makes it easy for would-be "wheel suckers" to follow. A slightly better choice is to accelerate so closely alongside the pack that skaters wishing to follow won't have room to accelerate until you (as the breakaway skater) have already gone by. Being so close also increases their risk of collision, and that may cause some rivals to hesitate. A close proximity is still not the best choice, however, because once skaters swing out of the pack to try to follow, they are directly behind the breakaway's initiator.

To accelerate on a break, the best option is to follow a trajectory that diverges from the pace line, forcing skaters who want to follow to travel an increased distance if they are to fall in behind and draft. When initiating an attack from the back of the pack, an effective method is to implement an extreme version of this tactic by moving all the way across the available road. This will force others not only to accelerate in chase, but also to cross the road to draft as they try to latch on. Doing this wider move can also place the break outside the peripheral vision of the skaters in front, ensuring the break gets as much momentum as possible before it is noticed.

Where to Break Away

The timing and origin of the breakaway, then, can affect the success of the maneuver. Beyond these factors, most racecourses provide certain good locations to initiate strategic breakaways. Hills are one of the best places to launch such an attack. Making a move on a hill is effective because speeds are fairly low and the effects of air resistance are minimal. Steep hills are therefore the best location for such a tactical assault on the field. Because hill-skating mechanics are quite different from straightaway technique, athletes who specifically train on inclines will have a decisive advantage.

An important hill-skating tactic involves pack positioning on steep inclines. When you are toward the back of the pack, particularly in a large group, it may be preferable to pull out to the side of the pace line and ascend the hill without any skaters directly in front of you. The slinky effect is much more pronounced on uphills, where even slight decreases in speed and forward momentum require high levels of effort to get back up to speed. Skating off to the side of the group, therefore, eliminates the risk of falling prey to this inevitable form of pack dynamics, and it has little consequence as to increased air resistance.

Another opportune place to initiate a break is the crest of a hill. Not only will other skaters be least expecting such a bold move at this point in a race, but also many members of the pack will be tired from climbing the hill. If you have sufficient energy available after ascending a hill, a breakaway attempt at the crest can pay big dividends.

Conversely, a downhill or a section of road preceding a downhill, are both very poor places to make a breakaway. Skaters who have experienced a pack's descent will understand why. Put quite simply, the physical and aerodynamic properties of a single-file line of skaters is far superior to those of a solo skater or smaller group. Because of the reduced drag associated with drafting, each skater in a pack begins to close up on the competitor in front. To avoid collision, skaters often place a hand on the lower back of the athlete in front, pushing them forward very slightly. This progressive compression begins from the back of the pack (since these skaters get the best draft), and becomes gradually more intense toward the front. What results is a compression and subsequent spring-like action. The effect is that the entire group accelerates faster and reaches a higher maximal speed than could be accomplished by gravity alone. On a steep descent, it is quite possible that a solo competitor, skating with considerable effort, could be caught by a large group of skaters who are simply gliding down the hill. Even if not caught, the pack's momentum carried over (conserved) onto the following flat section means that the pack can continue to glide, maintaining their velocity for some time. The solo skater, on the other hand, will decelerate very quickly, and will likely be caught.

Still another good place for making a breakaway is any section that presents "technical problems." Rough or uneven pavement, cracks, sewer grates, and the expanse of road preceding an area of wet pavement are all examples of such technical conditions. Not only will other racers be surprised by an attack in these areas, but those who feel threatened by treacherous conditions may also refrain from chasing or at least delay the pursuit of others who choose to follow.

Turns are a classic area for improving the likelihood of success in a breakaway, especially turns with a short radius or those that involve high speeds. Because it is easier for a group to go through a turn one at a time than as a mass, the pack will often funnel into single file just before the turn. This process, combined with the added general instability and fear of falling, normally causes the pack to slow. For this reason, a breakaway just before a turn can open a large gap between the breaker and the chasing members of the field.

When a skater crashes, competitors are almost always distracted by the chaos that such an incident leaves. When a main rival falls, a skater will sometimes attempt to capitalize on the misfortune of such an accident by initiating an attack. Although not contrary to the official rules of racing, this "vulture" tactic is poorly respected among many. If being regarded as a true sportsperson is your desire, this type of maneuver is strongly discouraged.

Defending Against Breakaways

For solo skaters, particularly ones who lack the skill or confidence to initiate attacks of their own, defending against breakaways (to avoid being left in the dust!) is a primary concern. Even for skaters who actively and repeatedly go on flyers, knowing which breaks to follow is a valuable asset. It would be far too fatiguing to chase down every attack that occurs. Knowing the competitors is a valuable asset in deciding whether to follow, but it is equally important to recognize and be able to respond to maneuvers that appear the most dangerous. For example, it is advisable to try to never let team skaters get together. If skaters on a team are assembling, try splitting them up by moving in front of one of them. Take notice of the activity of teams, especially during the latter stages of a race, and pick one skater to shadow. Even if the skater you choose to follow is not the one who will make the big break, being close to the action is essential if the goal is to be part of a tactical maneuver.

Deceptive Maneuvers

In a pack sport, part of an effective strategy is being able to trick, take advantage of, and deceive others. If you accept that deceptive maneuvers are part of the tactical game, then a broad range of options immediately becomes available. Here are just two such tactics.

Mock Breaks

A mock breakaway involves pulling out of the pack and briefly accelerating to lead your competitors into believing that a breakaway is in progress. This practice has three functions. For one, a mock break away can be used at slow times, when a skater does not actually want to break away alone, but instead wants to stimulate others to launch a counterattack that could be followed. Second, a mock break is useful to break up the group. Sometimes a pack falls into a rhythmic, almost hypnotic, state in which nothing is happening. Skaters will use the mock-break technique to wake up the field and try to stimulate an increased level of activity. And third, a mock break can be helpful when you want a certain position within the pack that is difficult to obtain. Because a mock break usually disrupts the pace line, gaps open, which can then be easily occupied by other skaters.

Playing Dead

Pretending to be tired is also an effective way to deceive other skaters (figure 13.4). Placing the hands on the knees or taking unusual amounts of stand-up rest can do one of two things. First, leading other skaters to believe that you are tired may lead

Jeff Dowling

13.4 Playing dead is an effective way to mislead the competition.

to a breakaway attempt by someone who assumes you will not be able to follow. But this deceptive tactic can also have the reverse effect of delaying the breakaway of a skater who may be thinking of launching an attack. The competitor may forgo the attack because she believes you will be an easy rival to beat in the finishing stretch. It is impossible to know the outcome of playing dead, but observing what happens and what does not can be useful information. In the first case, where the tactic initiates a breakaway, there may be little choice but to follow. This is acceptable, however, because it is a potential outcome you are seeking. Even if no break occurs, the tactic can still be successful because it can lead other competitors into believing you are tired. Their false sense of security (in no longer considering you a threat) can only help you later, if you initiate a breakaway or sprint to the finish.

Taking the Lead

Some skaters simply like to lead the race or the pack they are in. For many people, the thought of leading the group is just too exciting to resist. Some skaters feel more comfortable at the front where there is less risk of tangling skates. Others end up at the front simply because the continual cycling of the pack puts them there. Regardless, most skaters will spend some time "taking a pull" at the front of the group. In fact, performing this task is often expected, particularly when the group is small and cooperating for mutual benefit.

There are times during a race when heading up the front of the group is preferable. For example, it is better to lead with a tailwind rather than a headwind, or when the pace is slow rather than fast. And it can be advantageous to lead through treacherous road or environmental conditions, where the risk of falling is highest. Aside from this, taking the lead can be beneficial if you wish to control the pace of the pack. For example, if you find that the race is not unfolding in a manner that is conducive to your own race strategy, you may want to take the lead. You may also simply consider proximity to the front of the pack important for optimizing your finishing placement.

Bridging Gaps

Sometimes, a breakaway group forms and leads ahead of the main pack. An able skater may then attempt to bridge the gap in order to join the lead group. The first item to consider is whether the goal is to bridge up to the next group as a solo effort (with no intent of allowing others to follow) or with the cooperation of other skaters. In the solo case, it is important to feel confident that you have enough energy available to accomplish the task. Trying to bridge a gap only to run out of steam during the chase can result in disaster. If the bridge attempt fails, the skater may not even have energy enough to rejoin the chase group. You should also be confident in having enough energy to hang on to the lead group in the event they accelerate the instant you catch up. Getting immediately dropped by the lead group would render the entire effort a failure.

When you bridge a gap and pull the entire chase group up to a break, it is important to be sure that those behind you are willing and able to share in the effort. Usually, the chase group is more than willing to let one skater do all of the work. However, if the skater leading the bridge becomes too tired to accomplish this task alone, others in the group should be encouraged to help out. If you have any doubt, it is often best to try and make a solo bridge. In such an instance, the bridge should be considered a breakaway, and you should fully exploit the timing and element of surprise to maximize success.

Finishing-Sprint Tactics

There are basically two types of finishing sprints: a field sprint and a group sprint. A *field sprint* involves many skaters, who are usually in close proximity to each other (see figure 13.5). This is usually the main pack or a large chase group; it generally involves 10 or more skaters. A *group sprint*, on the other hand, involves a smaller number of skaters (the lead breakaway group), usually six or fewer. Once the final sprint begins, there is little you can do tactically. So your focus must be on what you do prior to the beginning of the sprint. In a mass field sprint, the most practical strategy is to stay close to the front, draft as long as possible, and sprint as hard as possible. However, the time preceding the finish line exemplifies the tactical nature of in-line racing. Skaters who repeatedly win races are not necessarily the strongest, but they do excel at using their heads, as well as their bodies, to ensure that they reach the finish line first.

There are two approaches to finishing-sprint strategy, each considerably different. Although it is important that you make some sort of decision about your finishing strategy near the end of the race, it is equally important to remain flexible. As with all other strategic elements, you must always be able to immediately adjust your finishing tactics in response to what others are doing.

Several general points may help you determine what approach to use. First, play up to your strengths. That is, do you have a high top speed or are you able to sustain a moderate sprint speed over a prolonged distance? Second, use surprise to your advantage. If a key opportunity arises (perhaps a time when the pack is not expecting an attack), take full advantage of it, even if the situation would be contrary to your initial plan. Execute the break, for example, without hesitation and with full effort.

Instigator Approach

As the name implies, this strategy relies on your being the one to initiate the final break to the finish. This tactic is often a gamble. You try to take the field by surprise in order to maximize the gap with the group. How far from the finish you initiate such a maneuver depends on two things: the instant that a good opportunity arises and your ability to sustain sprint speed. If top speed is not your strong point, it is advisable to attack from a considerable distance to the finish (400 to 600 meters). Conversely, if you excel at sprinting, it is best to wait as long as possible before making a break for the line. In some races, the lead group comes within 100 meters of the finish before a skater initiates the final sprint.

© Photo by Tom Cole

13.5 As the number of good skaters steadily increases, more and more races end in a mass field sprint.

The Respondent Approach

Some skaters choose to let another competitor initiate the terminal break near the finish with the intent of jumping in the skater's draft and making a pass just before the finish. If you choose this approach, you must try to determine those who will be most likely to launch the attack—and stay close to them. When the group is large, this can be a difficult task. Although the respondent approach is effective when it is executed properly, this tactic can fail if a competitor seizes an opportunity to surprise the field. Therefore, if you opt to let someone else make the break, you must be keenly aware of what everyone else is doing. In a large group, it is often best to stay close to the rear, from where you can see all the action, but not so far back that reacting to movement will be impossible.

OUTDOOR RACING—TEAM TACTICS

At the professional and elite levels, team skaters dominate the sport of in-line racing. The best skaters are usually selected to race for sponsored teams. Perhaps an even bigger part of why team skaters predominate, however, is that these athletes can successfully achieve strategic results by using team tactics. Decades of bicycle racing have yielded countless tactical methods that are widely applicable to in-line racing.

A team does not necessarily have to consist of four or five skaters. The fact is that even a team of two racers has a much broader range of tactics available to it than does any solo skater. If two skaters from a team compete against a solo skater of equal ability, it is almost impossible for the individual to win, provided the team skaters utilize effective tactical measures. Yet even solo skaters can benefit from an understanding of team tactics. Such knowledge is vital because it allows the individual skater to recognize and anticipate the very group tactics that might endanger his own chances for success.

Function of Teammates

Teammates can foster individual success in a variety of ways. They can block other skaters, let each other into the pace line, control the pace of the race for the benefit of other teammates, bridge gaps for the team leader, combine efforts in breakaway attempts, and cover counterattacks by rivals.

At the elite level, each skater on the team usually has a specific role to play. One skater is typically nominated as the leader, and the others function to protect and optimize the leader's chances of victory. Even for intermediate and advanced team skaters, prerace strategy often involves the decision to make one member the intended victor and to have the other team members serve as workhorses. This strategy is based on the premise that a victory for one team member is a victory for the entire team.

Team Breakaways

The breakaways that team skaters employ usually function the same way as those that solo skaters use. However, teammates can greatly increase the effectiveness of an attack. Teammates contribute a wider tactical base, so the breakaway methods then can involve more variety. Teams commonly use three basic breakaway tactics: the block and break, the alternating breakaway, and the lead-out breakaway.

Block and Break

The most basic tactic to enhance the effectiveness of a team's breakaway is to employ blocking techniques. It is unethical and illegal to impede other skaters with physical contact. So blocking techniques reduce the attractiveness of chasing a flyer by simply positioning one or more team skaters in a manner that will discourage and/or seriously delay rivals who choose to try and follow. It would take many pages to describe the myriad ways you can implement a block and break, so instead here is only one example (using three teammates).

One skater (A) occupies the front position of the pack, leading the group on the far left-hand side of the road. Two other teammates position themselves one ahead (B) of the other (C), a few spots back. These two skaters then pull out together and sprint hard along the right side of the pack. As the two approach the teammate who leads (A), the front team member (B) of the twosome continues to "hammer," while the teammate behind (C) slows and takes up position behind and to the side of the single teammate (A) who leads the pack. Both these two team members (A and C) not only cause a willfull slowing of the pack, but also pose a physical obstruction (block) to those other skaters who wish to pursue the breakaway. These two blocking skaters should take up as much road as possible without blatantly interfering with others. Even if other skaters try and follow the break, this maneuver is likely to give the breakaway skater at least a 10-meter buffer. The more team skaters there are available, the greater the ability to block and deter or delay others from chasing. Figure 13.6 illustrates the block and break maneuver.

Alternating Breakaways

This tactic is most effective for wearing down other skaters especially when the pack is small. It requires a minimum of two team skaters to execute. An alternating breakaway involves one skater going on a breakaway—forcing other skaters to chase—while a second teammate sits comfortably in the draft of those trying to catch the breakaway. Once the group has caught the flyer, the second teammate then pulls out of the pack and makes a break. This sequence can be repeated any number of times in an attempt to wear down non-teammates until the point when one of the

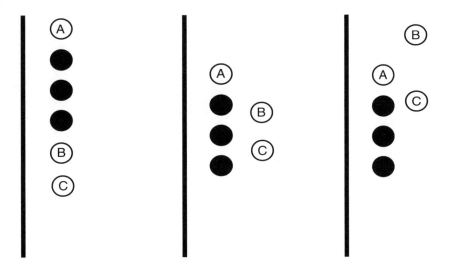

13.6 Block and break maneuver using three team skaters.

breaks can be sustained to the finish. If more than two skaters are available, the options increase dramatically. You might use this tactic in combination with blocking: two skaters could go on a (tandem) breakaway (see figure 13.7) while the remaining teammate slows the pace or all three teammates could take turns making breaks to wear down the pack.

Lead-Out Breakaway

Another tactic that team skaters commonly employ is the lead-out break. In this method, one skater is designated as a "rabbit," who essentially breaks away either at the start or very early on in the race. The idea is to tempt the pack to follow, keeping the pace exceptionally high while the other teammates draft. Once the pack catches the break, one of the other teammates can immediately launch another attack. Although a rare occurrence, sometimes the pack will allow a lead-out skater to get

USA Roller Skating

13.7 Two team skaters on a tandem breakaway.

away. In this event, the remaining teammates make every effort to ensure that the pace is kept slow by attempting to control the front of the pack. If a small group forms to chase down the breakaway, it is vital that one of the teammates be included in this group. Once in, the team skater can again try to slow the chase by either refusing to take the lead or slowing down when at the front of the chase pack.

Covering the Breaks

In some instances, breakaway attempts can be fast and furious, occurring one after another with little or no rest. Such successive maneuvers are called counterattacks. In a race with a great many flyers, it can be difficult to determine which one, if any, will be the terminal breakaway of the race. As a solo skater, it is impossible to follow each and every break. The beauty of racing in a team is that most breaks, if not all of them, can be represented by at least one team member. Once a team member is on the flyer, the other team members should do whatever they can to keep the pack from closing the gap. This tactic assures that whatever break proves to be the winning attack (by the skater staying in front) will involve a team member. Pro races often unfold this way, with the strong teams trading counterattacks in an attempt to wear each other out and determine which team members are most likely to win. Most often, a breakaway group forms containing a member of each of the main teams. Then the race for the chase pack is basically over, because none of the team skaters who remain in the pack will help others give chase. In fact, these skaters will often slow the pack to increase the gap of the breakaway group. If you are a solo skater, being aware of team tactics at least will enhance your personal performance by helping you determine which breakaways to attempt to go with and which ones to forfeit.

Dirty Tactics

At the elite and international levels, there are those who will do almost anything to win. These skaters employ tactics which are illegal, unethical, and sometimes dangerous. This win-at-all-costs mentality is detrimental to any sport, particularly a sport whose members aspire for eventual Olympic recognition of their sport.

Elite athletes, particularly those on teams, have been known to use unnecessary physical contact for the purpose of deceiving, obstructing, and even injuring rival skaters. Pushing, elbowing, clutching, grabbing, and tripping are examples of such infractions. The World Championships and Pan American Games are infamous for this level of contact and aggression among skaters, as well as the slack attitude of officials. United States world team skaters have even resorted to spraying aerosol cooking oil on their arms and clothing to make it difficult for rivals to grab them.

These negative behaviors tend to migrate back to the elite skating communities of participating countries, affecting the conduct and attitude of racers. Even worse, domestic coaches have been known to be the direct source for teaching these dirty tactics to young skaters.

For the most part, the novice and intermediate levels of domestic in-line racing are very clean. Ironically, as in many sports, it is the revered elite skaters whose actions prove most damaging to the credibility of the sport. If in-line racing is to be taken seriously as a sport worthy of Olympic credentials, the elite skaters will have to clean up their act considerably. At the same time, coaches must infuse young and developing skaters with the philosophy that winning is a worthy goal that is only satisfying if it can be achieved with respect for and compliance with the accepted rules of play, while demonstrating good sportsmanship toward one's rivals.

INDOOR RACING

Indoor in-line racing, governed in the United States by USA Rollerskating (USAC/RS), takes place on a 100-meter, asymmetrical track. The official championship track is illustrated in figure 13.8. Tactics and strategy with indoor racing are unique, differing considerably from the outdoor version. In fact, each metric distance involves distinct strategies. Table 13.2 shows distances for the various age categories in the United States.

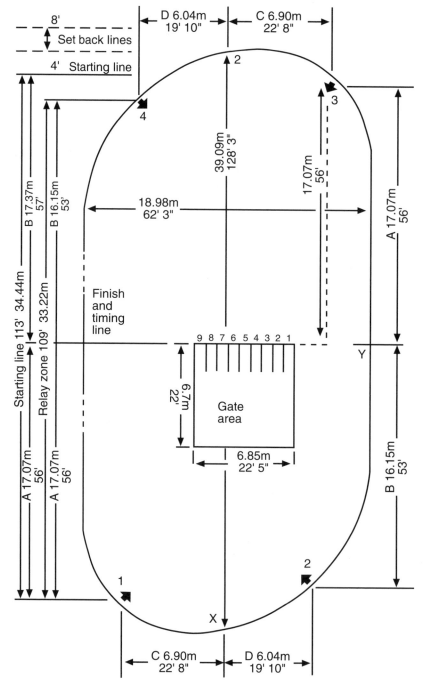

13.8 USA Roller Skating official championship 100m indoor track.

Reprinted, with permission, from United States Amateur Confederation of Roller Skating, 1995, *The speed book USAC/RS official rules of roller speedskating*. (Lincoln, NE: n.p.), 9.

Table 13.2

Age Group Divisions for Indoor Racing Used by the U.S. Amateur Confederation of Roller Skating (USAC/RS)

Division	Age (in years)	Race distances (in meters)
Primary boys and girls	<8	200, 300, 400
Juvenile boys and girls	8–9	200, 300, 500
Elementary boys and girls	10–12	300, 500, 700
Freshman boys and girls	12–13	300, 500, 1,000
Sophomore men and women	14–15	500, 1,000, 1,500
Junior men	16–17	500, 1,000, 2,000
Junior women	16–17	500, 1000, 1500
Senior men	Past 18	1,000, 1,500, 3,000
Senior women	Past 18	500, 1,000, 2,000
Classic men	Past 27	500, 1,000, 2,000
Classic women	Past 27	500, 1,000, 1,500
Masters men	>35	500, 1,000, 1,500
Masters women	>35	500, 700, 1,500
Veterans men and women	Past 45	500, 700, 1,000

Reprinted, with permission, from United States Amateur Confederation of Roller Skating, 1995. *The speed book USAC/RS official rules of roller speedskating.* (Lincoln, NE: n.p.), 6.

General Strategy

Although the focus of indoor racing tactics is primarily on passing methods, the distance being raced has the heaviest influence on the strategy and tactics. In the short sprint distances (i.e., < 500 meters), strategy is quite simple. The objective is to get out fast and try to be at or very near the front by the first corner. If you obtain the first position, the goal is to then stay there, skate as hard as possible, and make it difficult for others to pass. However, if you occupy the second or third position at the first corner, then the strategy must be to capitalize on a weakness or error on the part of any skater in front of you.

In longer races (more than 1,000 meters), however, the race is usually played out in a "cat-and-mouse" fashion. Even though the distances between 1,000 and 3,000 meters could be completed with sustained high-intensity effort, this rarely occurs unless one or more skaters choose to take the pace out hard and keep it there. Because the pace of these longer events will alternate between slow periods and those of near-maximal effort, there exist more opportunities to pass during slow moments. So passing ability and recognizing the optimal times and places to overtake another skater become the cornerstone tactical elements for implementing strategy.

Passing

Because indoor tracks are small in size (and therefore have tight turns) and are limited in surface traction, passing on them is very difficult, particularly at high speeds. Almost all passing is done somewhere in the short straightaways between turns. Skaters rely heavily on the corners, however, for building the speed necessary to pass. Effective turn technique combined with accelerating at the right moment can "slingshot" a skater out of the turn, yielding the required velocity to overtake an opponent in the straight.

The most basic corner pass occurs in the middle to end of the straight, as the next turn entry is being set up. Passing on the exit of the corner or in the early part of the straight, although possible, is increasingly difficult as speeds rise (figure 13.9). Because of the varying degree of traction on different surfaces, each track has characteristic areas where passing is easiest.

Inside Straightaway Pass

Given the small size of the track, passing in the straightaway is almost always the only good option available. An inside pass is very effective, but the pass must occur as early into the straight as possible, so that sufficient distance remains to prepare for the turn. Leaving the pass too late and entering the next corner too tight will either cause a fall or result in an excessively wide corner-exit trajectory, which immediately allows a rival skater to pass on the inside.

Because speed increases the difficulty of an inside pass, such a pass is usually saved for three conditions: when speeds are low, when the leading skater exits the corner wide, or when corner exit speed is low enough to overtake the skater in time to set up the next corner properly. A skater does not fully commit to making the pass to either the inside or the outside until the actual exit of the turn. Whenever possible,

13.9 With indoor skating, passing serves as the primary force behind strategy and tactics.

© Bob Justice/Mach Five Sports

however, a skater intending to pass should make a decision before entering the last corner before the pass. This approach is vital for maximizing acceleration by using as much force as possible within the slippage limits of the floor. Quick crossovers that do not fully extend are the most effective way for building speed in this regard.

Outside Straightaway Pass

A straightaway pass to the outside of the track is often easier to perform than the inside version. The skater does not have to swing out wide for the corner entry, and because of this the pass can occur much later in the straight. As you might expect, therefore, it is most commonly used at higher speeds.

Regardless of how the pass is executed, you must use the turn to build speed. Here are two options for building this speed:

1. Just before you enter the turn, fall back slightly from the competitor in front so that there is more room to accelerate. The gap must close up by the exit of the turn, at which point you will use the momentum and increased speed to pass the skater (or skaters) ahead.

2. Take a slightly wider path through the turn than those ahead are doing, attempting to skate immediately to the outside. To stay even with a skater to the inside requires more velocity because the outer skater is traveling a greater distance. This higher corner velocity will translate into more speed at the beginning of the straight, reducing the effort required to overtake the skaters ahead.

Defending Against the Pass

Having the ability to effectively defend against being passed is just as important as having good passing skills. Naturally, it is not possible to prevent every pass from occurring. But you can focus instead on defensive strategy—on making it as difficult as possible for competitors behind you to get past. Two specific methods have proved worthy in this defense. The first, and more effective, relates to the "line" that a skater takes around the track. This is particularly important before and immediately after the turns. Depending on how much traction the floor provides, there exists a superior trajectory that you should follow through each turn. The goal is to find not only the shortest and most stable path, but the one that allows you to build speed through each corner—while still "keeping the door shut" on others. By your skating the tightest possible inside line through a turn, you force passing skaters to make all their passes to the outside. Then you need guard against only one side.

The second method for defending against a pass involves trying to anticipate whether a skater is trying to pass to the inside or the outside. A skater must follow a reasonably straight course in the straightaway; she cannot block a passing skater by excessively weaving from side to side (side shuttling). However, she may slightly alter the exit path to make it difficult for another skater to pass. For example, if a skater is leading and notices that the competitor behind her is in the early stages of making an outside pass, she should exit the corner so that some space remains to the inside—but not enough to make an easy pass. Being slightly to the outside of the track in this way makes passing skaters go wider than they would have to if they were skating the tightest line. It is also possible to skate in a slightly random and unpredictable line, so that a passing skater cannot premeditate the maneuver (i.e., push the limits of the side shuttling rule). However, if you make this tactic flagrant, it will be considered an illegal block (foul), which would result in your being disqualified by the referee.

Counterpassing

It is often wise to force a passing skater to make the maneuver to the inside. This is because entering "tight" on the entry block often causes the skater to swing wide at the turn's exit. You should take advantage of his potential wide swing by anticipating the skater's exit trajectory and accelerating to pass on his inside as he swings wide. This tactic, called a counterpass, is an effective way to maintain pack position. But to be successful in the maneuver, you must be able to quickly recognize the optimal situation for applying it.

Implementing Race Strategy

Because of the nature of indoor racing, true breakaways—where one or more skaters open a gap on the pack—rarely happen. Longer races, which have a slower initial pace, certainly provide an environment that is more conducive to implementing such tactics. However, in indoor racing it is more common to see increases in tempo, where the entire pack responds.

When you formulate a strategy for an indoor event, you must be able to recognize and utilize your individual strengths and to avoid situations in which they may be vulnerable. For example, it is not always necessary for a skater who is especially adept at passing to be at the front. On the other hand, if a skater has poor passing abilities but a keen ability to maintain a high tempo, it is advisable for her to stay toward the front and never get too far back. Because it is difficult to pass more than one skater on each straight when the pace is high, you must always be aware of the distance remaining in the race, observe the activity of your competitors, and (as far as possible) plan each successive pass well beforehand.

A big part of being successful in short-track indoor skating is being able to anticipate the strategy of others in the pack. Then you can implement your own tactics at the most effective and appropriate times. These skills are the results of cumulative training and race experience. Becoming a good indoor tactician simply cannot happen overnight. Be patient, observe what tactics work well, and learn to avoid situations that led to previous errors.

IN-LINE SPEEDSKATING EQUIPMENT

For a newcomer to the sport, choosing the right equipment can be a daunting and frustrating experience. What makes selecting equipment especially complicated is that everybody has an opinion about what is best. From pushy salespeople to accomplished racers, people can be quite adamant in their views. This section highlights the types of equipment that are available, helps you to understand the pros and cons of each, and outlines important criteria for selecting equipment to fit your specific needs.

Speed Boots

Choosing the appropriate boot is the toughest choice a skater faces. New designs for speed boots enter the market each year, and each boot has a fairly specific fit. To make purchasing a simpler decision, you should first have an idea of the general characteristics of various types of boots, including short-track, long-track, hybrid, and custom-designed ones. Several types of speed boots are shown in figure 13.10.

13.10 Speed boots. From left to right: short-track, long-track, and hybrid boots.

Short-Track Speed Boots

Short-track boots borrow from the design and technology used by short-track ice speedskaters. In fact, companies that initially made boots primarily for ice usage now also make many of the boots used by in-liners. Some of the more popular boots carry labels by Bont, Simmons Verducci, and Miller. The design and construction of these boots are suitable for in-line use.

All short-track boots are designed in roughly the same manner. The boot's foundation is a hard, molded shell that encompasses the heel, sole, and lower portion of the sides of the boot. Short-track boots are considered high-cut because they rise up to enclose the entire ankle area. The shell of most early short-track boots was composed of fiberglass. Newer, lighter, and stronger materials (such as Kevlar, carbon fiber, and composite materials) are now used exclusively. Carbon fiber is the most common shell material currently, particularly in high-end boots.

Mounting Holes. A racing frame is attached to a short-track boot by threading bolts into aluminum mounting blocks embedded in the bottom of the shell. Short-track boots of the past had one or two mounting holes in the front and one or two in the back. Many manufacturers now have three mounting positions in the front and two or three in the back. This simple modification allows for a more lateral range of frame adjustment. It is important to realize that regardless of the size of short-track boots, the distance from the front to rear holes is six and a half inches, an industry standard (a few rare exceptions do exist). Although most five-wheel in-line frames are designed to match this measurement, it is important to note that there are a few exceptions.

Thermal Molding. Almost all short-track boots now have a heat-moldable area. Boots of the past employed thermoplastics in the ankle area to allow personalized molding. Today, high-end boots use space-age resins in the carbon fibers that actually allow portions of the shell to be manipulated when heated. This way, small pressure points in the boot can be alleviated with minor adjustments.

Because various boots have different thresholds at which they soften, heating should be done very gradually, one area at a time, using a heat gun or heat lamp. It is not advisable to put boots in the oven. When you mold a new boot, you should consult the manufacturer's instructions to ensure that you use an appropriate method.

Long-Track Racing Boots

Long-track boots are designed and specifically built for long-track and marathon ice skating. Most long-track skates come with a fixed, riveted blade. However, some European skate makers, such as Viking, build a "marathon" series of boots that can accept a bolt-on in-line frame or blade. Raps and Zandstra also manufacture boots with such a capability.

Boot Construction. Long-track boots are constructed very differently from their short-track cousins. These boots are described as "low-cut" because the rigid portion does not fully enclose the anklebone. In this respect, they feel more like shoes than skates, and are designed to allow more mobility in the ankle area. Instead of having a shell, long-track boots are made up of a hard sole and "counters" (supportive structures that encompass the lateral aspect of the boot). The size, strength, and material used in the counters can vary, but in high-end boots, the counters are made of a strong, heat-moldable thermoplastic or carbon fiber. These boots are usually easier to mold than short-track boots. The rest of the boot (the upper) is made of leather. Here, too, the type, quality, and thickness of the leather used in manufacturing the boot vary in overall quality.

Hole-Mount Spacing. Unlike short-track boots, there is no standard hole spacing with long-track boots. The distance between the holes varies, depending on the manufacturer and size of the boot. Because of this, a frame (or blade) must be purchased specifically to fit the make and size of the boot. Several makers, such as Mogema, build frames designed to match the hole spacing of long-track boots.

Hybrid Racing Boots

More and more, in-line racers are opting to buy what could be called a "hybrid" boot, one that shares qualities of short-track design, such as the use of a carbon-fiber shell for support, but also resembles a long-track skate in weight, sleekness of overall design, and (lower) ankle height. Hybrid boots are increasing in popularity because many skaters now realize the benefits to be gained by skating on a boot that allows greater ankle mobility than a high-cut short-track boot. Second, because hybrids can be used both for in-line and ice (short- and long-track) skating, they eliminate the necessity of buying a second pair of boots. Popular hybrid boots are made by companies such as Viking, Rollerblade (Equipe), and Miller (Criterium).

Custom-Designed Boots

There are many custom boot makers in the United States who make boots from a plaster cast and/or tracing of a skater's foot. Not only should custom-designing these boots assure a better fit than any stock product, but it should allow a skater to specify all aspects of the boot's design (e.g., ankle height, shell thickness, mounting-block type, color). Although having a custom-designed boot is often ideal, the cost is also significantly higher. A general observation is that only skaters with "unusual" feet should need to buy custom boots.

How to Choose

Ideally, choosing the right boot should be a simple matter. However, it can become a complex and confusing task, particularly for new skaters. With more variety of boots hitting the shops each year, the options continue to grow. For any skater wishing to buy a pair of speed boots, two factors are especially important to consider carefully: intended usage and fit.

Intended Usage. One reason that choosing boots can be complicated is because you must determine their overall usage: will you use the boots mainly for outdoor or indoor in-line skating or for short- or long-track ice skating? These days, many skaters participate in several disciplines. As a result, they seek a flexible, versatile boot that can accommodate the demands of more than one type of skating. The main factor in selection is basically the cut of the boot (high, medium, or low) and the subsequent level of support that it provides. Table 13.3 depicts six possible scenarios that help dictate the type of boot that will best match your purpose.

Fit. The fit should ultimately dictate what boot you purchase. It is important to ensure that the product's design will accommodate the shape of your feet. For example, Viking long-track skates are built very narrow, and would not suit a skater with a wide foot. Conversely, some boots are very wide, and would be a poor choice for a skater with narrow feet. It is often hard to cross off the boot you thought you wanted from your list of options, but if the fit isn't good, you should look for another brand. A poor-fitting boot can cause blistering, chronic foot pain, and acute injury to the foot, ankle, and supporting muscles of the lower leg.

Racing Frames

High-quality racing frames are made of aircraft-grade aluminum. The best frames are made by computer-controlled milling, where the product is extruded from a single billet of metal. When you face the many high-end racing frames available today, personal preference and aesthetics may primarily dictate your choice. Most frames boast superior durability, flex, and axle-system design, but the truth of the matter is that one frame will not allow a skater to go faster than another. The primary three factors that should go into frame selection are length, mounting compatibility, and profile height.

Table 13.3

Recommended Boot Type, Based on Skating Discipline

Skating discipline	Recommended boot design
In-line (indoor)	High-cut or hybrid boot
In-line (outdoor)	Long-track or hybrid boot
In-line (both disciplines)	Hybrid boot
In-line and short-track ice	High-cut or hybrid boot
In-line and long-track ice	Long-track or hybrid boot
All skating disciplines	Hybrid boot

Length

The current trend is to use as short a frame as possible that will accommodate five 80-millimeter (mm) wheels. A length of roughly 13 inches (more precisely, 12.8) is usually best. This short a frame facilitates a high stroke cadence, makes it easier to accelerate, makes crossover steps faster, and allows for better fine-tuning of velocity.

On the other hand, longer frames are preferable for those who are tall (over 6 feet 2 inches) or are big "pushers" (i.e., who use a slower stroke frequency and more force per stride)—usually skaters with an ice background. At the extreme end, there are skaters who seem to prefer frame lengths of up to 14.5 inches. For experienced skaters who have always skated on a short frame, trying a longer one can't hurt. If you're a new skater who doesn't know the difference, try a length of 12.8 or 13 inches, with 13.5 inches advisable for taller skaters (those over 6 feet 2 inches).

Profile Height

Racing frames come in two profile heights, high and low. Low-profile heights are sometimes preferred by long-distance skaters, those from a long-track ice background, and those who skate in-line on a long-track boot. In general, low-profile frames offer more stability and provide a more solid feeling of contact with the wheels.

High-profile frames, however, are used by most racers. Advocates of such frames argue that the increased height provides more boot clearance on corners, increases push displacement, and increases the range of angular leverage at the ankle.

Depending on the manufacturer, the difference in height between the two profiles can be as much as half an inch. Even this relatively small amount can result in significantly different sensory perceptions as you skate. Because frame heights differ between manufacturers, the high-profile version of one frame may be very close to the low-profile height of another. When you select a frame, decide which profile is desired and then compare the heights of the available options. See figure 13.11.

Mounting Positions

As mentioned earlier, it is crucial to have a frame that matches the boot. For long-track boots, this limits the choices somewhat. In North America, 98 percent of skaters likely have boots with a 6.5-inch hole spacing from front to rear. See figure 13.12

Most frames offer two or three lateral slots in the front and back, so that fore-aft boot position can be varied according to personal preference and the size of the boot. As a general rule, the boot should be positioned so that there is an equal amount of wheel protruding from the front of the boot as there is at the back. When you are purchasing a frame, place the boot on the frame to see if the mounting slots will allow for the desired fore-aft position. Figure 13.13 illustrates optimal fore-aft frame mounting.

Lateral Frame Positioning

The most desirable fore-aft frame position usually puts the boot in the middle of the wheelbase. As to the lateral position of the frame on the boot, however, there are several factors to consider. For starters, a frame's positioning is highly individual, and you may need a great deal of fine-tuning to find a comfortable position. When you attach the frame, start by "center-setting" it. This means positioning the front and back of the frame in the following manner: the middle of the front wheel (when

Barry Publow

13.11 High- versus low-profile frame height. Both frames pictured here are from Mogema.

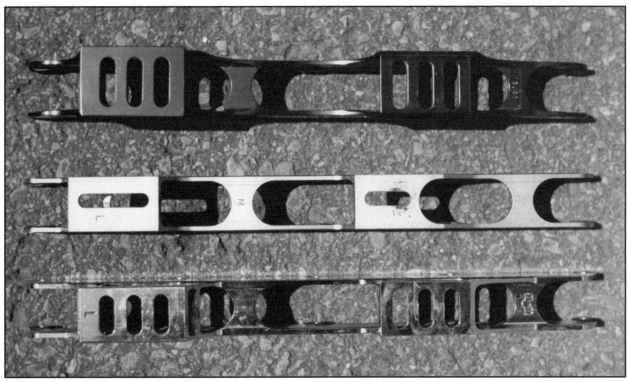

Barry Publow

13.12 Three different Mogema racing frames illustrate the variation in mounting slots. Top and bottom are 6.5-inch spacing. The middle frame is for a Viking (long-track) boot.

13.13   A fore-aft frame position with 50/50 wheel overlap in front and behind is considered optimal. Indoor skaters tend to prefer the boot in a slightly more forward position.

viewed from above) is aligned between the first and second toe of the foot; the tail of the frame should be positioned slightly inside the middle of the skate as viewed from behind.

Try skating with the frame in this position. If the ankles have a natural tendency to collapse inward, the frame should be moved more to the inside of the foot. When you initially make such an adjustment, it is advisable to move the toe and heel equally in very small increments (1 to 2 millimeters). The goal is to position the frame eventually so that when you stand with equal weight on both feet, the ankles naturally collapse slightly to the outside.

Once the frame is positioned to create slight outward ankle pressure, try skating. The position should be comfortable. However, lateral frame positioning is also highly specific to an individual's skating technique. For example, double-push skaters often position the frame to the extreme inside. Once a skating test has been performed, small adjustments should be made. At this point, the fine-tuning can take the form of moving either the heel or toe more inward than the other. Usually, the toe is moved inward proportionally more than the heel. The general rule is that when the skate points in the direction of travel, as viewed from above, the frame should be either pointing in the same direction or slightly more to the inside.

Finding the correct frame offset can be time-consuming. However, even minute adjustments can dramatically affect technical efficiency, and you should take the time to find the right position. Once this has been determined, it is best to never move the frame again. If removing the frame is necessary for some reason, mark the frame's position with tape so that you can duplicate it exactly at a later date.

Wheels

If you are confused about what wheels to buy, it may simply be because there is no one correct answer. Several wheel characteristics go into the equation, including the size, hardness (durometer), wheel profile, rebound, and core design. See figure 13.14 for several kinds of wheels.

Size

Wheel size for in-line racing ranges from 76 to 80 millimeters. Larger wheels are faster and offer less rolling resistance, but they also require marginally more effort to get up to top speed. Because of this, the smaller 76- or 78-millimeter wheels are commonly used for sprint races. However, 80-millimeter wheels are preferable for the majority of in-line races.

Durometer

The durometer is a standardized measure that uses what is called the "A" scale for increasing hardness. Durometers for in-line racing range from 78A to 85A, softer to harder. The primary factor in determining which wheel is superior is the condition of the pavement. Softer wheels (e.g., 78A) absorb shock forces more efficiently; therefore they are preferable for rough roads. Conversely, hard wheels have less rolling resistance, and are suitable for smoother pavements, where shock-absorbing

Anthony White

13.14 Most skaters race on wheels which are 80 millimeters in diameter. Durometer can range from 78A to 85A (see page 316).

capacity is less important. It is therefore ideal to own at least two sets of race wheels of different durometer (e.g., 78A and 82A).

Heavy individuals will cause a wheel to deform more than a lighter skater would. Because of this, heavy skaters should typically use a wheel that is harder than what might otherwise be selected for the type of pavement.

All skaters are likely aware that skating in the rain poses a major hazard because of the reduced traction. It is generally believed that soft wheels will provide the best grip of rain-soaked roads, and this is often true. However, you should know that soft wheels do not always perform the best on wet asphalt. The condition of the pavement and the actual urethane compound of the wheel will determine which wheel will perform the best. If roads are wet on race day and more than one durometer of wheel is available to you, spend some time testing your options, rather than automatically selecting the softest wheel.

If you don't have the time or inclination to perform such testing, at least try a simple traction test by holding the wheel at a slight angle (30 degrees), applying heavy pressure, and "scrubbing" the wheel against the road. The wheels that seem to grip the best when tested this way are not always the ones that will perform the best during skating, but using such a test is better than simply guessing.

Profile

Speed wheels have an elliptical profile. This shape provides as little surface contact as possible when the wheels are oriented vertically. The result is a decreased rolling resistance while gliding. As the wheels progressively angle (as in the push-off), the surface contact area increases, improving traction and control. For courses with few turns, a wheel with an extreme elliptical profile is best. Conversely, for skating on a track, indoors, or on a course where turn traction is important, a more rounded profile is desirable. To meet the demands of such venues, some companies make wheels specific for either indoor or banked-track skating.

Rebound

Wheel rebound refers to the amount of energy put into a wheel that is then returned to the wheel. Because every urethane compound produces a varying degree of rebound, wheels can vary slightly in this regard. A crude method for judging the rebound of a wheel is to simply drop it on a hard surface, so that it lands on the middle of the rolling portion and bounces back up. The higher the rebound of the wheel, the higher it will bounce back.

Although wheel manufacturers do not quantify rebound in measurable terms, all speed wheels are essentially of high rebound. Therefore, most skaters need not seriously consider rebound when choosing wheels.

Core Design

Until a few years ago, core (hub) design was given little attention in the research design of in-line wheels. Today, however, the design of the core is proving to be one of the most important elements in the performance of a wheel. Most speed wheels now use a large diameter, spoked core that decreases the weight of the wheel (because less urethane is used) and helps keep bearing temperatures low by increasing the air circulation. The structure of the core also helps absorb vibration, reducing the forces of shock which are eventually transmitted to the center of the wheel and bearing.

Bearings

All in-line skate bearings are referred to as 608s, a number that reflects the size and type of bearing. The issue of bearings invites much debate and personal opinion, so only basic information will be provided in this discussion. See figure 13.15.

Bearing quality is rated on the ABEC scale (which stands for annular bearing engineering committee). The ABEC rating system uses odd numbers, starting with one, to assess the overall quality of a bearing. For a bearing to even reach the ABEC scale, it must meet certain standards in the quality (hardness) of the chrome steel used and the tolerance of the bearing (a reflection of how tight the balls fit inside the raceway). Precision and semi-precision bearings are those that do not meet the minimum requirements of the ABEC scale.

Once a bearing gets on the ABEC scale, only the tolerance factor determines its rating. Logically, bearing quality should increase at higher ABEC ratings. However, a bearing with an ABEC-1 rating may be made of harder steel than one with an ABEC-5 rating. Because of this confusing fact, it is difficult to state conclusively that having higher ABEC-rated bearings is better than having lower-rated ones. In addition, you must question how much importance a high-bearing tolerance has, when in-line skating by nature is a sport that places angular load on the bearing. Most bearings are designed to operate in only one plane, with the resistive force to motion coming from a 90-degree angle to the axis of rotation. Because of this, skate manufacturers have specifically designed bearings with a different groove on the ball's raceway to better handle axial loading.

13.15 The debate continues over which bearing is best.

Anthony White

If you ask 10 elite skaters which they consider the best bearing, you will probably get four or five different answers. Still, if you can assume that pro skaters race on the best bearings, then you can conclude that the ABEC-5 rated or Swiss bearings, produced by one of the major skate companies, should be the first choice.

CHAPTER 14

Ice Competition

Ice speedskating is a versatile sport encompassing the disciplines of short-track, long-track (metric), and marathon racing. Each of these specific racing sports, although related to the others, is so distinct in format that it has a unique strategy and tactics. For this reason, each discipline will be discussed separately.

LONG-TRACK SPEEDSKATING

What makes long-track racing interesting is that time is the sole means for measuring success in performance. Although skaters race in twos, beating one's pair is not required unless placing first is the goal. Because of its solo nature, however, long-track skating does not involve the same strategic or tactical elements inherent in other forms of the sport.

Long-track ice skating always takes place on a 400-meter, symmetrical oval, which is divided into outer and inner lanes that are each five meters wide. Because a lap of the inside lane is shorter than an outer lap, some starts are staggered and skaters are required to change lanes every lap. The crossover zone constitutes the entire backstretch, from the exit of one turn to the beginning of the next turn. Skaters are required to use this area to switch lanes after each lap. Figure 14.1 shows the track and indicates the start and finish lines for each metric distance. In long-track races, pairings are based on performance in the 500-meter event. Therefore, skaters in most races are matched according to ability.

Most novice and intermediate long-track skaters compete in all distances designated for their age category. At the elite level, long-track skaters normally specialize in sprint events (500 and 1,000 meters), in one specific race, the distance events, or in all-around competition (where proficiency in several distances is most important). In World Cup and other international competitions, there are five distances for both men and women. These events are highlighted in table 14.1.

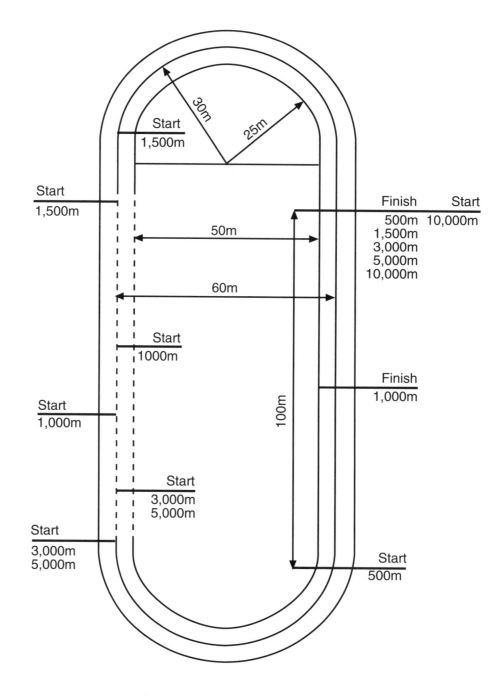

14.1 400-meter long-track ice oval. The dashed lines indicate the crossover zone.

Table 14.1

Men's and Women's Long-Track Distances Used for International Competition

Men	500m	1,000m	1,500m	5,000m	10,000m
Women	500m	1,000m	1,500m	3,000m	5,000m

World Championships

Long-track speedskating has three separate World Championships for sprint, single-distance, and all-around. For the single-distance competition, winners of each event are simply determined by the best time. The following section briefly discusses the scoring system used for the sprint and all-around competition.

Sprint World Championships

Each skater races two 500-meter events and two 1,000-meter events. The best time from each race is used to determine a *points total*. The lowest points total wins, and all further ranking is done by placing skaters by increasing points total.

The 500-meter time, in seconds, determines the number of points initially awarded to the skater. For example, a 500-meter time of 38.64 seconds is awarded 38.64 points. The 1,000-meter race is twice the distance, so the points are determined by converting the time into seconds and dividing by two. For example, a time of 1:13.62 (73.62 seconds) results in 36.81 points. Consider the following example in table 14.2 using two skaters.

In the example in table 14.2, Skater B recorded a 500-meter time 1.41 seconds faster, but was slower than Skater A by 1.24 seconds in the 1,000 meters. However, because of the greater relative importance of the 500-meter time, Skater B records a lower points total and is given the win.

All-Around World Championships

In the all-around competition, men and women both skate 500 meters and 1,500 meters. Women then skate a 3,000 meter and a 5,000 meter, while men do a 5,000 meter and a 10,000 meter. As in the sprint championships, a points total (also known as a sammelog) is used to determine the rankings. The 500-meter time in seconds

Table 14.2

Sample Points Totals for the Sprint Competition

| | 500m | | 1,000m | | |
	Time (seconds)	Points	Time (minutes and seconds)	Points	Points total
Skater A	38.64	38.64	1:13.62	36.81	75.45
Skater B	37.23	37.23	1:14.86	37.43	74.66

Table 14.3

Sample Points Totals for the All-Around Competition For Three Women

| | 500m | | 1500m | | 3,000m | | 5,000m | | Points | |
	Time	Pts.	Time	Pts.	Time	Pts.	Time	Pts.	total	Rank
Skater A	42.68	42.68	2:06.35	42.12	4:20.60	43.43	7:36.42	45.64	173.87	3
Skater B	43.20	43.20	2:05.58	41.86	4:16.66	42.78	7:31.15	45.11	172.95	1
Skater C	43.92	43.92	2:06.70	42.23	4:17.19	42.87	7:26.81	44.68	173.70	2

once again equates to an equal amount of points. The 1,500-meter time is converted into seconds and then divided by three, since it is three times longer than the 500 meter. For women, the 3,000- and 5,000-meter times are converted to seconds and divided by 6 and 10, respectively. For men, times (in seconds) for the 5,000 meter and 10,000 meter are divided by 10 and 20, respectively. Table 14.3 is an example that gives times for three female skaters.

Long-Track Tactics

Because metric ice skaters race against the clock in an attempt to record the best possible times, their tactics differ dramatically from those of other speedskating disciplines. Metric speedskating strategy is aimed to maximize *personal* performance by recording the fastest possible time. Since each metric distance involves specific strategic elements, each will be discussed separately.

500-Meter Sprint

The fastest skaters (i.e., those with the highest top speeds) do not always win in the 500-meter sprint. Rather, those who are able to accelerate up to maximal speed in the least amount of time often dominate this event. Race tactics therefore involve getting up to top speed quickly, maintaining control in the high-speed turns, and keeping the stroke cadence high as fatigue begins to set in during the last 100 meters. Skaters who start in the outside lane may be at a disadvantage, because negotiating the inner lane on the last turn can be difficult due to the combination of high speed and a tight turn radius. When this is the case, the final turn should be set up as wide as possible.

1,000-Meter Sprint

The 1,000-meter sprint is considered a sprint event because this race involves the same high speeds as the 500 meter does. In fact, some skaters record a 1000-meter time faster than twice their personal best for the shorter distance. For example, consider a skater whose personal bests for the 500 and 1,000 meter are 36.22 and 1:11.78, respectively. The latter time is faster (lower) than twice their 500-meter best. This is possible because in the 1,000 meter, the skater does not need to accelerate up to speed for the second half of the race. Therefore, the actual splits would look something like this: first 500 meters—37.88 seconds; second 500 meters—33.9 seconds (total of 71.78 seconds, or 1:11.78).

Because the 1,000-meter sprint requires that a skater maintain near top speed for an extended period of time, pacing is very important. The 200-meter "opener" indicates the ability of the skater to accelerate up to maximum velocity, while the 600-meter split reflects the degree to which top speed is sustained. The final 400 meters should involve very little drop-off in time. Race strategy for this event should therefore be to explode off the start the same way as in the 500 meter, relaxing very slightly during the straights but working every corner with maximal effort.

This is the only race event where the athletes skate an uneven number of inner and outer turns, an interesting fact. That is, the skater who starts in the inner lane will skate a total of three inner turns and two outer turns, while the skater in the outer lane skates two outer turns and three inner turns.

1,500-Meter Race

The 1,500 meter is perhaps the most intriguing event because it requires a delicate balance between sprint speed and pacing (the ability to skate consistent lap times). It also results in the highest lactic acid levels of any speedskating race. In this event, a skater has little time to settle into a comfortable rhythm, but must be able to relax and use strides that are at once smooth, yet powerful. According to Diane Holum (1984), the coach of five-time Olympic gold medalist Eric Heiden, the strategy for this event should involve careful pacing. Make an initial start effort of between 80 and 85 percent. Once up to speed, the second lap should be skated as relaxed as possible. At the 700-meter mark, the skater begins to increase velocity by building acceleration through the turns with near-maximal effort. Then, to maintain speed during the last lap as fatigue sets in, effort must be at 100 percent, concentrating on proper technique.

Starting out too fast in this event creates a high level of oxygen debt early in the race that will make it almost impossible to maintain steady lap times throughout the race. Lap times should always be within one second of each other. To achieve this pacing, the skater must continually "change gears" and consciously increase the degree of effort being applied (to overcome the process of progressively accumulating lactic acid). The best skaters are able to skate lap times consistently within two- to three-tenths of a second, steadily increasing speed in the last few laps.

Distance Events

For women, the distance events are 3,000 meters and 5,000 meters, whereas for men they are 5,000 meters and 10,000 meters. Although there are considerable differences between these events and the times required to cover the distances, each shares strategic and tactical considerations. The most important technical modifications to make in skating distance races are a slightly higher body position, a decreased push displacement (shallower knee angle) and power per stroke, and a slower stroke frequency (i.e., longer glide).

In distance skating, the primary tactical element is pacing. The best skaters demonstrate this by recording successive lap times within one second of each other. As in the 1,500-meter distance, a skater should start out conservatively to avoid excessive early-energy contribution from the anaerobic system. Many coaches instruct their athletes to record a negative split—that is, to skate the second half of the race faster than the first half. Performing a negative split, and even keeping lap times consistent, requires a steady increase in effort throughout the race to combat the progressive effects of fatigue and lactic acid accumulation.

Skating the distance events requires athletes to be as efficient as possible. Relaxing the upper body and maintaining proper technique in the latter stages of the race are crucial to avoid wasting energy. In skating, you should gradually accelerate through each turn, using a slightly elevated leg tempo, so that your exit velocity is higher than entry speed. Exiting the corner with a slight—but significant—elevation in speed will allow you to relax for the first half-dozen strides, as slight deceleration occurs in the straight. The rest of the straight should serve as an opportunity to simply maintain velocity. Once you enter the next corner, rebuild your acceleration and repeat the process.

SHORT-TRACK SPEEDSKATING

Short-track ice racing is a relatively new (and still evolving) speedskating discipline. At the 1988 Winter Olympics in Calgary, short-track skating was introduced as a demonstration sport. At the next Olympic games in Albertville, France, short-track had already become a recognized medal sport. An annual World Championship also is held to determine the best individual and team skaters in the young sport. Table 14.4 lists the elite-level distances used by men and women.

Short-track skating events take place on a 111-meter, symmetrical oval track, as depicted in figure 14.2. Short-track events are skated in heats, semifinals, and finals (or just heats and finals). Usually four or five skaters compete in each race. The exception is the 3,000 meter, in which up to seven skaters are allowed.

Much as with indoor in-line racing methods, short-track tactics vary widely, depending on the distance being skated and the pack's level of aggression. Passing is again the basic skill behind the execution of strategy. However, because the traction of a sharp blade on ice is not compromised—unlike wheels on a slick floor—short-track skaters are able to execute passes in ways and places that indoor in-line racers could only dream of.

Passing

Being able to pass other skaters in short-track is a vital skill. The best skaters not only make passing look easy, but also can execute such maneuvers in very tight places. Passing in short-track skating, as with indoor in-line skating, almost always occurs on the straights. But a short-track skate has a blade that allows the athlete to pivot and turn in a very small radius when necessary, so the pass can take place late in the straightaway and, in rare instances, through the corner. The pass can occur either to the inside or outside of the track, and its precise location can vary greatly. Still, we can distinguish essentially two categories of passes.

Table 14.4

Short-Track Distances for Men and Women

WORLD CHAMPIONSHIP			
500m	1,000m	1,500m	3,000m
OLYMPICS			
500m	1,000m		

Note: The International Skating Union has changed the rules governing Olympic competition. Beginning in 1998, men and women will skate only the 500m and the 1,000m race distances.

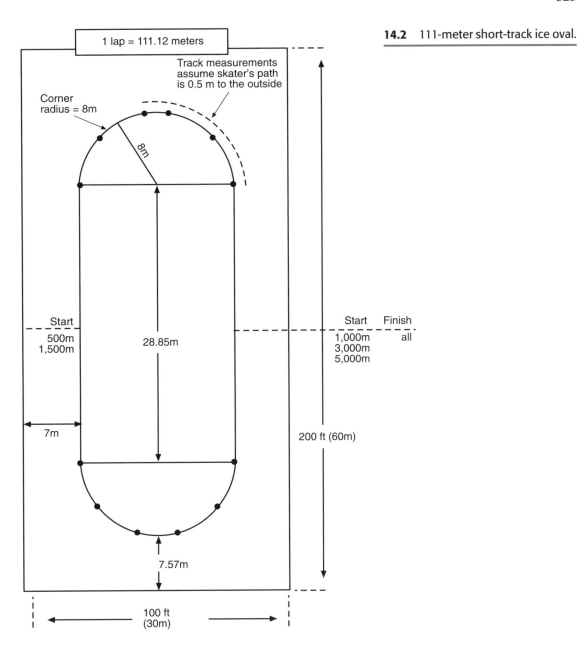

14.2 111-meter short-track ice oval.

1 lap = 111.12 meters

Track measurements assume skater's path is 0.5 m to the outside

Corner radius = 8m

8m

Start
500m
1,500m

28.85m

Start   Finish
1,000m   all
3,000m
5,000m

7m

200 ft (60m)

7.57m

100 ft
(30m)

Early Pass

An early pass occurs between the exit of the turn and the first half of the straight (figure 14.3). You must plan such a tactic ahead of time and use the corner to accelerate and build speed if you wish to minimize the effort required to overtake the skater ahead. To accomplish this tactical passing, you can increase speed throughout the entire corner or wait until after the apex (center) of the turn to start accelerating. If you're skating at a slower pace, you can wait for the apex. At more moderate speeds, it is better to "work" the entire corner to ensure that your exit speed will exceed that of the skater in front whom you will pass.

Most often, the skater planning to pass has already decided or has intentions to go either to the inside or outside of the track. However, you must remain flexible enough in your strategy so that you can make a last-minute change in your decision. Once you have the required velocity to overtake the skater ahead, your exit trajectory must be slightly wider for an outside pass—and tighter for an inside pass.

14.3 Early pass.

Which maneuver you implement will depend essentially on the position of the skater ahead. For example, if the skater to be passed is holding tight to the corner blocks, an inside pass will be difficult. If the skater falters, however, and swings wide as she exits the corner, you (as the passing skater) should take full advantage, because in such a case an inside pass would be easier.

Late Pass

Overall, the early pass is used most often when the race pace is slow, but at higher speeds it becomes increasingly difficult to pass early in the straight. When the pack begins to pick up speed, passing may be easiest in the last few meters of the straightaway or between the corner entry and the first corner block. Passing in this area is called the late pass (figure 14.4).

One of the key differences between making a late pass in short-track racing compared with indoor in-line racing is that ice skaters need not always set up the corner wide. Because in-line skaters have limited traction, entering the corner tight would undoubtedly force them wide on the turn's exit, making them vulnerable to a counterpass. With ice skaters, in contrast, a pass can be done very late, when the passing skater is on the most extreme inside of the track. A "pivoting" technique may be used to remain tight throughout the turn, and it reduces the risk of a wide corner exit. At high speeds, even a late pass on the outside may require the passing skater to pivot and cut in front of the competitor ahead in order to execute the pass before the middle (apex) of the turn.

The same strategy you used for the early pass is fine for passing late in the straight. That is, you build acceleration in the preceding corner. If you decide to pass

© S. Hicks/Photo

14.4 Late pass.

once you are already on the straight, accelerating enough to overtake the skater ahead is very difficult, especially when the pace is fast. All passes must be premeditated!

General Race Strategy

It is normally safe to assume that all skaters in a short-track race are of similar caliber. The skater who takes the victory in short track is not always the one who is the fastest. Rather, he or she is the one who combines the best overall fitness, technique, and passing ability with (perhaps most importantly) a sound and well-implemented strategy.

The 500-meter event is an all-out sprint. The goal should always be to get off the start line as quickly as possible and aim to get into the first or second position by the end of the first corner. Once you're in the lead, the strategy is to try and stay there by avoiding mistakes and defending against competitors trying to pass. When you're not leading, it is pointless to waste energy by trying to pass on every corner or straightaway. Rather, wait to take advantage of an error on the part of another skater, or plan every passing attempt to maximize the chances for success.

In spite of the moderate increases in race distance, all the other short-track distances are usually skated in "cat-and-mouse" fashion. Even in the 1,000 meter, the first half of the race is often slow, picking up pace slowly to end in a sprint for the last five or six laps. Occasionally, a skater will push the pace early on, trying to burn out his or her competitors. For skaters who are good at sustaining a near-maximal effort for prolonged periods, this strategy can succeed in taking the edge off those competitors with a higher top speed. For skaters who have superior passing ability and speed, the best strategy is to relax during most of the race—without ever getting too far to the back in the pack. Once the end of the race nears and the pace picks up, the goal for such a skater is then to either lead or sit in second place, waiting for an opportune moment to pass. The primary focus in determining your race strategy is always to take full advantage of individual strengths. This means doing whatever you can to dictate how the race unfolds, so you can implement your desired tactics and develop optimal chances for success.

MARATHON SKATING

Marathon skate racing is a pack-style event that typically involves distances from 40 to 100 or even 200 kilometers. Admittedly, marathon racing is the least popular ice discipline in North America. In many northern European and Scandinavian countries, on the other hand, it is common for marathon races to involve hundreds of competitors and draw thousands of spectators. In Holland, marathon racing is immensely popular, sometimes with two such races each week.

Marathon races take place on a 400-meter oval on a canal, lake, or river. In North America, what few marathons there are take place on an oval, with only a few on natural ice. Because of the low interest in marathon skating in the United States and Canada, those who participate in such long-distance events almost always skate in at least one other skating discipline. There are few who specialize in marathon skating. In the Netherlands, however, many athletes specifically train for and compete in marathon-distance races. There speedskating is a way of life, and athletes in their 40s and 50s routinely compete in—and often win—marathons. In fact, many older Dutch marathon skaters could humble the best of North America's marathon athletes.

Being a successful marathon skater requires a high aerobic output, a strong resistance to muscular fatigue, and an unbridled technical efficiency. Because marathon races are pack-style, strategy and tactics are also vitally important for success in them. In countries where marathon skating is popular, many teams battle head-to-head for top honors of the day. Even for those who compete without the benefit of teammates, race strategy can play an important role in determining success. The strategy and tactical elements employed in marathon skating are essentially the same as those described for in-line racing. Because the distances being skated are greater, long solo breakaways are extremely rare, and the intensity of most tactical maneuvers is significantly lower than with the shorter, more intense in-line events.

It is unlikely that marathon skating will ever become widely popular in North America, not only because of a general lack of interest, but also because the United States and Canada have had such a successful history in short-track and long-track skating. The lack of speedskating ovals and appropriate natural ice venues also makes it difficult to stage such marathon events. In the foreseeable future, marathon skating will remain the less well-represented speedskating discipline in most countries. A few skaters who are passionate about the event and others who may aspire to travel to other countries to pursue their love of the sport will certainly carry it on.

ICE SPEEDSKATING EQUIPMENT

The workmanship, production methods, and quality of the materials used to make ice speedskates have improved over the years, but the basic design has changed little.

The difference between short-track, long-track, and hybrid boots has already been discussed thoroughly (see chapter 13), and this section will only discuss the differences in blades among the ice disciplines.

Long-Track Blades

The traditional blades used for long-track speedskating are composed of a runner (the blade itself), a tube (that portion of the blade that houses the runner), cups (the attachments between the tube and the sole plate), and a sole plate (the part that physically attaches the blade to the boot). Most long-track skates have blades that are riveted directly to the boot. Although this provides a very strong mount, the center-set, stationary position of the blade can pose problems for some skaters who would prefer the blade to be adjustable. For these people, the blade can be remounted in the desired fixed position, or the skater can use a boot that allows lateral adjustments in the blade.

Blade Length—The length of the blade is primarily a matter of personal preference. Most big, strong skaters use a longer blade, while smaller skaters usually choose a blade correspondingly on the smaller end of the spectrum. Although there is no rule limiting blade length, the common range is from 15.5 inches to 18 inches.

Blade Thickness—Long-track blades are the thinnest speed blades. Most of them are between 1 and 1.2 millimeters thick to provide a low running resistance.

Blade Material—Speedskating blades are made of steel. The type and hardness of the steel can vary slightly, but stainless steel is used in many good-quality blades to prevent rusting. Harder steel is more time-consuming to sharpen, but it stays sharp longer and is generally believed to provide a lower running resistance. Some blades have a bimetal runner, in which two grades of steel are electronically welded together. The steel that touches the ice is harder, while the upper part of the runner is composed of softer steel. These blades are believed to be superior because the harder steel's contact with the ice provides a lower running resistance, while the softer steel increases the overall comfort by absorbing small vibrations.

Blade Rocker—The degree to which the blade deviates from being perfectly flat is called its rocker, and it can be observed by placing a straight edge along the bottom of the blade and checking the clearance at each end. The rocker is measured in meters, reflecting the radius of the circle that would be drawn if the arc of the blade were used to determine the size of the circle. For long-track skates, the blade's radius ranges from 19 to 24 meters (62 to 79 feet). Sprinters prefer to use a smaller blade radius to better negotiate the high-speed turns, and distance specialists typically use a blade with a comparatively larger rocker. See figure 14.5

Klap Blades

Although a relatively simple concept, from a biomechanical perspective, the klap blade is an engineering marvel. This blade, which continues to rewrite the long-track record book, was discussed in chapter 2. This section outlines the design and construction of these blades. It should be noted that early on in their use, the klap blade has only proven superior for long-track and marathon skaters. Although special short-track klap blades do exist, athletes of this discipline are still experimenting with this technology. Until the blade undergoes further evolution, it is doubtful it will infiltrate into the competitive short-track arena the way it has the other ice disciplines. The klap blade is essentially made up of three parts: the blade, the return mechanism, and the stabilizer bar. Figure 14.6 compares klapskates and fixed-blade skates.

14.5 Short-track (left) and long-track skates.

Anthony White

The Blade

The blade portion of the klapskate, made up of the runner and tube, is identical to that of a traditional long-track blade. The front cup of the traditional blade is replaced by a hinged joint assembly, while the heel cup is replaced by some form of interface acting between the rear of the blade and tail end of the boot.

The Return Mechanism

The return mechanism is designed to return the blade to its resting position during the regrouping of the push leg. It is important that the resistance to blade extension is minimal, while ensuring the tension of the return mechanism is sufficient to retract the blade before the skate is set down for the following stride. Early on in the skate's design, two types of return mechanisms have surfaced. Both involve the use of a spring, but the location and orientation of the spring differs between models. Some use a longitudinally-mounted spring which spans from the front hinge to roughly the midpoint of the stabilizer bar. The Finn, Maple, Marchese, Easton, and Bont klaps employ such a similar design. On the Viking klap blade, the spring design differs considerably. Here, the spring is mounted laterally, and is embedded within the front hinge assembly. The klap blade made by SSS is similar to this design. Despite their differences, both designs accomplish the same thing—they return the extended blade to the boot. It is difficult, if not impossible, to declare one design superior to the other.

The Stabilizer Bar

While the design of the stabilizer bar differs between manufacturer, its function remains unchanged. This piece of metal, usually aluminum, runs from the front

Anthony White

14.6 Klap (left) and fixed blade long-track skates.

hinge assembly to the rear cup. Its purpose is twofold: to eliminate lateral movement and torquing between the boot and blade, and to increase the overall strength and durability of the boot/blade unit.

The klap blades presently on the market are essentially first generation. They signify, however, the onset of a technological revolution in blade functioning that is likely to continue into the near future. The meteoric rise and dominance of klap-clad skaters has raised many questions about the future direction of the sport. The only certainty is that the klap blade is here stay. If the sport of speedskating is to maintain its present level of purity, however, the International Skating Union must soon develop decisive limitations relating to all further developments of blade design.

Short-Track Blades

Short-track and long-track blades are distinct but nevertheless share several common points. A short-track blade consists of a runner, tube, and the cups. It is bolted to the bottom of the boot. This attachment, however, provides for about an inch and a half of lateral adjustment: if the bolts are simply loosened, the blade cups can slide to the desired position. Most blades also allow fore and aft adjustment by offering several holes to attach the blade tube to the mounting cups. Overall, the cups of short-track boots are considerably higher than their long-track cousins. This gives the skater more boot clearance when cornering. Refer to figure 14.5.

Blade Length—Historically, short-track blades have been shorter than those used for long-track skating. The current trend among elite skaters is to use longer blades, up to 18 inches. Most novice and intermediate skaters should look for blades between 15 and 16.5 inches.

Blade Thickness—Because of the increased demand for strength and stability, short-track blades are thicker than long-track ones. The normal range is between 1.1 and 1.4 millimeters.

Blade Material—The steel used in making short-track blades is much the same as for their long-track cousins. It can involve varying degrees of hardness and quality. The tube of most short-track blades is made of aluminum, as are the cups. This material helps to reduce weight while still maintaining the necessary strength in the blade.

Blade Rocker—Because short-track skaters must perform tight corners and tricky passing maneuvers, the rocker used on short-track blades is much smaller. Most short-track skaters use a rocker of about eight meters. Some elite skaters will actually sculpt the blades so that there is a different rocker used on certain parts of it. For example, the back half of the blade often has a smaller rocker than the front half. Regardless of the specific rocker used, the idea is that a more extreme deviation from flat provides a more defined peak, or high point, that allows pivoting and tight turning.

Blade Bend—Elite short-track skaters discovered that bending the blade into a very subtle banana shape in the direction of the turn facilitates tight cornering. Most often, the blade's bend is more pronounced for the left, inside skate. Until recently, skaters wishing to bend their blades had to rely on rather crude methods, and once the blade was bent, it was impossible to ever straighten again. Today, some blade manufacturers offer a short-track blade with an internal bending system, whereby the blade can be bent to differing degrees by simply turning a small screw in one end. This not only allows the skater to determine optimal blade bend, but also provides a means to vary the desired bend, depending on the distance to be skated. It should be noted that some long-track sprinters also bend their blades very slightly. This is believed to make the last inner turn of the 500-meter more negotiable.

CLOSING REMARKS

Like many other athletes, both ice and in-line speedskaters consistently strive to improve performance through hard work, discipline, and a solid commitment to the achievement of personal success. Although solid technical ability is vital for the full benefits of physical conditioning to be realized, the quality of your training time also has a primary importance in determining the value of a given workout or training program.

It has been my intent in each of the preceding chapters to illustrate the roles that various technical and training-related factors have in the overall conditioning process. Optimal training for speedskating is a carefully blended mix of strength, power, endurance, and technical finesse. Success builds also from a host of secondary factors, such as pack awareness, mobility skills, the implementation of effective tactics, and dynamic coping skills that are specific to one's event. In this sense, speedskating is a worthwhile, challenging athletic endeavor. Improvements in equipment, technique, and training methods are likely to pave the way for tomorrow's athletes to surpass the level of accomplishment now displayed by top speedskaters. Until then it is my hope that *Speed on Skates* will represent the best source of specific technical and training information available for the developing athlete.

Appendix 1

Associations and Governing Bodies—In-line

Name	Phone	Fax	Email
USA Roller Skating	(402) 483-7551	(402) 483-1465	usacrs@usacrs.com
USA Inline Racing	(407) 682-2328	(407) 682-2388	tjmartin@sprintmail.com
Canadian In-line & Roller Skating Assoc.	(416) 260-0018	(416) 260-0798	cirsa@ican.net
Roller Sports Canada	(403) 938-4018	(403) 938-4910	execdir@rollersports.com

Associations and Governing Bodies—Ice

Amateur Skating Union	(708) 790-3230	(630) 790-3235 (Fax)
US Speedskating	(216) 221-6137	(216) 899-9577 (Fax)
Speed Skating Canada	(613) 748-5669	
International Skating Union (Switzerland)	011-41-681-410-06-00	

Appendix 2

400m Artificial Ice Ovals in North America

U.S High Altitude Sports Center: Butte, Montana
Ice Facilities: Outdoor 400-meter long track oval; outdoor, non-refrigerated 85 × 200 foot rink for short-track skating
Ice Season: November 1 to March 1, weather permitting
Clubs: Montana Amateur Speedskating Association, Chuck Durkin (406) 723-8005

Olympic Oval: Calgary, Alberta
Ice Facilities: Indoor 400-meter long-track oval; two indoor international-size rinks for short-track
Ice Season: July 1 to April 1
Clubs: Alberta Amateur Speedskating Association, (403) 220-7911; Calgary Speedskating Club, (403) 220-4417; Ichiban Speedskating Club, (403) 220-7910

Oquirrh Park Speedskating Oval: Kearns, Utah
Ice Facilities: Outdoor 400-meter long-track oval; outdoor international-size rinks for short-track
Ice Season: December 1 to March 1
Clubs: Rocky Mountain Speedskating, Boris Leiken, (801) 277-3043; North Utah Speedskating Club, J. Glad, (801) 479-4486; Wasatch Speed Skating Club, K. Keller, (801) 532-5539

U.S. Olympic Training Center: Lake Placid, New York
Ice Facilities: Outdoor 400-meter long-track oval; two indoor international-size rinks for short-track and one 85 × 200 indoor rink for short-track skating
Ice Season: Late November to early March
In-line season: April 1 to November 1
Clubs: Adirondack Speed Skating Club, Thomas Miller, (518) 891-3499

John Rose Minnesota Oval: Roseville, Minnesota
Ice Facilities: Outdoor 400-meter long-track oval; infield ice available for short-track practices (no boards), 85 × 200 indoor rink for short-track speedskating
Ice Season: November 1 to April 1
In-line season: Mid-April to Mid-October
Clubs: Minnesota Skating Association, Gene Casler, (612) 646-7058; Midway Speed Skating Club, (612) 484-4916; Plymouth Speedskating Club, Becky Oly, (612) 729-4066; Powderhorn Speed Skating Club, John Martin, (612) 888-7704; Shoreview Speed Skating Club, Becky Brooks, (612) 729-7302

Pettit National Ice Center: West Allis, Wisconsin
Ice Facilities: Indoor 400-meter long-track oval; two international-size rinks for short-track speed skating
Ice Season: September 1 to April 1; Short track rinks open year-round.
Clubs: W. Allis Speedskating Club, Rick Martin, (414) 965-2241; Badger Speedskating Club, Tony Arena, (414) 549-1630; Wisconsin Speedskating Association, Elayne Riley, (608) 837-7704

Anneau Gaetan Boucher: Ste-Foy (Quebec City), Quebec, Canada
Ice Facilities: Outdoor 400-meter long track oval, 2 ice hockey rinks
Ice Season: mid November to mid March
Clubs: Quebec Speedskating Federation: Robert Dubreuil (418) 651-1973; Fax (418) 651-1977

Bibliography

American College of Sports Medicine. 1990. The recommended quantity and quality of exercise for developing and maintaining cardiorespiratory and muscular fitness in healthy adults. *Medicine and Science in Sports and Exercise*. 265-274.

Åstrand, P.O., and K. Rodahl. 1986. *Textbook of work physiology*. NY: McGraw-Hill.

Bompa, T. 1983. *Theory and methodology of training*. Dubuque, IA: Kendall/Hunt.

Bompa, T. 1993. *Power training for sport*. Oakville, Ontario: Mosaic Press.

Chu, D. 1992. *Jumping into plyometrics*. Champaign, Ill: Human Kinetics.

de Boer, R.W., G. de Groot, J. de Koning, A.J. Sargeant, and G.J. van Ingen Schenau. 1987a. A peculiar pattern of muscular contraction during human locomotion: Speedskating. *Journal of Applied Physiology*. 394: 74.

de Boer, R.W., E. Vos., W. Hutter, G. de Groot, and G.J. van Ingen Schenau. 1987b. Physiological and biomechanical comparison of roller skating and speed skating on ice. *European Journal of Applied Physiology*. 56: 562-569.

Eckblom, B., L. Hermansen, and B. Saltin. 1967. Hastighetsakning pa skridskor. *Idrottsfysiologi* rapport nr. 5.

Foster, C. 1993. *Physiological perspectives in speedskating*. Unpublished manuscript.

Foster, C. 1995. Getting the most out of strength training. *Speedskating Times*. June-July: 7.

Foster, C., N. Thompson, and C. Snyder. 1993. Ergometric studies with speed skaters: evolution of laboratory methods. *Journal of Strength and Conditioning Research*. 7(4): 1993-2000.

Hedrick, A. 1994. Strength/power training for the National Speed Skating Team. *Strength and Conditioning*. October: 33-39.

Holum, D. 1984. *The complete handbook of speed skating*. Hillside, N.J.: Enslow.

Janssen, P. 1987. *Training lactate pulse-rate* (5th edition). Oulu, Finland: Polar electro oy.

Kahn, J.F, and H. Monod. 1989. Fatigue induced by static work. *Ergonomics*. 32(7): 839-846.

Kandou, T.W.A., I.L.D. Houtman, E.V.D. Bol, R.W. de Boer, G. de Groot, and G.J. van Ingen Schenau. 1987. Comparison of physiology and biomechanics of speedskating with cycling and with skateboard exercise. *Canadian Journal of Sport Science* 12(1): 31-36.

MacDougall, J.D. and D. Sale. 1981. Continuous vs. interval training: a review for the athlete and the coach. *Canadian Journal of Applied Sport Science* 6(2): 93-97.

MacDougall, J.D. and D. Sale.1993. Lecture prepared for Human Physiology 4C6, McMaster University, Hamilton, ON, Canada.

MacDougall, J.D., H.A. Wenger, and H.J. Green, eds. 1991. *Physiological testing of the high-performance athlete*. 2nd ed. Champaign, Ill: Human Kinetics.

Matveev, L.P. 1965. Periodization of sports training. *Fizkultura i sport*. Moscow.

Pedemonte, J. 1983. A new approach in selecting proper power loads for power development. *National Strength and Conditioning Association Journal* 5(3): 47.

Prampero, P.E., G. di Cortini, P. Mognoni, and F. Saibene. 1976. Energy cost of speed skating and efficiency of work against air resistance. *Journal of Applied Physiology* 40(4), 584-591.

Shepley, B., J.D. MacDougall, N. Cipriano, J.R. Sutton, M.A. Tarnopolsky, and G. Coates. 1992. Physiological effects of tapering in highly trained athletes. *Journal of Applied Physiology* 72(2): 706-711.

Snyder, A.C., K.P. O'Hagan, P.S. Clifford, M.D. Hoffman, and C. Foster. 1993. Exercise responses to inline skating: Comparisons to running and cycling. *International Journal of Sports Medicine* 14: 38-42.

United States Amateur Confederation of Roller Skating. 1995. *The speed book: USAC/RS official rules of roller speed skating*. Lincoln, NE: USAC/RS.

van Ingen Schenau, G.J., and K. Bakker. 1980. A biomechanical model of speed skating. *Journal of Human Movement Studies* 6:1-18.

van Ingen Schenau, G.J., G. de Groot, and R.W. de Boer. 1985. The control of speed in elite female speed skaters. *Journal of Biomechanics* 18(2): 91-96.

van Ingen Schenau, G.J., G. de Groot, A. Wim Scheurs, H. Meester, and Jos J. de Koning. 1996. A new skate allowing powerful plantar flexion improves performance. *Medicine and Science in Sports and Exercise* 28(4): 531-535.

van Ingen Schenau, G.J., G. de Groot, and A.P. Hollander. 1983. Some technical, physiological, and anthropometrical aspects of speed skating. *European Journal of Applied Physiology* 50:343-354.

Verkoshansky, V. 1969. Perspectives in the improvement of strength-speed preparation in jumpers. *Review of Soviet Education and Sports* 4(2): 28-29.

Zanon, S. 1977. Consideration for determining some parametric values of the relations between maximum isometric relative strength and elastic relative strength for planning and controlling the long jumpers conditioning training. *Athletic Coach* 11(4): 14-20.

Index

Please note: *f* indicates a reference to a figure and *t* refers to a table.

About the Author

Barry Publow—one of the most respected in-line coaches and athletes in Canada—is world-renowned for his expertise in the areas of technique and training application. He is the director of the Miller Canada Race Team as well as a team skater. He is also a two-time member of Canada's National Inline Speed Team, with whom he participated in the 1994 World Championships. Since 1993 he has been consistently ranked as one of the top five elite male skaters in Canada.

As the National Inline Speed Team coach at the 1995 Pan American Games, Publow led his Canadian senior skaters to their best finish ever at an international event. And as the coach of the Toronto and Ottawa Inline Speedskating Clubs, he has worked with many of Canada's top elite and age-group skaters.

Publow is also an accomplished ice speedskater and a fully certified ice speedskating coach. A regular staff writer for *Fitness and Speed Skating Times*, Publow makes his home in Ottawa, Ontario.